'This book offe[illegible] to the role and implications of th[illegible] reform. Focusing primarily on England, although with international comparisons, it provides an engaging and well-informed exploration of the divergence between the world of education as seen through the lens of public legislation, and the operation of the schools system, under the influence of policy reform, on the ground.'

Professor Neville Harris, University of Manchester

'The field of law-based education reform has received insufficient attention as a framework for the analysis and understanding of education policy. This is no longer the case with this riveting account of the interplay between legislation and education policy in England. The book is a must-read to understand the emergence of the most contested education policies of our time.'

Professor Ellen Goldring, Vanderbilt University, USA

Law, Education, Politics, Fairness

IOE Press

The Bedford Way Papers Series

24 *Theorising Quality in Higher Education*
Louise Morley

25 *Music Psychology in Education*
Susan Hallam

26 *Policy-making and Policy Learning in 14–19 Education*
Edited by David Raffe and Ken Spours

27 *New Designs for Teachers' Professional Learning*
Edited by Jon Pickering, Caroline Daly and Norbert Pachler

28 *The Dearing Report: Ten years on*
Edited By David Watson and Michael Amoah

29 *History, Politics and Policy-making in Education: A festschrift presented to Richard Aldrich*
David Crook and Gary McCulloch

30 *Public Sector Reform: Principles for improving the education system*
Frank Coffield, Richard Steer, Rebecca Allen, Anna Vignoles, Gemma Moss and Carol Vincent

31 *Educational Resource Management: An international perspective*
Derek Glover and Rosalind Levačić

32 *Education in a Global City: Essays from London*
Edited by Tim Brighouse and Leisha Fullick

33 *Exploring Professionalism*
Edited by Bryan Cunningham

34 *Music Education in the 21st Century in the United Kingdom: Achievements, analysis and aspirations*
Edited by Susan Hallam and Andrea Creech

35 *Critical Practice in Teacher Education: A study of professional learning*
Edited by Ruth Heilbronn and John Yandell

36 *Accelerated Leadership Development: Fast tracking school leaders*
Peter Earley and Jeff Jones

37 *Post-Compulsory Education and Lifelong Learning across the United Kingdom: Policy, organisation and governance*
Edited by Ann Hodgson, Ken Spours and Martyn Waring

38 *From Exam Factories to Communities of Discovery: The democratic route*
Frank Coffield and Bill Williamson

39 *An Aims-based Curriculum: The significance of human flourishing for schools*
Michael Reiss and John White

A full list of Bedford Way Papers, including earlier books in the series, can be requested by emailing ioepress@ioe.ac.uk

Law, Education, Politics, Fairness

England's extreme legislation for education reform

Dan Gibton

Institute of Education Press
Bedford Way Papers

First published in 2013 by the Institute of Education, University of London,
20 Bedford Way, London WC1H 0AL

www.ioe.ac.uk/ioepress

British Library Cataloguing in Publication Data:
A catalogue record for this publication is available from the British Library

ISBNs
978-0-85473-922-6 (paperback)
978-1-78277-037-4 (PDF eBook)
978-1-78277-038-1 (ePub eBook)
978-1-78277-039-8 (Kindle eBook)

Typeset by Quadrant Infotech (India) Pvt Ltd
Printed by CPI Group (UK) Ltd, Croydon, CR0 4YY

Contents

Part 3: Analysis and implications of England's law-based reform

To my parents, Joab and Dinah

List of figures and tables

List of abbreviations

ACSL:	Association of College and School Leaders (formerly SHA: Secondary Heads Association)
ALB:	Arms-Length Body
ATL:	Association of Teachers and Leaders
BSF:	Building Schools for the Future
CTC:	City Technology College
DfE:	Department for Education
DfEE:	Department for Education and Employment
DfES:	Department for Education and Skills
DCSF:	Department for Children, Schools, and Families
EA:	Education Act (from various years)
EAZ:	Education Action Zone
EBacc:	English Baccalaureate
EIA:	Education and Inspections Act (2006)
EIC:	Excellence in Cities
ERA:	Education Reform Act (1988)
EMG:	Education Maintenance Grants
EU:	European Union
FSM:	Free School Meals
GCSE:	General Certificate of Secondary Education
GM:	Grant-Maintained
GTCE:	General Teaching Council for England
HMI:	Her Majesty's Inspector
HMCI:	Her Majesty's Chief Inspector

K-12:	a common term for 13 years of public education from kindergarten (K) to the end of the 12th year of secondary schooling (also known as 6th Form or Year 12 in England)
KS:	Key Stages
LA:	Local Authority
LEA:	Local Education Authority
LMS:	Local Management of Schools
NAHT:	National Association of Headteachers
NC:	National Curriculum
NCLB:	No Child Left Behind
NCSL:	National College for School Leaders
NGO:	Non-Government Organization
NUT:	National Union of Teachers
OfQUAL:	Office of Qualifications and Examinations Regulation
Ofsted:	Office for Standards in Education
QCDA:	Quality and Curriculum Development Agency
QUANGO:	Quasi-Non-Government Organization
PFI:	Private Finance Initiative
PPP:	Public–Private Partnership
SEAL:	Social and Emotional Aspects of Learning
SEF:	Self-evaluation Form
SES:	Socio Economic Status
SIP:	School Improvement Partner
STA:	Standards and Testing Agency
TDA:	Training and Development Agency for Schools

Acknowledgements

My gratitude to the Institute of Education, University of London, for its help in three periods of study between 2000 and 2011: to Director Emeritus Professor Geoff Whitty and current Director Professor Chris Husbands; to Professors Stephen Ball, David Gillborn, David Hopkins, Ron Glatter, and Carol Vincent; and to Doctors Sara Bubb and Marie Lull.

My deepest thanks to the London Centre for Leadership in Learning (LCLL), under Doctor Hilary Emery, Professor Alma Harris, and, currently, Ms Vivienne Porritt, for its kind help and support. Many thanks to Professors Louise Stoll and Kathryn Riley and Dr Karen Edge for their sound advice. Thanks to Mr Max Coates, Ms Elizabeth Wood, and Doctor Rob Higham. Many thanks to the LCLL administrative staff for their assistance.

Thanks to the British Foreign Office for its help in funding the 2000–01 fellowship at the Institute of Education, under the auspices of the Chevening Award Scholarships, and to the British Council for its administrative support.

Thanks to my alma mater, Tel-Aviv University, for its continuous support of my research. Thanks to the Jaime and Joan Constantiner School of Education, where I am a tenured member of the senior staff, and the Buchmann Faculty of Law where I am adjunct lecturer.

Thanks to colleagues and friends from my department, Professors Abraham Yogev, Avner Ben-Amos, Izhar Oplatka, and Doctors Uri Cohen and, last but not least, Audrey Addi-Raccah, who each helped in their own way. Many thanks to my friend and mentor Professor Yuval Dror.

I appreciate the generous help given to the study by the Israel Polak Unit for Sociology of Education and Community, chair: Professor Abraham Yogev.

Special thanks to my host and dear friend Professor Peter Earley, from the Institute of Education, for his continuous help, advice, and contributions to this study and to my work. Thanks to Professor (Emeritus) Ros Levačić for her wise guidance.

Thanks to my mentors and colleagues Professor Naama Sabar, Tel-Aviv University, and Professor Ellen Goldring, Vanderbilt University, for all that I have learned from them on educational research.

Thanks to Ms Yael Schlezinger and Adv. Tamar Livni-Huberman, my dedicated and thorough research assistants, for their important inputs.

Thanks to my mom, Dinah Gibton, for her essential help.

Loads of thanks to Mr Jim Collins, editor, who taught me, in his unique 'cool' manner and in a very short time, important things about writing and publishing (and would probably comment that this sentence is too long); and to Ms Sally Sigmund and Mr Jonathan Dore of the Institute of Education Press team for their good ideas and efficient production.

Finally, thanks to the participants who dedicated some of their precious time to take part in this study. For obvious ethical reasons I cannot mention your names but you will always have a place in my heart.

About the author

Dan Gibton is tenured senior lecturer, Constantiner School of Education, and adjunct lecturer, Buchmann Faculty of Law, at Tel-Aviv University, where he has worked since 2000 teaching educational law and policy at the Department of Educational Policy and Administration, the School of Education, and the Faculty of Law. Areas of interest include trends in educational law-based policy and reform. In particular his work attempts, through qualitative research methods, to study how educational law influences education policy and reform, and the role of education law in affecting fairness and equality in the globalized economy. During 2000–1 (when he received the Chevening Award Scholarship for 2000), 2005–6, and 2010–11, he was visiting fellow with the Policy Studies Group and with the London Centre for Leadership in Learning, both at the Institute of Education, University of London. Since 2007 he has been tutor on the University of London External MA international programme in Applied Educational Leadership and Management. He is the author of *Legalized Leadership: Law-based educational reform in England and its effect on headteachers* (Institute of Education, 2004).

Foreword

When Dan Gibton told me he was writing a book on law and education, I was not entirely convinced that this would be a book I would warm to. But I now realize that I was envisaging a book about what he terms 'educational law' rather than 'law-based reform'. The latter is actually the focus of his book, and its intellectual roots are in socio-legal studies and the sociology of education policy.

The American commentators John Chubb and Terry Moe once suggested that radical reform in education was much easier in the United Kingdom than in the United States because our parliamentary form of government allowed it to proceed faster and farther. Leaving aside the fact that it was never entirely that simple, and certainly not since the devolution of powers to Scotland, Wales, and Northern Ireland, legislation passed at Westminster is anyway only a small part of the story about how educational reform gets done.

On the other hand, there has been a tendency in some recent sociological studies of education policy inspired by Stephen Ball to move so far away from a 'command and control' understanding of how reform gets done that the legislative aspect of the 'policy cycle' has come to be somewhat neglected in favour of policy 'messiness' and governance through networks.

Gibton's book helps us understand the place of law in education reform, not so much as a 'top-down' guarantor of desired change but nevertheless as an important part of the policy cycle that frames reform at all levels in myriad subtle and not so subtle ways. He demonstrates this largely with reference to the English case over the past thirty years or so, but he also makes comparative reference to the United States and Israel, the other jurisdictions that he knows well. This enables him to throw some light on the strengths and weaknesses of the English approach to reform.

The book's legislative focus is the 2006 Education and Inspections Act and the 2011 Education Act. These pieces of legislation were enacted during the second and third of Gibton's three sojourns in England, the first of which was in 2000–01. This allows him to comment on the continuities and discontinuities of English reform under successive governments. The empirical meat of his study is a hundred in-depth interviews with senior figures in education reform, some of whom he interviewed more than once. He then distils these into four imaginary policy actors – a civil servant, the head of an academy chain, a director of education in a local authority, and the CEO of a think tank – and six imaginary 'superheads' active not only in school leadership but also in the network governance of education. All are eerily – even scarily – familiar to those of us who have been close to education reform in recent years!

Contrary to my initial concern, Gibton's book is not in any sense dry or disinterested. Indeed, he positively takes sides. He adopts the view that policy is a public expression of values and he is clearly personally disturbed by some of the values embodied in the neoliberal turn in policy. Yet he also recognizes the limitations of the previously dominant social democratic tendency in English education policy. The fourth term in his book's title is 'fairness' and it is clear throughout that Gibton regards equity as a key test of reform, whatever its political provenance.

What we have here is necessarily an unfinished story. Gibton has now become such a seasoned observer and analyst of the English scene that it is be hoped that it will not be long before he returns to these shores to see how the story unfolds and offer us further insights into the possibilities and problems of law-based education reform on the English model.

Professor Geoff Whitty
Director, Institute of Education,
University of London, 2000–2010

Chapter 1

Introduction: Why study law-based education reform in England, and how to do so

> *... Yet if hope has flown away*
> *In a night, or in a day,*
> *In a vision, or in none,*
> *Is it therefore the less gone?*
> *All that we see or seem*
> *Is but a dream within a dream. ...*
>
> (Edgar Allan Poe, 1849)

Approaching and entering Sanctuary buildings, the huge home of England's Ministry of Education (known, in 2011, as the DfE),[1] one encounters a contrast between the formal, old-fashioned, slightly drab exterior, and the smart, modern, business-like, interior. The ten-storey open atrium is surrounded by uniform open-floor planning, in which even senior civil servants settle for a cubicle, perhaps with partitions that are just a bit higher or a bit more closed and private than those of the more junior officials. Going into the building one receives a message of modernity, efficiency, power, and control: a bustling hub of activity, running, planning, and controlling the more than 24,000 schools that comprise England's public education. However, this uncluttered, organized façade hides a colourful quilt of policies, programmes, power melees, and controversies. Since 1988 England has had a major new education law (known as an act in England) about every two years. Such amount, scope, and frequency of educational law are unprecedented in the world. This book attempts to understand how and why this situation happened, the politics and mechanisms of education policy and reform that fuelled it and were fuelled by it, and the figures and organizations involved in it and that bear its impact.

A ten-minute walk from the Ministry of Education, Portcullis House, with its huge Cornish granite and aluminium-bronze exterior, opens up to a modern interior – very much like that of the ministry and many official buildings in England. Again, this has a ten-storey high open atrium that offers both space, light, a feeling of openness and of transparency combined with efficiency and control. In this building a senior MP involved in education legislation told me:

> Do you know why we legislate? Because we can. New education legislation is somehow embedded in the DNA of administrations and secretaries of state. We simply have to come up with a new education bill every second year or so, and if there's a new government, even if it's run by the same

> party and headed by the same Prime Minister as the previous one, it still has to come up with a new education bill in its first six months.

These two buildings represent the realm, the place where things 'happen', where decisions are made. But the actual map of legislation is a colourful, intricate, and complex bricolage that tinkers towards change. When we look more closely, the linear disguise of policy and of legislation is quickly replaced by a maze, a dream within a dream, a riddle wrapped in a secret. The findings in this study show that there is a schema among policymakers who draft and influence legislation. The schema is that legislation modifies the educational world, the school, the LEA, and the work of headteachers and teachers, in a positivistic manner that can be isolated, consistent with independent and dependent variables. The schema also depicts a situation in which legislation is nearly the *end* of the policy cycle and not its starting point. This can be one explanation of the frequency of legislation. Other components of the explanation are related to the education policy debate but are, in reality, more about the English legal and government system, which will be discussed in this book only marginally as it is outside my area of expertise and distant from the empirical evidence gathered in this study. Not only is the linearity of legislation disparate from what it seems, but political alliances and identities take something of a liquid form. As Kingdon (2003: 206) notes, government agendas are the result 'of considerable doses of messiness, accident, fortuitous coupling and dumb luck'. This process of luck will also be explored in this book, and findings show that luck is not a valid policy tool. Legislation in England's education is deeply rooted in a political culture and is inherent to the law's whole existence. Feuer (2006) cautions that unreasonable expectations from school reform create constant anxiety, requiring policymakers:

> ...to adjust the theory of action underlying education reform and research, from one with implicit tones of optimization and objective rationality toward one that assumes conditions of complexity coupled with cognitive limits of educational decision-makers; from one that inevitably disappoints researchers and reformers to one that embraces without shame or embarrassment the ideal of reasonable strategies based on appropriate deliberation; from one that sees inevitable failure in every imperfect proposal to one that tolerates incremental improvement, steady albeit slow progress, and continual evaluation.
>
> (Ibid. 39)

The legislation language and content of education law is extremely complex and difficult to handle. It models the education field, whilst at the same time creating a separate, parallel, existence beside it. It also creates expectations in its strict mandatory character. Both these dimensions will be analysed in the book, including comparative analysis on how some other countries address the issue of education reform through reform.

People, policymakers, managers of education, and laypersons alike tend to comprehend legislation as more vast and influential than it really is, believing that it touches on every area of educational life. A lot of what is done through directives or through budgetary control is perceived as if it were legislated. That is, I think, one of the downsides of the large amounts of legislation that exist: a tsunami effect that amplifies the sheer weight of legislation in England, which is already more than exists anywhere else. This does not mean that legislation has no bearing on policy; it moulds the culture, the discourse, the structure, and the practice of education in many ways that will be presented in this book. First, my findings show that it creates a unique type of discourse (Ball, 1994) among policymakers and educators. Second, as the system becomes more and more decentralized, legislation constructs a framework necessary for school reform. Third, legislation generates public debate, within the profession and beyond.

The people I have talked to in this study are both the formal and the informal designers of educational reform legislation in England, and its formal and informal interpreters and implementers. Therefore their perceptions of the law, of the legislation process, and of what they see as covert or overt agendas in its planning, are of importance to what happens in the education field in England. Their viewpoints, their feelings, and the perspectives and thoughts they attribute to the legislators, are denominators that mould their reaction to the law, their action upon the law, and their own attitudes towards it. The field (Bourdieu, 1987; Galligan, 2010; Hacker, 2008) of figures and views will be portrayed and analysed. This is the hidden 'commonplace' (Ewick and Silbey, 1998) of education legislation reform in England and it is this field and these arenas that this book intends to present and study.

Studying the legislators, policymakers, and educators who were interviewed, and their stories, shows that their alliances and identities shift dramatically over the years. For instance, in 2005–6 there was a strong Social Democrat propensity among the recipients of educational law. It was perceived by educators as generally doing some right things in an attempt to minimize achievement gaps that were correlated with socio-economic and ethnic gaps, combined with critique that policies were too neoliberal and did not travel the 'extra mile' towards more equity and less segregation. Meanwhile the levels of critique that policy has weakened local – both municipal and school-level control – can be seen to rise steadily as we move forward along the decade from 2001 to 2011. In 2011, the interviewees – some of them from the same cohort as the one interviewed in 2005–6 – have become disenchanted with what they saw as a controlled management of schooling that disenfranchised educators of their powers and their professional authority, without a justifying trade-off. Such a trade-off could include improving equity and minimizing SES (Socio Economic Status) or ethnic-based gaps. Remarkably, many of the fierce opponents of New Labour, who saw it as being too neoliberal, have themselves moved on. Some now head or run academies, or work for privately-financed organizations that embody the ideology of the current Conservative–Liberal-Democrat administration in the Ministry of Education:

> I think New Labour were disappointed with the long-term effects of their policy. In a way they felt they were let down by implementers and the receiving end of policy. There was a difference between them and the Conservatives: they were more pragmatic, not as ideological, more laid-back, relaxed, but also much more interventionist. New Labour legislated as if they were in power for ever. The Conservatives act as if they are here only temporarily.
>
> (NGO CEO, 2011)

Finally, the investigation of law-based reform, legislation, and the views of legislators, policymakers and educators, will ask the main questions of this book. The first question touches on the following issues: What are the politics of law-based reform, and what power and hegemony issues prevail? Whom does the law strengthen and whom does it weaken? This discussion will include issues such as launching and eradicating various categories (perhaps brands?) of schools and school organizations (for example EAZs, chains, federations, and so on); how legislation shapes the principal arrangements of the education system; and to what incidences and crises legislation responds. The second question is: How do law-based reform and legislation serve as an equitable tool, and reinforce or deteriorate equality and fairness in education and schools? In exploring this question the place of legislation in areas such as admissions policy, segregation and choice, and school improvement will be considered.

The conceptual framework

The core of the book is positioned within the fields of law-based education reform and the evolving interest in how legislation shapes education, and how it is applied as a policy tool (Gibton, 2004b; Smrekar and Goldring, 2009; Harris, 2007; Heubert, 1999). Conceptually, several fields of research feed the theoretical framework of this book (see figure 1.1).

First, this is a socio-political legal study (Ewick and Silbey, 1998; Hacker, 2008; Harris, 2007) that maps the bodies, the agencies, and the people who make education law and law-based education reform in England. Two points of view will be presented. The first is that of lawmakers and policymakers, and the second is that of the recipients, the clients, the users of law-based education reform, and the people and agencies that are influenced by the law.

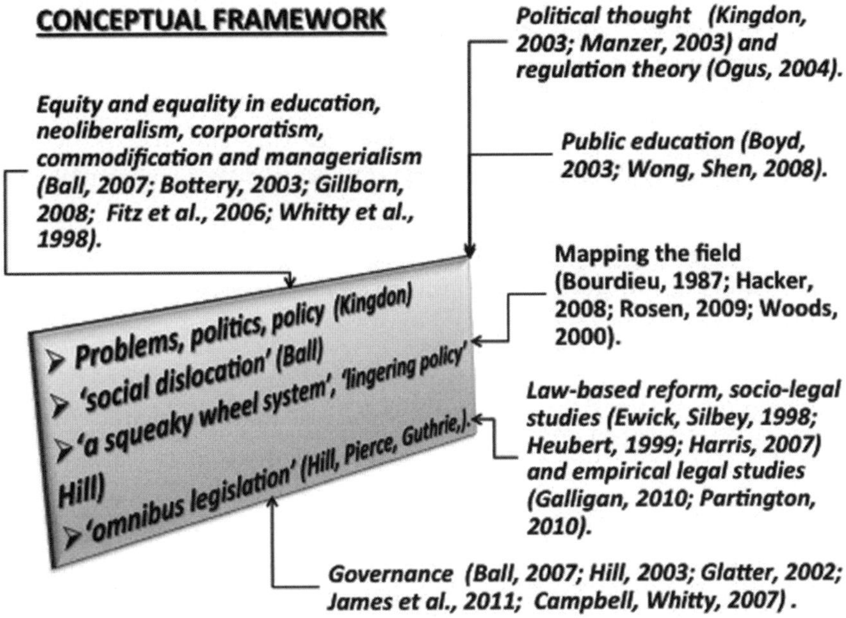

Figure 1.1: The conceptual framework of the study

Second, the book draws upon literature and research on public policy (Kingdon, 2003; Young, 2006), public policy in education (Manzer, 2003; McDonnell, 2009), and especially governance and education policy (Ball, 1994, 2007; Glatter, 2002; Balarin *et al.*, 2008) in light of a globalized economy (Bottery, 2003). The study complements the literature on governance (Campbell and Whitty, 2007; James *et. al.*, 2011; Ranson, 2011; Woods *et al.*, 2007) through the analysis of legislation. The book also discusses the compliance and appropriateness of legislation in relation to crises in government and politics (such as the legislation on social cohesion following the July 2005 bombings in London); the targeting, or missing, of 'policy windows' (Kingdon, 2003, for example the Academies Act of 2010 in the early days of the Conservative–Liberal-Democrat government); and the unique combinations of 'problems, politics, and policies' (Kingdon, 2003) indispensable for moving ideas and turning them into policy. The specific place of education law in this maze will be studied. Special attention will be given in this sub-area of the conceptual framework to the issue of legislation (Ogus, 2004) and legislation's role in regulation. The ability or shortcomings of legislation in respect of creating effective and fair agencies and tools of regulation will be analysed.

Third, the tension between neoliberal and Social Democrat ideologies will be explored, in regard to the legislation, its content, and its results. A strong stand will be made in support of social justice and equity in education (Barry, 2005; Dworkin, 2000; Fitz *et al.*, 2006; Gillborn, 2008; Whitty *et al.*, 1998). Special emphasis will be placed on the issue of school choice (Berends *et al.*, 2009; Berends *et al.*, 2011), segregation, desegregation, and resegregation, and their reflection in legislation and the legislative process. This will include the depiction of *public education* (Boyd, 2003; Hill, 2003), as a basic term in the discussion on equity in education – the ethos of which is rooted in US education policy research – and in England's education law. The place of law-based policies (such as Education Maintenance Allowances, the introduction of free schools, the legal shift in the powers of the school adjudicator and the admissions code and other types of change in the strengthening or weakening of equity and equality in education) will be discussed extensively.

The design and method of the study

Methodologically, this is a qualitative interpretive study (Bernard, 2010; Charmaz, 2006; Smith *et al.*, 2009) that consists of two distinct parts.

The first part is a socio-political analysis of educational legislation regarding K-12 school reform,[2] with some references to earlier relevant laws, going back to the 1988 Education Reform Act and perhaps earlier. These are only points of reference as they have been analysed and studied thoroughly in other literature (for example Ball, 2007; Harris, 1993; Whitty *et al.*, 1998; Whitty, 2008).

The second part includes over one hundred in-depth interviews with senior figures. These cover the following strata: beginning with the planning aspect, such as MPs and DfE civil servants; then the influencing and advisory tier, including NGOs, QUANGOs, and ALB CEOs; onwards through the implementing middle level of governance, relating to LEAs and, again, NGOs, QUANGOs, and ALB CEOs; and finally the receiving end – 'superheads', and CEOs of heads' and teachers' unions, and other individuals such as academics involved in policymaking. The interviews were carried out in three phases: in the year 2000–1, in the year 2005–6 and in the year 2010–11. Some figures were interviewed several times, to allow for an analysis of any change in their views over a decade. Content analysis included a three-stage process: phrases, vignettes (episodes), and complete stories were analysed through *emic* (from within) and *etic* concepts (emerging from literature).

The plan of the book

Following this introductory chapter, the book is divided into three parts. Part 1, 'Law-based education reform', sets the conceptual foundations and outlines a legal analysis of education legislation in England. It begins with Chapter 2, which explains what law-based education reform is and offers some definitions and models. Chapter 3 presents three examples of law-based reform: England, the US, and Israel. The comparison will evolve around issues of structure, role, the relationship with Supreme Court rulings, and legislation's role in achieving equity and social justice, including a proposed 'social justice meter' of education law in the three countries. Chapter

4 presents England's law-based reform, and tells the story behind two education bills – the 2006 Education and Inspections Act and the 2011 Education Bill that exemplify the remarkable phenomenon of educational legislation.[3] The questions at the core of this chapter deal with whether, how, and to what extent the last big education act under New Labour was a forbearer of the dramatic change introduced by the 2011 Education Act under a different, Conservative–Liberal-Democrat government in terms of the system's structure and equity. It also asks whether the 2011 Education Act is revolutionary rather than evolutionary. Part 2, 'Who is involved in England's law-based reform, and how?', presents the empirical evidence. It begins with Chapter 5, which maps the field of the key figures and organizations involved in, or influenced by, law-based reforms, and then moves on to present their views on this outstanding English phenomenon (that is, the scope and frequency of legislation). This empirical section of the book continues with Chapter 6, which maps the various contributors and participants in England's law-based educational reform ideologically, from democratic socialism, on to social democracy, then to 'third way' and finally to neoliberalism. Chapter 6 further analyses and sharpens the debate, the similarities and dissimilarities between New Labour and Conservative (including the current Conservative–Liberal-Democrat government) regarding the role, content, and forming of educational legislation. Chapter 7 presents an accrued imaginary template of four figures involved in education law, namely: the civil servant; the head of a trust that organizes new types of schools; the head of education for an LEA; and the CEO of a think tank. Chapter 8, which concludes the second part of the book, focuses on the unique role of school headteachers in shaping educational policy and law. The third part of the book, 'Analysis and implications of England's law-based reform', begins with Chapter 9, which examines legislation's declarative role versus its function as a lever for change in the long-term planning of school reform, and the perils of adhocracy and symbolism in education law. Chapter 10 explores whether legislation is pragmatic or ideological, how it presents the outsiders' impact on legislation – NGOs, QUANGOs (recently nicknamed 'QUANGOes), and ALBs,[4] with a focus on think tanks versus local government – and the career shifts and alliances, coalitions, and oppositions of figures within the emerging 'issue network' (Deleon, 2006). Finally, Chapter 11 concludes by offering a longitudinal comparative framework for assessing legislation's role in promoting or weakening equity, equality, and social justice, and asks what can be learned from the English case on the pros and cons of legislation as a policy tool in education, including how problems can perhaps best be confronted.

Notes

[1] Remarkably, the ministry's title has changed five times in the last two decades: Department for Education (DfE); Department for Education and Employment (DfEE); Department for Education and Skills (DfES); Department for Children and Schools (DfCS); and finally in 2010, Department for Education (DfE) once again.

[2] A common international term for 13 public/compulsory years of education, from kindergarten/pre-school to 12 years of schooling.

[3] As of August 2011– under impact assessment in Parliament.

[4] Arms-Length Bodies.

Part 1

Law-based education reform

Chapter 2

Law-based education reform: The term, its origins, and its context

The conceptual framework of the study

As explained in the Introduction, the conceptual framework of this book is based on several main clusters of literature and theory, not all of which can be presented in detail here. Rather, I have chosen some core theories that I believe are at the heart of studying England's law-based education reform. Other literature will be mentioned later in the book, whenever necessary, to explain and discuss findings. At the beginning I will present and analyse three principles of education reform from the last two decades. These principles will earmark the analysis of four conceptual foundations of this book: law-based reform in neoliberal ideology and the globalized economy; law-based reform in political thought, education policy research, governance, and regulation; and law-based reform in ethics, social justice, and public education. Finally, the fundamentals of law-based reform will be presented.

The three principles of education reform in neoliberal systems

School reform in the last two decades or so has been based, generally, on three principles that appear and reappear and may take on different forms and shapes, but are fundamentally consistent.

The first principle is that equality can be retained in a system with open enrolment and choice (Berends *et al.*, 2011). The second principle is that micro-processes in the classroom – that is, teaching and learning – can be controlled, changed, and improved by financial, organizational, and legal macro-processes (Bottery, 2000; Ball, 2007). The third principle is that a neoclassic market (Houser, 1996; Ogus, 2004) can exist in education.

Understanding these principles is essential to the understanding of school reform and perhaps of its failure (Payne, 2008). Summing up research (Ball, 2007; Fitz *et al.*, 2006; Berends *et al.*, 2009) on the three principles that dominate managerialist education reform in neoliberal-based administrations yields a disturbing conclusion. The scientific base for these principles is, at best, disputable and, at worst, weak.

We now have sufficient evidence to substantiate claims that school choice in its various forms (for example open enrolment or vouchers), coupled with quasi-privatization and further distinction between commission and delivery/provision of education services, has contributed to increasing inequality and a widening of socio-economic gaps in many societies. In the United States, the 2007 landmark court case, 'Parents Involved in Community Schools v. Seattle School District No. 1/Meredith v. Jefferson County Board of Education', combined with some two decades of introducing competition between schools, has deepened these gaps. In England, educational sociologists (Ball, 2007; Fitz *et al.*, 2006; Gillborn, 2008; Whitty *et al.*, 1998) have warned repeatedly that choice and relaxed admissions policies have severe repercussions, in terms of equality.

The second principle is a major trait in school reform under neoliberal regimes (Ball, 2007; Bottery, 2000; 2003; Manzer, 2003). It stems primarily from the base of neoliberal economic ideas that schools should be managed like any other organization, and that they are generally mismanaged or suffer from a management deficiency. According to this theory, management is universal, typical, and standard in its nature (Gibton, 2003). This means that knowledge about management of one type of organization (such as an IT firm, a bank, an NGO) is principally the same as managing a human service organization such as a school. The problems – and therefore the means to solve them – are similar, as are the 'types' or models of management. This also means that managing in one culture is the same as managing in any other, and that the standards of good or bad management will be the same in any type of organization or culture. This leads to a managerialist culture in the management of school systems.

The third principle of education reform is that a neoclassic market (Houser, 1996; Ogus, 2004) can exist in education (Houser, 1996). In order for such a market to exist there are five pre-conditions. The first condition is the 'liquidity' of the product or service. This means that its qualities allow it to change hands easily, through an apparatus that makes getting rid of the service and acquiring an alternative technically and legally easy, but it also means that the whole market is open to all consumers. The second condition is what Houser calls a 'situation of faceless sellers and buyers', which means that the loyalty of the consumer to a specific product or service, or to a given supplier of a product or service, is low. The third condition is that there is sufficient information to reach a learned decision. The fourth condition is the existence of, and accessibility to, knowledge that allows the consumer to interpret the information. The fifth condition is that the consumers' actions are rational.

The problem is that a neoclassic market rarely exists, even with regard to financial instruments or products such as stocks, but when a human service such as education is involved, a neoclassic market is implausible. Due to distance, the complete 'market' of schools will never be available to any one receiver of the service. Loyalty to a school can be really low, and there is usually a complex web of pros and cons associated with choosing one school over another. However, relocating a child to a new school is problematic, and the price paid for such re-adjustments can be high, emotionally and pedagogically. Fixing the damage is difficult, and there is a shelf-life for the opportunities and options available to correct the implications of bad education. The information necessary to reach a sound decision is, at best, incomplete, though information and communications technologies and powerful audit mechanisms that publish their inspection reports and results help to improve this situation. Knowledge on how to interpret and analyse the information is scarce, certainly among laypersons, and the endless arguments among policymakers and researchers regarding the interpretation of education data do not leave much room for optimism in this scenario. Finally, human behaviour, especially when dealing with such a complex, value-laden, critical, and ideologically-driven area as education, is hardly ever rational. At best we might achieve what (Ogus, 2004) defines as 'bounded rationality' – that is, limited by a small market, by limited liquidity, by limited information, and by limited capacity to interpret it, in addition to the emotional constraints, beliefs, rumours, fashion, and gossip that often influence school choice (Ben-Porath, 2010; Stein *et al.,* 2011).

How is it, then, that the three conditions are noticeably present in determining the structure and content of education reform, when their scientific validity is so low? The answer, again, lies within the influence of neoliberal ideology and that of the globalized economy, their principles becoming something of a religion.

The socio-political context of law-based education reform

Bottery explains that, according to the neoliberal ideology:

1. social progress lies in the achievement of continuing increases in economically defined productivity
2. management is a distinct organizational function which plays the crucial role in planning and measuring the necessary improvements in productivity
3. such productivity increases will come about through the creation of a labour force installed with this productivity ideal, who are vigorously tied into such corporate aims
4. to reform this crucial role managers must be granted the right to manage proactively available resources, both material and human.

(Bottery, 2000: 63)

This universal, typical, and standardized idea of management is related to the larger concept of a globalized economy, which itself is closely connected to neoliberal philosophy. From an economic and political point of view, globalization is connected with the term 'ideology' and control of neoliberalism:

> To guard against their greatest fears – fascism, communism, socialism, authoritarian populism, and even majority rule – the neoliberals have to put strong limits on democratic governance, relying instead upon undemocratic and unaccountable institutions (such as the federal reserve or the IMF) to make key decisions. This creates the paradox of intense state interventions and government by elites and 'experts' in a world where the state is supposed not to be interventionist.
>
> (Harvey, 2005: 69)

Neoliberal ideology is strengthened and spread by the force of globalization and of the globalized economy (Ball, 2007; Bottery, 2000), defined by Plank and Keesler (2009) as the 'shrinking state'. As a result of globalization it becomes ever more difficult to retain localized systems that do not comply with international educational standards. Emerging international chains of secondary schools show that this phenomenon is slowly seeping into the lower tiers of education – the European Council of International Schools (ECIS) and the Schola Europaea being two such examples. Baker (2009) explains that globalization has created and advanced a global educational culture that has produced specific reforms and policies that are being distributed worldwide, in what Ball defines as a 'policy epidemic' (Ball, 2008a: 39). The global education culture (Baker 2009: 962–3) is based on four values that often contradict each other:

1. *Equality of opportunity and social justice*: Through the promotion of widespread mass education up to university and college level, and advancing the understanding that education cannot, and should not, solely be the asset of the upper classes.

2. *Development of modern individuals for the collective good*: This managerialist idea presupposes that education benefits society as a whole more than it benefits the individual. This is an important principle of neoliberalism that gives this dominant ideology a twist and explains why ultra-capitalist regimes put special emphasis on investment in education reform.

3. *Dominance of academic intelligence*: Making this knowledge the primary tool for social mobility, as opposed to social capital and class. This means a standardization of academic curricula including the emergence of international baccalaureates of various kinds.

4. *Meritocratic achievement and education credentialism*: This dictates certain uniform structures and practices in education systems world-wide.

Law-based education reform is an example of such intensive state intervention. Neoliberalism is an updated form of capitalism that relies on market forces and concurrently relies on regulatory state intervention and investment in public services, while at the same time attempting to deconstruct public services and replace them with a regulated quasi-privatized market (Ball, 2007). The forces of globalized economy and policy are often based on neoliberal views that are translated into education policy and reform that are imposed, even forced, upon national school systems by international financial organizations (Harvey, 2005; Ball, 2007).

This supports an interventionist culture that treats teachers and headteachers with growing suspicion. Therefore the second principle is based on the assumption that the teaching and treatment of pupils can only change through coercive mega-changes in the organizational, legal, and financial conditions of schooling. Economic theories on cost-effectiveness state that dissemination and other slow forms of cultural change are unworthy and impractical, and produce the framework of the second principle (that is, that micro-processes in the classroom can be controlled, changed, and improved by financial, organizational, and legal macro-processes). This principle means that teaching will change through threat of school closure and headteacher replacement, and through encouraging and reinforcing practice of the deepest intricate quality, often through behaviourist strategies such as financial compensation and competition.

Heyneman (2009) completes this issue in his analysis of school choice worldwide. Congruent with Baker's globalized educational values, Heyneman suggests that choice is the manifestation of free-market ideology and practice in education policy but is also a common demand by parents and is strongly correlated with social cohesion. This is one of the most controversial issues in the field of education policy. One argument is that parents do not want to choose a school, having to immerse themselves in a complex process of understanding the relevant data. What they want is a decent school nearby:

> Decent schools are those where pupils learn a lot about real things, generally enjoy school, do reasonably well in their tests ... behave well, feel safe, and are properly guided and cared for by teachers and adults around them.
>
> (Green, 2005: 5)

Contrary to this, neoliberal researchers such as Le Grand (2005) assert that it is only in a choice-quasi-market situation, that equality of choice will be available for the disenfranchised and marginalized groups, for the well-to-do always have choice even in a controlled system that assigns specific schools to specific students.

According to Ball, this:

> ... unstable, uneven but apparently unstoppable flood of closely interrelated reform ideas is permeating and reorienting education systems in diverse social and political locations with very different histories. This convergence has given rise to what can be called a *generic global policy ensemble* that rests on a set of basic and common *policy technologies* ... the

> components of this ensemble and the workings of these technologies [are] ... *the market, management* and *performativity*.
>
> (Ball, 2008a: 39)

This paradigm, Ball (2008a: 40) explains, is based on the following principles:

1. efficiency, effectiveness and quality
2. decentralization of power to schools
3. cost-effectiveness in the provision of public funds
4. setting targets and standards – also known as a high-stakes system
5. centralized strategies to respond to external pressures and demands.

All this could not have been accomplished without the major role of technology (Baker, 2009; Zhao and Lei, 2009). Technology facilitates free, swift streams of large amounts of information on educational achievement and statistics that help international and national organizations, as well as the general public, to closely monitor and compare education policy outcomes in various countries, and hold politicians and decision-makers accountable – whether in reality or theoretically. This can create a false sense of control in a system that is sometimes controlled more by powerful external forces than by local ones.

One of the results of the convergence of neoliberalism and globalization in policymaking, and of widespread neoliberal ideas, is, as mentioned earlier, 'a paradox of intense state interventions and government by elites and "experts" in a world where the state is supposed not to be interventionist' (Harvey, 2005: 69). Such interventions occur in the field of education policy that is harnessed to the task of disseminating neoliberal ideas and managerial ideology. This controlled planning of education aimed to achieve ideological and political goals is new, and is connected to the forces of the globalized economy.

Neoliberalism and globalization are gradually becoming the antithesis of Social Democracy and localism. When translated into the language and practice of education reform, this means the international, standardized, one-size-fits-all, decentralized competitive systems, versus local, tailored, bottom-up solutions crafted and led by professionals in the field and by communities with a 'soft' approach to accountability and blame culture. Figure 2.1 shows this growing dichotomy.

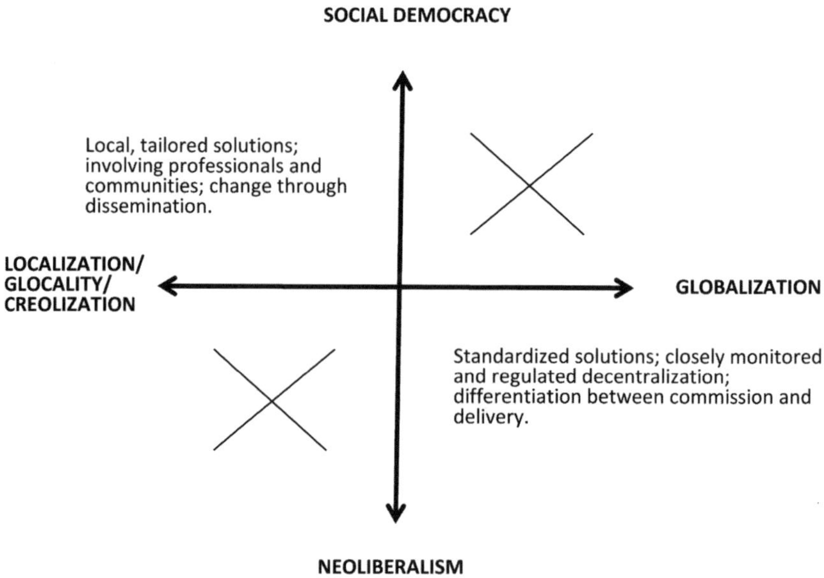

Figure 2.1: Law-based reform between ideology and locality

The ethical and philosophical foundation of law-based education reform

The late William Boyd, a leading researcher on education policy in the US, has been a champion of the idea, ideal, and policy of public education. According to Boyd (2003):

> The ideology of the governance of public schools is deeply committed to a belief in a democratic system of 'common' public schools, operated as well as financed by the government, that provides a standardized curriculum, treats everyone equally (irrespective of social class, culture, race or religion) and is accountable to a publicly elected school board. As part of a nonprofit public organization, public schools are (ideally) supposed to be insulated from both politics and competition. They should not compete with one another for students or resources, or use selective or 'elitist' admission policies ... This makes 'magnet' schools, charter schools, and other departures from the norm problematic.
>
> (Boyd, 2003: 5)

This powerful statement epitomizes the romantic perception of public education in the United States, a perception less evident in England, but a useful one for the study of law-based reform. Nevertheless, empirical evidence for the information in this statement is at best questionable. The commitment to a democratic system of common public schools and a standardized curriculum may exist. However, three decades of research – from the basic US studies by Coleman *et al.* (1966) and Jencks (1972) to the most advanced and updated UK research (Fitz *et al.*, 2006; Gillborn, 2008) – cast serious doubts on this 'equal treatment'. Public education *was* perhaps insulated from politics, relatively, which is another agreeable point. But indeed the main virtue of this system – equality – was challenged even when systems were centralized and uniform. Perhaps the best example for a rude awakening from this myth is to be found in the sombre words of Stephen Ball:

> There is no going back to a past in which the public sector as a whole worked well and worked fairly in the interests of all learners. There was no such past. ... it is difficult to deny that some education businesses do some things well, and perhaps better than some of the public sector, and do enhance the lives and opportunities of some young and not-so-young people. This is not a defence of the private sector as a whole but it may involve an acceptance that some kinds of private sector participation are more defensible than others and that some public sector 'work' is not as defensible as all that.
>
> (Ball, 2007: 187)

Ball further calls to 'Move beyond the tyrannies of improvement, efficiency, and standards to recover a language of and for education articulated in terms of ethics, moral obligations and values' (ibid. 191).

This is an important declaration from a leading critical sociologist, and, what is more important with regard to the above words, from someone who has been a leading opponent of decentralization, privatization, and managerialist policies in education reform for at least two decades. But Ball de-mystifies the romantic idea of public education as Boyd expressed it, and in a way tears the mask from the debate on decentralization. This does not mean that Ball is for managerialist and neoliberal practices, but that things are far more complicated and less straightforward than they seem, the solutions being out of our immediate grasp and the divisions between good and bad not being as trivial as they are sometimes presented by either side of the dispute. Still, public education advocates believe in the Dworkinian value of 'equality of resources' (Dworkin, 2000) as the underpinning of 'sovereign virtue'. Dworkin is a strong supporter of affirmative-action admissions policy. He argues that acceptance to an educational institution should be based not on the background and previous achievements of candidates but on their prospective academic future:

> In a racist society people are indeed rejected absolutely for who they are and it is therefore natural that racial classifications should be seen as capable of inflicting a special form of injury. But it would nevertheless be perverse to disallow the use of such classifications to help combat the

> racism that is the true and continuing cause for that injury. The special psychological character of race is not a fixed fact to which policy must always defer. It is a product and sign of racism and it must not be permitted to protect the racism that has generated it.
>
> (Dworkin, 2000: 407)

The call for social justice is also at the core of Barry's (2005) thinking:

> Manifestly in a society dedicated to the pursuit of social justice, intensive research efforts would be devoted to finding out the best ways to overcome the disadvantages that children carry with them into the school system – and continue to suffer from – as a consequence of their home and neighbourhood environment. In fact, the conventional (and convenient) wisdom has been that 'there is almost nothing that money spent on schools can do to improve outcomes'.
>
> (Ibid. 55)

Barry sums up the debate on social justice as a key desirable virtue of capitalist societies:

> The left has one enormous advantage over the right: the case for radical change … can be shown to flow from widely accepted premises without any need to indulge in obfuscation or lies. All that has to be done is to clarify the logical implications of the principles that people maintain they espouse and relate them to facts. In contrast, the only honest case that can be made for the agenda of the right is that it suits the people who benefit from it very nicely.
>
> (Ibid. 234)

Law-based education reform drifts, therefore, between the two poles. One pole is that of a neoliberal globalized economy that dictates school denaturalization and managerialism. This needs legislation to re-regulate and reorganize the system, as will be presented onwards in this chapter. The other pole is that of social justice where legislation can weaken or control savage competition and minimize unfair advantages among those who are more well-off, in acquiring education through public funds.

The political, organizational and institutional context of law-based education reform

The results of the three principles of education reform, and the growing influence of neoliberalism and the globalized economy, shape education systems worldwide (Cohen *et al.*, 2007). This is where the concept of 'educational regimes' (Manzer, 2003) comes in. Reaching over and beyond the professionals' control and involvement in education, and directly addressing these three groups: upper classes, the 'articulate middle class' (Brighouse *et al.*, 2002), and ethnic minorities, the regime offers to 'free' them, and perhaps the public as a whole, from the 'clutches' of public education. This is done by a mixture of legislation and managerial practices that view ethical and pedagogical issues as bureaucratic and technical:

> An educational regime is a stable ordering of political principles and public authority for the governance of education. An educational regime is instituted, first, as a collective response to a primary problem of political economy. Second, its coherence and purpose depend on widespread acceptance of a core of political ideas that may derive from a dominant political ideology but more often will be created from conflict and compromise among the proponents of opposing doctrinal positions. Third, an educational regime implies a distinctive set of public policies covering both the governance and the provision of education.
>
> (Manzer, 2003: 3–4)

This conflict is part of a growing debate on how education should be run. Manzer differentiates between social democracy, conservatism, and liberalism; the latter is also divided by Manzer into 'utilitarian liberalism' and 'ethical liberalism' ideologies *within* educational regimes. Utilitarians focus on markets as the driving force of change, and shun ideas that look at society as a mosaic of groups that do not receive an equal shot at the goods handed-out. Bottery (2000) deepens this analysis, using the metaphor of 'steering and rowing' (ibid. 31). While social democracy sees its role as committed to both, and sees markets as being opposed to the public good, Conservatives ('New Right') see markets as the 'natural, moral, and economic way' by which education should be governed; and 'new modernizers' ('ethical utilitarians' according to Manzer) believe in 'steering, limited rowing' – that is, regulated markets within strong centralized frameworks. The uniform model, connected to the idea of 'public instruction' or public education, is embedded in:

> The ideas of universality and inequality that constituted the core commitment to public education as social policy within the welfare state …
>
> (Manzer, 2003: 248)

Meanwhile, the 'multiform model', also called 'communitarian':

> … adopted policies of separate schools and communal self-governance to create educational regimes that would be consociations of denominational, linguistic, or racial and ethnic communities.
>
> (Ibid. 325)

This de-professionalization of education and its harnessing to neoliberal politics and agendas is a central facilitator to further educational legislation. Legislation allows governments to circumvent both civil servants and professionals, and to implement reforms swiftly in large systems – in harmony with the second principle of education reform. Legislation also helps in the regulation of a decentralized system, and in governing in such a system in which many central agencies are no longer part of the government itself but often some kind of 'outsourced' power and control. Decentralized, quasi-marketized (Levačić and Woods, 2000), and quasi-privatized (Ball, 2007) education needs a good deal more supplementary regulatory attention than a system where both commission and also delivery of education services rest in the hands of national or local government, where schools are owned and run by national or local governments that are also the employers of teachers and headteachers. The government is implementing reform that is underlain by an ideology that public education should be run not by publicly-elected institutions and authorities (in other words, the ministry of education or the local education authorities) but by a maze of private or semi-private organizations.

Why has there been more educational law in the last few decades, certainly in England but elsewhere as well? The answer lies within the change in education policy, for instance decentralization, and in managerialist patterns that evolve from the traits of globalization and need further regulation. Regulation is an important part of modern legal and economic theory. Anthony Ogus, a leading theorist on regulation, presents education as an 'impure public good' that benefits both the individual and society:

> Clearly a person who receives such a commodity is the primary beneficiary and the price that she is willing to pay for it should, in theory at least, reflect that benefit ... But other members of society also gain from the provision of education ... there are assumed to be material gains to present and future generations from a better-trained workforce, education may encourage socially responsible behaviour and political stability through a more informed electorate, and ... cultural heritage may be enriched.
>
> (Ogus, 2004: 35)

The public interest requires, therefore, not only public funds but forms of regulation that monitor the quality of the service implemented, as this type of public service is prone to market failure (Ogus, 2004; Teubner, 1986). Such a failure can be the result of various variables and progressions. One is the difficulty of creating a neoclassic market as described earlier, with people reaching decisions based on 'bounded rationality' (Ogus, 2004), a term that represents the limited capability of the consumer to 'receive, store, and process information' (Ogus, 2004: 41). Other difficulties egress from legislation being over-politicized and over-socialized (Teubner, 1986). All these can be summed up as the tendency among legislators to adopt a one-dimensional viewpoint of the regulated arena, and a linear theory on legislation that presupposes the power of legislation to be one that can control all relevant variables – whether independent, dependent, or mediating – so as to reach a certain planned, expected or desired outcome. Ogus explains that not only do consumers lack the necessary knowledge to reach rational decisions, but legislators also lack such knowledge, and often do not realize the intricacies, complexities, social forces, or behaviour that 'tint' the processes of reform and change and their outcomes. This is categorized by Ogus as a 'synoptic delusion' in which:

> ... the centralized pool of information on which rulers must rely for regulatory measures could never replicate the widely dispersed fragments of knowledge which individuals use in pursuance of their own ends and therefore could never be adequate to anticipate all the variety of circumstances to which specific regulation must be applied.
>
> (Ogus, 2004: 57)

Governing through non-government agencies, a common trait of law-based reform in education, is therefore sometimes a fad, as the mere formation of the regulatory body creates considerable 'hype' and sometimes a public feeling of freshness and control over institutions and officials – LEAs, schools, and headteachers, for instance – that will, once and for all, 'teach them a lesson'. The fantasy is that the regulatory body will supply the consumers with accurate information that is simple to understand and use, and that it will praise the worthy and blame the incompetent. But after a while, Ogus explains, this might change:

> Attention is transferred to other subjects, public support is lacking and the agency becomes vulnerable to domination by the regulated interests. ... the information required by the agency may be obtainable only from the regulated industries; lack of expertise in the subject-matter may mean that the agency has to recruit its officials from those industries; and the industries may threaten the agency with costly time wasting appeals should it fail to be 'cooperative'.
>
> (Ogus, 2004: 58)

In addition, regulation of complex social services – where process (for example admissions policies, regulation, or types of schools) can itself be harmful, quite independently of any harm or benefits caused by outcomes, and where it is difficult to agree on the 'common' characters of what constitutes success or failure (such as minimizing SES-based gaps, excellence, and so on) – is rarely simple or unobtrusive. Regulation itself carries burdens of bureaucracy, costly audit, and reporting mechanisms that: (1) minimize the resources left for carrying out the service itself (the latter often being constantly short on funding); and (2) change the culture of the regulated institution to a point where the delivery of the service is jeopardized. The more decentralized the system, and the more quasi-privatization and quasi-marketization are becoming fundamentals of education policy and reform, the more the government needs to consider issues of regulation and governance.

Governance has become a major concern of educational policy research in the last decade, as findings show that the planned or envisaged outcomes of policy disappoint policymakers and politicians over and over again (Glatter, 2002, 2003; Hill, 2003; Payne, 2008), as Hill explains:

> Optimists about governance think rules can control just enough to allow professional judgment to be used effectively. Standards-based reform, today's mainstream approach to improvement of public education, takes this 'just enough guidance' approach. Its supporters urge states and localities to strip away all requirements that do not promote good instruction ... Supporters ... criticize the extant governance system for getting in the way of good instruction. Pessimists about governance doubt that rules can be so perfectly aligned ... What is not controlled – what is literally left to chance – is whether teachers, principals, and parents retain the capacity, resources, and freedom required to provide and to support good instruction. Pessimists ... view governance as inevitably a squeaky wheel system.
>
> (Ibid. 62)

One of the most stimulating theories of governance with regard to policy initiative and change is that of Kingdon. In his ground-breaking study, Kingdon (2003: 206) concluded that government agendas are the result 'of considerable doses of messiness, accident, fortuitous coupling and dumb luck'. Change is not the result of careful planning and translation of agendas to law and budgets, but occurs when 'policy windows' open. Such windows of opportunity are crucial for new policy enterprises that can only occur when a convolutedly woven quilt of discerned problems meets alternative solutions, and when policy communities (made up of interest groups, academics, and consultants) advocate proposals that produce streams of ideas that eventually take form when policy windows open.

Glatter's definition of governance, 'governing without government' (Glatter, 2002: 226), is helpful because it grasps, in a short phrase, the sometimes necessary but futile attempts of governments and public authorities to regulate public services under a threat or trend or even public demand (from a social-democratic viewpoint) to decentralize and privatize services to allow choice and accountability (from a neoliberal and globalized economy viewpoint).

What is law-based education reform?

The area, or field of study, of law-based reform appeared in educational research mainly in the 1990s and mainly in the US (DeMitchell and Fossey, 1997; Heubert

1997, 1999) and in the UK (Gibton, 2004b; Harris 1993; 2007). Figure 2.2 (based on Gibton, 2004b), presents the disciplinary and conceptual roots of law-based education reform.

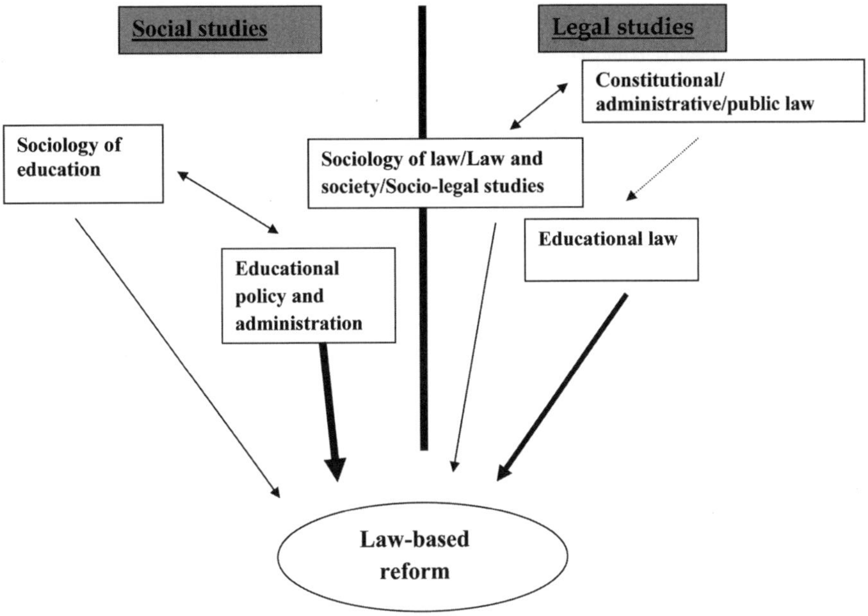

Note: arrow widths represent strength of affinity.

Figure 2.2: Law-based reform and its disciplinary, theoretical and conceptual origins

The field is quite separate from the adjacent area of educational law. Educational law (sometimes referred to in the US as 'school law') is the legal field that deals with legal aspects of education (Ford, *et al.*, 2005; Imber and van Geel, 2010; Ruff, 1999; La Morte, 2011). Most of it is derived from the larger fields of constitutional and administrative law, both part of public law. From the constitutional point of view, educational law is related to issues such as human and civil rights, children's rights, and also the evident connection between education, enlightenment, knowledge, and democracy. As education is a public service in most – and sometimes all – of its aspects, running, and finance, it is part of administrative law. Other areas of educational law are derived from civil and criminal law, for instance, issues of pupil safety that have to do with criminal and civil negligence. But education law is, just like other fields studied and taught in law faculties, about legislation and litigation. Law-based education reform is an interdisciplinary field of study, situated between law and social studies, specifically socio-legal studies (Ewick and Silbey, 1998). I believe the sociological side is stronger than the legal side. Law-based reform, as a field, is interested in the sociology of how educational law is involved, both formally and informally, in an overt and covert manner, in the fields of educational policy and administration. It is concerned with the question of how educational law becomes a policy tool, and how it influences structures and practice in education. It is also interested in the political aspects of educational law. The sociology of educational policy and the sociology of law are therefore related: (1) in the sense that both fields are concerned with the politics of legal language and process; (2) in the sense that both fields look into the gaps between the perceived, 'sacred', and 'perfect' images that law produces among laypersons, and often among members of the legal and educational professions as well; and (3) from the critical viewpoint of sociology that looks at the law from a perspective of power relations, hegemony, and oppression.

Both the sociology of law (Jackson, 1985) and the sociology of education (Ball, 1994; Boyd, 1988; Hannaway, 2003; Smrekar and Goldring, 2009) treat educational law and educational policy, consecutively, as a type of discourse. Both are treated as part of politics. This insight is often looked upon with dismay, not to say anger or perhaps despair, by large audiences. Education policy and, even more so, law, are often seen as the stronghold, or possibly the last resort, of any likelihood of changing the important field of education. The idea that law and policy can influence education a lot less than people think, and that the correlation between structures and procedures that are advanced by legislation and policy, is, at best, problematic, causes a grim awakening among many (Ogus, 2004). Consequently the study of law-based reform evolved from all these concerns. The field is intersected *in the seams* between law-making, policy, and politics. Traditionally, socio-legal studies have long been interested in how people's perception of the law and of legality impact on the law's capability to influence, in return, human behaviour, and institutional or organizational structures:

> This formulation of consciousness as cultural practice and specifically as participation in the construction of social relations attempts to keep alive the tension between structure and agency, constraint and choice. It seeks to capture people's sense of purposes, stakes, and constraints within a broad ethnographic domain. ... Every time a person interprets some event in terms of legal concepts or terminology – whether to applaud or to criticize, whether to appropriate or to resist – legality is produced. The production may include innovations as well as faithful replication. Either way, repeated invocation of the law sustains its capacity to comprise social relations.
>
> (Ewick and Silbey, 1998: 45)

Such conceptualization and perception, structuring and restructuring, are closely connected to both ideology and hegemony, two terms that will be used in the analysis of findings further on in this study. These terms are explained by Ewick and Silbey in their already classic work that set the ground for qualitative research on how people see and act upon their perspicacity of law and legality:

> To what extent are structures ideological, or, to put it differently, to what extent do structures embed power? How does the distribution of resources and relative access to legitimating cultural schemas produce and preserve social inequality and relative powerlessness? A related question concerns the extent to which structures are hegemonic.
>
> (Ibid. 225)

The researchers and theoreticians in the field of law-based education reform are usually trained in law (as understanding the unique language of law may be important) and often in social studies and/or educational administration as well. They habitually belong to faculties of education but are also adjunct lecturers, or permanent staff, in faculties of law.

Conclusion: the conflicts of law-based education reform

Summing up the motivations for law-based education reform shows that they are twofold. On the one hand, decentralization and standards-based reform, and the introduction of quasi-privatized forms of schooling (such as charter schools, academies, free schools, vouchers, and so on), the decline of public education in its Boydian sense, and the deepening involvement of non-government and non-LA organizations in education (for example NGOs, academic institutions, businesses, or denominational organizations), require legislation for reasons of regulation and control of non-government and non-public provision of education. On the other hand, a social justice approach to education (Barry, 2005; Dworkin, 2000), and especially desegregation and equal funding policies, require legislation to ensure equitable procedures that advance equality in the provision of education. This means that both types of reform, whether managerialist or centralized – however contradictory in their ideological backgrounds and implementation – require legislation. As education is a necessity for the existence and flourishing of democratic society, equipping its citizens with the necessary tools to judge and choose – including between agendas, policies, and public figures – legislation is a tool that plays a vital role in assuring that this service is provided for all. In the near past, theories such as John Rawls's (1971) notion of fairness dominated legal thought on democracy. Nussbaum, who offers an updated model of 'capability' that challenges the Rawlsian contractual definition of justice, presents ten 'human capabilities' (ibid. 76–8), some of which are exceptionally relevant to public education's goals:

> Senses, imagination and thought ... and to do these things in a 'truly human' way, a way informed and cultivated by an adequate education,

> including, and by no means limited to, literacy and basic mathematical and scientific training. ... experiencing and producing works and events of one's own choice, religious, literary, musical ... Being able to use one's mind in ways protected by guarantees of freedom of expression with respect to both political and artistic speech, and freedom of religion exercise ...
>
> Emotions ... not having one's emotional development blighted by overwhelming fear and anxiety ... (supporting this capability means supporting forms of human association that can be shown to be crucial in their development.)
>
> Practical reason. Being able to form a conception of the good and to engage in critical reflection about the planning of one's life.
>
> Affiliation. Being able to live with and towards others ... to engage in various forms of social interaction; to be able to imagine the situation of another ... Having the social bases of self-respect and non-humiliation; being able to be treated as a dignified being whose worth is equal to that of others. This entails provisions of nondiscrimination on the basis of race, sex, sexual orientation, ethnicity, caste, religion, national origin.
>
> (Nussbaum, 2006: 76–8)

Nussbaum's main argument against the Rawlsian (Rawls, 1971) conception of justice is that its definition should be freed from mutuality:

> The capabilities approach denies that principals of justice have to secure mutual advantage. Even when noncooperation is possible and even habitual (because domination is so easy), justice is good for everyone. ... Justice is also one of our ends and we limit our pursuit of it too much when we think of it as the outcome of a contract for mutual advantage, however morally constructed and constrained.
>
> (Ibid. 90)

This foundation of a theory of justice in general is tightened by H. Brighouse's (2006) critique of the 'human capital theory approach' that assumes general benefits for all as the result of training pupils to be productive workers. Instead, he offers an alternative, much wider, set of goals, very much in the footsteps of Nussbaum, based on striving for autonomy and a flourishing life for all. Under these goals schools should, Brighouse explains, attempt to educate for a self-sufficient economic life, but this should be the entering precondition for good education, and absolutely not its ultimate goal:

> ... even if we knew how to design schooling to promote growth (which we don't) we'd do better to use schooling to enable children to interact with the economy in ways that facilitate their flourishing ...
>
> (Ibid. 41)

Such advanced theories of justice place a heavy burden on law-based education reform, because they view the provision of education as insufficient unless it benefits all to their highest capabilities. Neoliberal ideology sees education in a much more restricted capacity. Chubb and Moe's (1990) classic work did an important job in emphasizing these contradictions:

> Democratic institutions allocate decisionmaking rights by attaching public authority to elected and appointed positions of government ... and by setting out rules that specify who can occupy these positions and how the authority attached to them must be exercised. ... In this sense, democracy is essentially coercive. The winners get to use public authority to impose their policies on the losers. ... What makes this peculiar form of coercion broadly acceptable is that public authority does not belong to any individual or group. It is up for grabs.
>
> (Ibid. 28–9)

While Rawls and Nussbaum emphasize the 'justice' aspect of democratic institutions, Chubb and Moe focus on the political aspect. Chubb's and Moe's important contribution to this discussion is the distinction between 'politics' and 'markets', in which:

> Governments must create a legal framework that specifies and enforces property rights. They must use their public authority, in other words, to impose a system of rules for determining who owns what property and for assigning to owners the authority to make certain choices about its disposition.
>
> (Ibid. 29)

In the book he edited, Heubert (1999), who is one of the founders of research on law-based education reform and perhaps coined the term, gathered together a formidable group of writers and researchers in the field (such as Gary Orfield who writes on desegregation, Paul Weckstein on quality education, and Molly McUsic on school finance). According to Heubert, US education has benefited from the outcomes of law-based reform, which can be an effective tool for advancing values in education. This is especially true when decentralization and standards-based reforms are the crux of change. When equity and fairness are jeopardized, legislation may indeed be the remedy. He does, however, point at problems. One problem is the gap between lawmakers and educators – the gap between policy, law, and pedagogy

(Reglin, 1992; Weckstein, 1999). Legislators tend to see the educators as conservative and outdated in the ways of the world, especially in the economic and managerial ways of thinking that are so pronounced these days. Meanwhile, educators feel that policymakers have little understanding of life in schools and the constraints of their work. Heubert insists that:

> Poor collaboration between educators, lawyers, researchers and parents makes it difficult to use the law to advance important educational aims. Poor collaboration also leads to unnecessary lawsuits, which can cost thousands or even millions of dollars and can reduce significantly the funds that would otherwise be available for other purposes. Court orders and consent decrees, usually entered when school authorities are unwilling or unable to address problems on their own, can hamstring educators for decades, dramatically reducing discretion and flexibility in addressing central questions of education and school leadership …
>
> (Heubert, 1999: 7)

Weckstein is also cautiously optimistic on the ability of law-based reform to effect fundamental changes in school reform. He cautions that the problematic experiences educators have with school reform prompt them to circumvent it as a tool for success. The increased emphasis on legislative mandates is part of the attempt by policymakers to succeed better in implementing reform and forcing educators to comply. This vicious cycle should be broken – and the sooner the better. So in the face of this messy situation of mutual mistrust and suspicion, the solution lies in the adoption of a three-stage process:

> 1. Stimulating demand for change by parents who, aided by educators and advocates, understand what to look for in schools and their rights to obtain it; 2. Building school and staff capacity – by combining adequate resources with a committed focus on the kinds of pedagogy, curriculum-embedded assessment, teacher preparation … supporting structures … that the research shows stimulate high-level student learning; and 3. Enforcing accountability for implementing policy …
>
> (Weckstein, 1999: 363)

These conflicts will be the main pathway for exploring law-based reform in England in this book. The next chapter presents and analyses, through these conflicts and theories, three cases of law-based education reform: England, the United States, and Israel.

Chapter 3

Law-based education reform from theory to practice: Three cases

Introduction

This chapter provides a concise analysis and comparison of three examples of law-based education reform, from England, the US, and Israel. The grounds for this choice are twofold. First, all three are under the apparent 'rule' of an 'educational regime' (Manzer, 2003), as their governments attempt to harness education policy and reform to neoliberal agendas, promoted by international organizations, such as the OECD, of which the three countries are members. Second, their localized versions of law-based reform are quite distinct from each other, therefore providing a worthwhile case for comparison and discussion. While English education policy is dominated by frequent and extensive legislation, with hardly any intervention by high courts in government policy, the US model balances between updated legislation and an active intervention of supreme courts, at both state and federal level. In Israel, scarce and outdated legislation is often overshadowed by active courts and policy that occurs outside of the law. The three countries also have very dissimilar models of central versus municipal/local control over education. The presentation of the three cases is not merely informative, but is rather a combination of information and structure together with socio-legal comments, the latter being the main point of this chapter. The analysis will attempt to show how uniform international and global forces bear upon legislation on education policy in the three countries, and also how glocalization or creolization (Phillips and Ochs, 2004; Robertson, 1995; Stewart, 2007) occurs in law-based reform. Special attention is given to the theme of this book: law, politics, and fairness.

England

England has by far the most frequent and comprehensive education legislation of any country in the world. The following table presents the major pieces of legislation, between 1988 and 2011.

Table 3.1: Law-based reform in England 1988–2011: Main components

Legislation	Type	Main contents/policy	Politics
1988 Education Reform Act (ERA)	Primary	Establishing GM schools; parental choice; establishing National Curriculum.	Conservative governments wanted to weaken LEA control over schools.
1992 Education (Schools) Act	Primary	Establishing Ofsted in practice – by defining HMCI's authority and responsibilities; further powers and arrangements for GM schools.	The fourth side of the square of change under the Conservatives: the NC, 'opting-out' and GM schools, school choice and standards.
1993 Education Act (EA)	Primary	Strengthening Ofsted (power of special measures etc.); setting funding authorities; further definitions of GM schools.	Re-centralization of school inspection and control.
1996 Education Act (EA)	Primary	Establishing Key Stages 1–4 and standardized assessment of achievement in schools, ages 5–16.	Attempts by the new Conservative administration (Major) to boost schools' results and hold them accountable.
1997 DfEE white paper 'Excellence in Schools'	Primary	Six principles of education policy for the Labour administration: 'there will be unrelenting pressure on schools and teachers for improvement' (art. 4) and 'standards matter more than structures' (art. 17).	Labour government proposes yet another revolution in educational policy that 'previews' 1998 SSFA.

Table 3.1 cont.

Legislation	Type	Main contents/policy	Politics
1998 Standards & Frameworks Act (SSFA) (and Circular 10/99 'Social Inclusion – Pupil Support')	Primary	Increasing and widening Ofsted powers (including placing schools under 'special measures'); appeal procedures regarding admissions; new policy regarding permanent exclusions including appeal procedures establishing school governing bodies; setting Educational Action Zones (EAZs).	Labour government begins a 4th major policy change in a decade: government turns regulator.
1998–1999 QCA publications	Circulars, directives	Establishing National Literacy & Numeracy strategies as part of the National Curriculum and requirements in Key Stages 1–4.	Further Labour government pressure on schools and teachers and introduction of standards.
2000 Education (School Teacher Appraisal) (England) Regulations	Secondary	Establishing performance management and threshold assessment procedures.	Fulfilling the promise of relentless pressure on teachers – responsibility for educational results now lies within the school.
Learning and Skills Act, 2000	Primary	Established City Academies as a version of CTCs. Improving inspections and teaching in post-16 FE. Establishing Learning and Skills Councils for FE.	

Table 3.1 cont.

Legislation	Type	Main contents/policy	Politics
Education Act, 2002	Primary	Defining the powers and structure of City Academies (formerly CTCs and Specialized Schools, now renamed academies – sec. 67). Strengthening and defining the powers of schools' governing bodies as the actual 'board of directors' of the school. Allowing federations of schools.	Strengthening the further splits in England's school system, lessening the role of comprehensive schooling and strengthening the segregated and elitist trends in the post-2000 law-based reforms.
Children Act, 2004	Primary	Consolidation of child services under the Local Authority (LA), creating a 'one-stop-shop' of childcare and education. The act began a process of placing these services under Ofsted inspections, later strengthened by the EIA, 2006.	Extending the influence and power of the ministry (then DfES) on new services.
Higher Standards, Better Schools For All: More choice for parents and pupils (white paper, 10/05) presented to parliament 01/06/2005	Primary	Establishing Trust Schools; further admissions freedom to secondary schools; encouraging banding; LEA to become commissioner rather than provider.	Weakening the LEA, strengthening school networks. Further segregation.

Table 3.1 cont.

Legislation	Type	Main contents/policy	Politics
Education Act 2005	Primary	Impotent additions and definitions of the power of Ofsted, HMCI, HMIs, the nature of school and LEA inspections, schools causing concern placed under special measures. Renaming the TTA as the TDA, and strengthen its independence as a QUANGO.	Reasserting and widening central government's powers of audit, supervision, and inspection.
Childcare Act, 2006	Primary	Implementing and broadening 'every child matters' policy to early years education and creating arrangements for childcare of working parents.	Further extension of education responsibility of the state to early years. Lately (July 2010) discussed by the Childcare Commission (the Teather/Miller commission).
Education and Inspections Act, 2006	Primary	Balancing between academies and LEAs, beginning the inspections policy of charter-types schools (academies and trust schools). Strengthening the admissions code and the schools adjudicators. Naming Ofsted and formalizing its statutory status on top of that granted in 1992–3 to HMCI (sec. 118).	The last act between the Blair and Brown administrations.

Table 3.1 cont.

Legislation	Type	Main contents/policy	Politics
Education and Skills Act 2008	Primary	LEA's roles on attendance and standards; SEN and transport; parental contracts (part 4 secs. 41–5); adult and FE education; raising the age of compulsory education to 18 (part 1 secs 1–9).	An extension of the Brown administration's policy that included extended school days and 'Sure Start' (launched 1998).
Apprenticeships, Skills, Children and Learning Act 2009	Primary	Establishing OfQUAL, establishing the post and appointing the Chief Executive of Skills Funding; establishing The Young People's Learning Agency For England.	Strengthening FE opportunities. Widening the range of LEA responsibilities in 14–19 education.
Academies Act, 2010	Primary	Further spread of academies, establishing free schools, freeing academies and free schools of training, curricular, and enrolment (admissions) requirements.	A swift move of 'branding' the system by the Conservative–Liberal-Democrat government.
The Importance of Teaching – white paper 2010	Primary	Further autonomy of schools, heads, and teachers. Powers of discipline on pupils. Introducing teaching schools and free schools. Introducing EBacc.	Implementation of Conservative political and educational ideology.

Table 3.1 cont.

Legislation	Type	Main contents/policy	Politics
Education Act, 2011	Primary	Implement the white paper. Weaken the powers of schools adjudication and the admissions code.	Further weakening of LAs and introduction of new types of LA-free schools.

This is perhaps the ultimate and most far-reaching example of an 'educational regime' (Manzer, 2003). Although English education legislation is, traditionally, attributed to the Thatcher Conservative administration period, its sources are rooted in the last Labour government before the Conservatives took power. Prime Minister Callaghan's notable speech, delivered at Oxford's Ruskin College on 18 October 1976, provided a presentiment of the changing times – perhaps overdue as the impending change of administration proved – and carried a sombre foreboding all at once. His words lay the foundation of England's law-based reform that began only during the following Conservative government and was adopted some 20 years later by his own Labour party (by then under its new title, 'New Labour' – not entirely disconnected from issues of education policy):

> I must thank all those who have inundated me with advice: some helpful and others telling me less politely to keep off the grass, to watch my language ... It is almost as though some people would wish that the subject matter and purpose of education should not have public attention focused on it: nor that profane hands should be allowed to touch it. ... I cannot believe that this is a considered reaction.

These words are the beginning of the realization, later the neoliberal draught, that sees education as something too vital to be left in the hands of educators, and holds that government should reach 'above' and 'over' educators to change education according to some real or presumed public opinion. Callaghan continues:

> If everything is reduced to such phrases as 'educational freedom' versus state control, we shall get nowhere. I repeat that parents, teachers, learned and professional bodies, representatives of higher education and both sides of industry, together with the government, all have an important part to play in formulating and expressing the purpose of education and the standards that we need.

These words also predict and suggest a new form of governance. The beginning of the business world's growing influence on education policy is also becoming a pathway to change:

> I recognise that teachers occupy a special place in these discussions because of their real sense of professionalism and vocation about their work. But I am concerned on my journeys to find complaints from industry that new recruits from the schools sometimes do not have the basic tools to do the job that is required. ... To the teachers I would say that you must satisfy the parents and industry that what you are doing meets their requirements and the needs of our children. For if the public is not convinced then the profession will be laying up trouble for itself in the future.

Finally, Prime Minister Callaghan ironically lays out the poignant basics of law-based reform under Prime Minister Thatcher:

> Let me repeat some of the fields that need study because they cause concern. There are the methods and aims of informal instruction, the strong case for the so-called 'core curriculum' of basic knowledge; next, what is the proper way of monitoring the use of resources in order to maintain a proper national standard of performance; then there is the role of the inspectorate in relation to national standards; and there is the need to improve relations between industry and education.

These words outline the foundations of a high-stakes monitored system with a national curriculum. The important factors of the future reforms that are not mentioned in this 1976 Ruskin speech are decentralization, 'freeing' schools from the powers of local authorities and local government, and open enrolment.

The resemblance between Callaghan's speech and the subsequent education policy of the Conservatives is echoed in the interviews that were conducted in this study. There was a disagreement between interviewees, beginning in 2001, as to whether New Labour's policy differed from that of its Conservative predecessors, but in 2011 a senior DfE civil servant said:

> It really depends how far one moves away in time, and adopts a satellite-view of education. At a smaller resolution one can trace a common set of denominators from Callaghan's Ruskin speech to Thatcher and Major, onwards to Blair, Blunkett, Barber, Adonis, and Brown, and right up to Gove's current office and Cameron's government.

Such an opinion certainly does not represent that of all interviewees and there was indeed a rift among them regarding the continuum or contrast between the various administrations and the two main political parties. Nevertheless this is a powerful statement that can be corroborated by the text of the Ruskin speech, and corresponds with Manzer's (2003), Bottery's (2000), and Ball's (2007) writing on globalized identical processes in education policy under neoliberal governments. This issue will be explored in depth later on in this book.

The Education Reform Act (ERA) of 1988 set the precedent for the postmodern wave of legislation, in a truly revolutionary manner (Harris, 1993; Whitty *et al.*, 1998). Distinctly, England's education system would never be the same after this law, that included both a 'mission statement' and an actual new policy setting. Since then, a new comprehensive education act has been presented to parliament every two and a half years, on average. Looking at these acts can tell the story of education policy in England in the last three decades. Harris (1993) noted that the 1988 ERA added several hundred new powers to those that were already part of the Secretary of State's authority and responsibility. Most major policy changes in England in the last 25 years have been introduced in white papers and, later on, in primary legislation. Not only has legislation been a major policy tool, but it has also been a declarative device for informing the public on planned change, alerting the media, perhaps igniting public debate, and advertising government engagement in, and concern for, education. Arrangements anchored in legislation have included: open enrolment and Grant-Maintained schools; the National curriculum; Ofsted and HMI's increased powers and involvement in inspection; admissions authorities and policies; the office and role of the Schools Adjudicator; Key Stages; and National Strategies.[1]

However, some important policy initiatives were not constituted through and by primary legislation. Two apparent examples, one from the Blair–Brown period and one from the Conservative–Liberal-Democrat government, are the Building Schools for the Future (BSF) project, and Pupil Premiums.[2,3] Others are partly embedded in primary legislation, with their main components implemented through regulative administrative and financial tools, such as community cohesion, and, again, admissions and admissions' appeals policy and directives. All of these involve lengthy documents, sometimes hundreds of pages long, containing hundreds of articles. Despite their size they are frequently replaced not only when a new government takes over, headed by the opposition party, but also within the administration of one party and even within one government's term and under the control of the same secretary of state. It is quite unimaginable that any officials, be they headteachers or heads of education for a local authority, not to mention heads of a board of school governors, who volunteer to perform the duty of governor, or senior staff members (such as heads of year or of a department) would be able to master all the relevant legal documents to perform their office.

The frequency of legislation is not the only problem for English policy implementers and educators. With it come contradictions and tensions that derive from the swift changes and revolutions meeting resistance from school culture – which moves at a much slower pace – and being converted into more gradual evolution and development, particularly when new laws set in. Of all the laws listed in Table 3.1, the most striking reform in terms of short-lasting substantial change was that of the Children Act, 2004. This law subordinated a range of major child services to the ministry (up until then called the Department for Education and Skills

– DfES – and from then to 2010 Department for Children, Schools, and Families – DCSF). Significantly, this subordination was further followed down along the system's hierarchy, from the department to local authorities and further on to schools. In one swift strike, case workers, doctors, and police became part of the school and the local education department. This happened in a situation where educators had very little idea or experience of how to handle the new authority and responsibility, each carrying with it a world of professional discourses and traditions, and with minimal instruction on how to organize people and roles. In light of this huge volume of change the system veered towards the new policy, embedded and anchored in legislation. Traditions, working methods, and habits that had evolved over decades, perhaps longer, were required to change immediately. Any basic understanding of public policy or organizational reform could easily predict the inherent hardships and therefore the period required to truly implement this reform – regardless, at this point, of its necessity or logic, which I have little expertise to comment on. But for the purpose of this book the amazing fact is that as early as 2006 this reform had begun to wither away when the Brown–Balls administration attempted to rearrange power once again. The final blow came with the Conservatives in 2010 when they reversed the role to their pre-2004 definitions, which meant a reinstatement of the various departments' previous powers (again without capability to judge this reform or its reversal), including the wry re-titling of the ministry to the straightforward 'Department for Education' (DfE) that it had been in 1996. One can only imagine the deep organizational, cultural, and normative repercussions of this change cycle.

Weighing up the situation in England's law-based education reform in 2012 leaves little hope of any restructuring of the fundamental rules of this deterministic system that mandates a new education law every two years as the basis for education policy and policy debate.

The United States

As the United States has fifty separate education systems, each under its own education legislation and often with an education clause in its constitution (in addition to federal education law, federal and state case-law), and over 14,000 independent school districts (Fuhrman *et al.*, 2007), mapping law-based education reform in its entirety in this chapter is inconceivable. Therefore after a short overview I will present several cases that are relevant to the particular study presented in this book.

> Educational policy ... must be based on such appropriate legal authority as federal or state constitutional or statutory provisions, state board of education or state department of education regulations, case law, or local school board policy. Several forces operate, however, that at times make it difficult for those who administer public schools to function in a lawful manner. These forces include a federal system of government composed of several levels and corresponding branches that bear on the educational

> enterprise, engaging and sometimes conflicting laws or policies emanating from these levels and branches, and a climate of legal uncertainty surrounding certain controversial issues that become highly politicized.
>
> (La Morte, 2002: 1)

Constitutional supervision of legislation and policy, that exists both at the federal and at the state levels, is a distinct characteristic of the US legal system. This means that the high courts can, and do, provide binding interpretation of legal arrangements and policy, and sometimes cancel legislation when they see it as opposed to higher constitutional provisions. The courts also proactively produce and implement education policy through extensive case law. The most dramatic of both the former and the latter is undeniably the historic decision of Brown v. Board of Education Topeka, dated 1954 (Thompson Ford, 2004; Balkin, 2002) in which the Supreme Court of the United States ruled that segregation between black and white pupils in public schools was unconstitutional, and stood contrary to the 14th Amendment's 'equal protection clause'.[4] In this case Chief Justice Earl Warren explained, somewhat dryly, why segregation was unacceptable in a twentieth century liberal democracy:

> Today, education is perhaps the most important function of state and local governments. Compulsory school attendance laws and the great expenditures for education both demonstrate our recognition of the importance of education to our democratic society. It is required in the performance of our most basic public responsibilities, even service in the armed forces. It is the very foundation of good citizenship. Today it is a principal instrument in awakening the child to cultural values, in preparing him for later professional training, and in helping him to adjust normally to his environment. In these days, it is doubtful that any child may reasonably be expected to succeed in life if he is denied the opportunity of an education. Such an opportunity, where the state has undertaken to provide it, is a right which must be made available to all on equal terms.
>
> We come then to the question presented: Does segregation of children in public schools solely on the basis of race, even though the physical facilities and other 'tangible' factors may be equal, deprive the children of the minority group of equal educational opportunities? We believe that it does.
>
> (Brown: 493)

In this simple paragraph Chief Justice Warren set a standard for fairness in education. It is romantic and debatable yet impregnable, and I will return to issues of integration many times in this book that alludes to 'fairness' in law-based reform in its title. The years following the Brown case showed that when desegregation policies moved from the deep south, where segregation was forbidden de jure, to North Eastern and Western states, where segregation was de facto, the federal courts were more reluctant to spread the Brown-based policy, and many court cases were local, and not as all-encompassing as Brown's (Perea, 2004; Thompson Ford, 2004; Minow, 2001; McUsic, 2004).[5] Nevertheless, two decades after Brown its results became unmistakable. When American demographics changed in the 1980s and onwards, as large numbers of African-Americans moved to Midwestern states and the growing Latino population and other immigrant groups caused the Brown 'formula' to become obsolete, new constructions became essential. When the court passed the ruling in 1954, integrating black and white pupils meant, to a satisfying degree of exactitude, integrating low and high SES populations. However, by the 1980s all this had changed, partly because of the success of the Brown-based policies (Wilkins, 2004). This meant that a different type of ruling became necessary, and indeed, new decisions, such as *Missouri v. Jenkins* (1995)[6] and Abbott v. Burke (1990)[7] replaced the actual bussing of pupil populations with monetary transfers from affluent communities to less affluent ones. But this was done only partially as federal courts have refused, since as far back as 1985, to compensate poor communities that received poor education due to low property-based taxation. The original Brown decision never went beyond municipal (district) boundaries, thus granting affluent groups of parents that turned to 'white flight' – and later 'bright flight' by affluent non-whites too – a form of 'immunity' from Brown-based desegregation bussing policies. The controversy is ongoing in American education policy research (Smrekar and Goldring, 2009) but has been somewhat finalized by another recent dramatic court decision,[8] in which an increasingly conservative court minimized the Brown precedent and ended a fragmentary process of 'freeing' school districts from the mandatory approval of their desegregation and attendance programmes, with the result that school districts turned 'unitary'.

Parallel to intensive policy-related case law, legislation has played an important role in education policy as well. All states have extensive school policy legislation that, from the mid-1960s onwards, has been overshadowed by extensive federal law-based reform that has become increasingly influential since the beginning of the millennium. Education was traditionally an inner-state matter, but in 1965 came the Elementary and Secondary Education Act (ESEA – Fuhrman *et al.*, 2007; Hess and Petrilli, 2006)[9] that stated in its illustrious Title I:

> Congress hereby declares: it to be the policy of the United States to provide financial assistance (as set forth in this title) to local educational agencies serving areas with concentrations of children from low-income families to expand and improve their educational programs by various means (including preschool programs) which contribute predominantly to meeting the special educational needs of educationally deprived children.[10]

This commitment that began rather declaratively (Hess and Petrilli, 2006) was the result of a decade of debates and of policy initiatives that followed the Brown ruling and the democratic administrations of Presidents Kennedy and Johnson. Several versions of this law followed, accompanied by more federal law-based intervention in policy.[11] This breakthrough legislation that was re-authorized several times subsequent to 1965 reached its pinnacle in its 2001 version under the title 'No Child Left Behind' (NCLB). A huge piece of legislation, NCLB moved ESEA from a general commitment and provision of funds, to a highly regulatory phase that mandated, as a precondition for existing and further funding, the implementation of a whole-system and whole-high-stakes accountability-based reform. In return for federal funds, states were required to build programmes that would bring their pupils up to three consecutive grades of attainment accountability and achievement (basic, proficient, and advanced – the level of each determined in each state to reach proficiency by 2014) and under Section 1111, NCLB: 'demonstrate that the state has adopted challenging academic content standards and challenging student academic achievement standards'. NCLB kindled a tremendous controversy among educators (Darling-Hammond, 2010; LaFever, 2006; Payne, 2008), policymakers (DeBray, 2006), and legal scholars (Hess and Petrilli, 2006; La Morte, 2011). The debate ran the gamut between issues of professionalism and fear of a takeover of standards of teachers' professional authority, to issues of embedding an untruthful culture that encourages 'teaching to the test' and getting rid of weak students, to general issues of federal involvement versus state, district, staff, community, and parental control over education. Among education researchers there was a secondary debate due to NCLB's demand that reform would be based on rigour and evidence, phrases that gave preference if not cliquishness to quantitative research methods,[12] thus limiting possibilities for socio-political and culturally-based critical theory qualitative studies. This was not just an argument on methodology, but on judging law-based reform according to sub-texts and hidden agendas, and linking reform to neoliberal globalized-economy principles – part of what this book aspires to do as well. These respective debates have not ceased and are reflected in the current administration's plan for the re-authorization of NCLB (namely ESEA):

> Over time, districts will be required to ensure that their high-poverty schools receive state and local funding levels (for personnel and relevant nonpersonnel expenditures) comparable to those received by their low-poverty schools. In addition, districts that use their resources to provide strong support to disadvantaged students will be given additional flexibility to provide such support. States will be asked to measure and report on resource disparities and develop a plan to tackle them.
>
> (US Department of Education, 2010: 11)

Analysis of this ambitious document reveals many important points. A 'white paper' (in English terms) is, just like its English counterparts, a policy declaration. In this case it builds upon the controversial but substantial NCLB legislation and converges into it the politics and ideology of the Obama administration and perhaps addresses some of the critique against NCLB. However, the document still embraces a high-stakes evidence-based platform combined with new paragraphs on equity and teaching English as a second language to immigrants.

Although the United States Constitution (Hess and Petrilli, 2006; Imber and van Geel, 2010; Reilly, 2000) does not have a specific education clause, many state constitutions do (Tractenberg, 2006). An important ingredient of these is often an 'adequacy' clause that allows, through judicial interpretation and implementation, state supreme courts to intervene in education policy issues including admissions policy, desegregation and equal school funding.[13] These rulings are often the cause for heated arguments and are sometimes criticized and challenged as opposing the democratic process of legislation in state legislatures and, when school finance is involved, as contradictory to property rights (Cohen *et al.*, 2007; DeMitchell and Fossey, 1997; Imber and van Geel, 2010; La Morte, 2011). As the issue of equal distribution of funds was left to the states' discretion at a relatively early stage (DeMitchell and Fossey, 1997; McUsic, 1999; La Morte, 2011), several of these had their legal systems – both through legislation and through case-law – dwell extensively on issues of equity and equity-related school finance. The core of these cases – which have not appeared in England or in Israel so far – is connected to the structure of school finance in the US that is based heavily on local (municipal, district) property taxes, resulting in big gaps in the quality and abundance of education services among schools, ethnic groups, and communities.

As in other issues in this chapter, the scope of writing in this book does not intend to cover all examples but to provide an overview that will allow analysis of England's law-based reform from a fairness standpoint. So I will present one striking case: that of New Jersey. Following the US Supreme Court's milestone 1973 decision of *San Antonio v. Rodriguez*,[14] (that, as mentioned before, decided not to intervene in the district tax-based gaps in education provision) state courts did intercede, sometimes dramatically so, in this matter. New Jersey had a traditionally (Liss *et al.*, 2006) unequal system with large SES-based gaps between school districts and segregated (homogenous) within-district characteristics. Early in the 1970s, Rutgers University's Newark campus law school established, under Professor Paul Tractenberg (a leading figure in the study and promotion of law-based education reform in the US) an Institute on Education, Law, and Policy. This centre (there are others that do similar work elsewhere in the US)[15] has launched, since its inception, over forty court petitions to the supreme court of New Jersey, most of them under the already famed 'brand' names *Robinson v. Cahill* and *Abbott v. Burke.*[16] Summing up these cases reveals an amazing example, perhaps the most comprehensive and consistent that has ever been documented. The forty-year history of case-law began with a dramatic decision that mandated the state of New Jersey to fund the weakest group of school districts to the equivalent level that children received in the strongest group of districts. Further decisions mandated the weaker districts (nicknamed for a long time 'Abbott districts') to choose and implement certain reforms that were found successful elsewhere in the US, and ordered the legislature to seek court approval for new legislation to ensure that it was consistent with the case law. This is an unusual case of ongoing court supervision that is traditionally contrary to the Anglo-American legal legacy. Although the Brown case itself is such an example – as it placed many school districts under federal court supervision and authorization of attendance boundaries and desegregation plans for over five decades – it is still the exception and not the rule. Of course the New Jersey example also demonstrates the downsides of this phenomenon. For instance, when the courts ordered extra funds for the weaker 'Abbott' districts, the mid-range districts that were not affluent, on the one hand, but did not qualify for the equalizing funds, on the other hand, were left with less money. At the same time, the Abbott districts were afraid to improve to such a degree where they lost the extra funding and other benefits. Of course a fierce public, political, and legal argument seethed around the contentious issue of court intervention in democratically-accepted arrangements. Given these serious reservations on the limits of court-based reform, the New Jersey example shows how courts can challenge legislation and intervene in situations that are obviously fundamentally unfair and that the politically strong groups in power, that control the legislative process, decide to ignore.

The United States is far from positioning an ideal example of law-based equitable reform. Its stratified and multi-layered structure limits the possibilities and widens gaps. Notwithstanding, the US model contributes two important points of reference to the study in this book. The first point is the balancing power of legislation and of case law in policymaking, the latter offering a 'third rail' for weak groups and also making the public and the legislators pause and think before implementing certain types of unfair reforms. The second point is the strong law-based and case-based pledge for integration and equality – regardless of results at this point in time, but more from a romanticized, ideological and conceptual standpoint. These points of reference will be explored further when discussing the English case of law-based reform.

Israel

Israel's schools are governed by occasional, outdated, educational law in a formerly centralized system (Gibton and Goldring, 2002) that is rapidly becoming decentralized (informally, outside the scope of the law). Problems of SES-based achievement gaps, and challenging relations between Jews and Arabs, between religious and secular groups, and between new immigrants and natives (Yogev, 1997) have prompted the

Supreme Court to intervene over and again in equity-related policy issues. Some 18 per cent of Israeli citizens are Arab–Palestinians who can be considered as an indigenous nation and certainly a distinctive ethnic and religious minority. They suffer from ongoing discrimination in terms of funds and degrees of autonomy in curriculum planning (especially in teaching their narrative on the political situation) although they have schools that teach in Arabic throughout the K-12 years (Abu-Asba, 2006). They also experience inner tensions (that is, between a large Muslim majority and Christians, and between affluent and educated and poor areas). Gaps in standards of living, including in education, between the financial and cultural centres in big cities and immigration towns in the periphery, add to a persistent debate on equality, while the sheer diversity of the population enhances arguments over religion, multiculturalism, and hegemony.

Israel's education law is orthodox in its structure, and does not, as of now, suffer or enjoy – depending on one's opinion – the characteristics of the new education regime-type legislation that was described in the English and American cases presented in this chapter. This does not mean, however, that Israel's governments did not adopt the views of such regimes, as will be explained.

In Israel's early years, the government enacted two important Education Acts – the National Education Act, 1953 (Dror, 2007) and the Compulsory Learning Act, 1949, that practically nationalized various politically and religiously affiliated semi-private chains of schools that existed from the time of the British mandate. The Acts established three tiers of schools. The first tier involved the majority of public (that is, maintained) schools labelled 'National-Formal', and included two sub-groups: one secular, which included separate schools for Jews and Arabs; and one religious, Jewish modern–orthodox. All of the National-Formal schools were owned and run by the state or by local authorities, administered a mandatory National Curriculum, and received full public funding. The second tier included a tiny independent ultra-orthodox Jewish group of schools that received limited government funding, if any, as their pupils were exempt from public education, and congregated under the title of 'educational institutions' – not even named as schools by law. Finally, Article 11 of the National Education Act allowed the Minister a residual power to give formal recognition to a third tier of non-state schools, to impose and implement the National Curriculum in them, to define their governance arrangements, and to determine the government's funding. Through this option, after sixty years of the National Education Act, many types of schools were established up to a point where in 2011 over one-quarter of Israel's schools and students were operating and studying in this third tier (Gibton, 2011). This group, called 'Recognized Schools', includes over 15 types of schools: secular and religious, Jewish and Arab, Muslim and Christian, vocational and academic, and owned and governed by a mosaic of organizations, NGOs, QUANGOs, churches, and other agencies. Although the 1953 Act links the Recognized Schools' compliance with government policy – and especially with the

National Curriculum – to public funding, in practice this was followed only loosely by the governments. A large number of the Recognized Schools became so due to coalition agreements with political parties, as part of attempts to form multi-party cabinets.

In 1968, in the wake of the Brown era in the US, the government initiated an SES-based integration policy throughout the system that was quite comprehensive at first. The integration reform was not anchored in law but was implemented through the governments' control over the National-Formal schools and the employment of their headteachers. But when, in the 1980s, Israel underwent a social and political change towards neoliberalism, and when the winds of globalization blew in the 1990s, large groups of Israelis began to look for a way to 'opt out' of integration (Ichilov, 2010). Without mandatory, de jure, integration the Recognized schools, not owned by the government, and partly out of its control, became the obvious selective escape-route and thus grew in numbers. They now represent two-thirds of the secondary system, and about a third of the system as a whole. The groups of Recognized schools vary in nearly every conceivable educational denominator: their affiliation to local or national government; their ownership; their relation to faith; their forms of funding – public and private; their pedagogical agenda; parts of their curriculum; and their admissions policy.

It is in this setting that several important legislative changes have occurred since 2007. As far back as 1992, Israel's parliament, the Knesset, replaced an outdated system that allowed the government to allocate large sums of money to non-government education organizations without clear guidelines (Gibton, 2011).[17] An amendment in the Budget Fundamentals Act, 1985 (1992) allowed certain ultra-orthodox school networks to retain full government funding while safeguarding their 'character and status'. This clause was declared unconstitutional by Israel's Supreme Court in 2002,[18] forcing government to precondition its funding via compliance with the National Curriculum. As a result the religious parties in the Knesset mounted a five-year campaign that would ground their privileges in primary legislation. Their efforts paid off as, between 2007 and 2009, educational legislation was passed, despite sizeable public outcry. The new legislation included the following:

1. An amendment to Section 11 of the National Education Act, 1953, mandates LEAs to match whatever ministry funding has allocated to Recognized Schools.[19]

2. An amendment to the National Education Act established a new group of government-maintained and run schools offering 'National curriculum education that accommodates in its program enhanced studies of Judaism and Jewish identity…'.[20] This allowed a new type of religious–liberal school to receive government funding.

3. The Cultural Education Institutions Act, 2008, allows government to fully fund schools that 'provide systematic education that evolves from the distinct life-style of the unique cultural group that study in it according to its unique characteristics, and that received recognition from the Minister ...' (Section 1). This formalized government funding to the most extreme Jewish–Orthodox institutions.

These three pieces of legislation are the first attempts to formalize the rogue or autonomous (according to one's standpoint) sections of Israel's public education system, not through control, but through recognition of their freedom from government control and their public funding.

The courts supported the 1968 integration reform strongly for over two decades. Court cases, a trickle at first and then a steady flow, criticized the allocation of public funds to schools that were not under comprehensive public supervision as being unconstitutional. Meanwhile, Israel's Supreme Court began gradually to weaken its grip on equality-based integration policies.[21,22] Scholars attribute this change to the wider transformations in Israel's society, politics, and economy, that have not skipped the supreme court that adopted some neoliberal opinions on school choice. This critique was intensified by a negative opinion of the court towards the government's inconsistent policy that allowed the 'Recognized' sector to do as it pleased.[23] Based on equal-treatment judicial policy, the courts found it difficult to defend government-established integration when the government itself, especially due to the political agreements referred-to beforehand, freed groups of schools from compliance with admissions codes.

This means that in 2012, the de jure situation in Israel changed radically, if gradually. Although the large regulatory laws I have described in England and the US's law-based reforms do not exist in Israel, nevertheless it has incorporated and adopted many of their educational regimes' traits and trends. Israel's acceptance into the OECD and its neoliberal drive, backed, encouraged, and sometimes coerced, by international financial organizations (such as the World Bank, the WEF, and the IMF) and international consultancy firms (for example McKinsey), have finalized its relocation away from an equality-inspired system. Instead, Israel is shifting to a system that is characterized by numerous types of schools and governance, and that is fast becoming segregated. Therefore Israel presents a third model to those of England and the US. Holding fast to the old-fashioned scant legislation, without a written constitution but with an active supreme court that has adopted some of the neoliberal discourse, it is entering a zone of decentralization with minimal regulation and balancing powers.

Comparison and conclusions

Analysis of the three cases – England, the US, and Israel – produces some worthwhile insights. Table 3.2 compares the three countries in terms of law-based reform. The table presents the three cases according to three denominators: the first is legislation and case-law, and the relations between them; the second is the influence of legislation on macro-processes and micro-processes in schools; and the third is the role of law-based reform in building up equity tools and reaching or promoting equality.

Table 3.2: Law-based reform: A comparison of three cases

Denominator/ factor	**England**	**United States**	**Israel**	**Implications for politics and fairness**
Legislation and case law: the relations between them	Massive legislation, with minimal supreme court intervention in policy. Modern legislation that 'upgrades' secondary legislation and bylaws to primary legislation, and relies heavily on regulatory bodies to minimize inequitable trends (Ogus, 2004; Harris, 2007).	A chain of federal legislation that increases the influence and involvement of federal authorities. A traditional abundance of court cases, in federal and state constitutional courts that balance legislation and offer 'third rail' (Welner, 2000; 2012) policy.	Scant, haphazard legislation (Gibton and Goldring, 2002; Gibton, 2011). Intensive supreme court intervention, weakening court support for desegregation and growing support for school choice and neoliberal policies.	Strong coordination between legislation and litigation can be helpful in a stressful area such as education policy. Unexpected results of legislation are a cross-cultural pandemic.

Table 3.2 cont.

Denominator/ factor	**England**	**United States**	**Israel**	**Implications for politics and fairness**
Influence of legislation on macro-processes and micro-processes in schools	Quite dramatic. Legislation has had enculturation influence on teaching and learning; on admissions policy and segregation/ desegregation; and on types and structures of schools.	Quite dramatic. In the last decade a high-stakes standards system has influenced anything from teaching and learning to enrolment policies.	Legislation is more and more disconnected from processes in the field, leaving important issues for the courts to decide.	In England and the US legislation quickly changed the scene of education policy by implementing the ideologies of educational regimes.
The role of law-based reform in building up equity tools and reaching or promoting equality	A steady drive towards a neoliberal managerialist system, with disregard for segregation, produced an equity-deficient system regulated by market forces.	The withdrawal from *Brown* creates doubts about their system's commitment to equality and the law as an equitable tool.	An unintended but clear drive to quasi-privatisation and withdrawal from former equitable trends such as SES-based and multicultural integration.	The balance between legislation and strong constitutional case-law is necessary to make law an equitable tool, but courts too can easily surrender to neoliberal values.

Table 3.2 shows three distinguishable models of law-based reform. The American model offers two parallel, often contradicting and sometimes complementary and supporting, pathways – namely legislation (at federal and state level), and case-law (in the federal courts and in the state courts). The English model relies heavily on extensive, intensive, and frequent legislation, with minimal court intervention in government policy arrangements, and zero intervention in policy-moulding. Finally, we have the Israeli model, somewhat chaotic, with minimal, accidental legislation, limited governance, and hesitant and inadvertent case-law that certainly can be proactive in policymaking and policy-restriction. However, all three models have their limitations and attributes. The parallel policymaking through legislation and

case-law has significant advantages. According to Welner (2000; 2011), Heubert (1999) and Weckstein (1999), such a mix offers the most conciliatory formula between the democratic majority reflection of power-based interests and 'third rail' equality (Welner, 2000) forces:

> Americans have historically looked to schools as, in Horace Mann's words 'the great equalizer of the conditions of men' ... If the schools fail to act as such an equalizer, instead indulging the inequities of political power, then they will tend to project those same inequities onto schooling opportunities. ... Political decisions designed to benefit children of the politically powerful will usually stir less opposition (and receive more vocal support) than will decisions designed to benefit the children of those with less political power ... Equity then can be thought of as the universalisation of third-rail treatment: the treatment of less powerful people and groups in ways that confer benefits equal to those obtained by more powerful people and groups.
>
> (Welner, 2000: 6)

This does mean that this book will present the American model as inherently fair, albeit Welner explains that the result of third-rail court-based policy influence would 'in all likelihood, be only a rough approximation of fairness' (ibid. 7). This is a note to keep in mind when comparing the three models of law-based reform presented here. Figure 3.1 offers a preliminary 'social justice meter' for assessing the fluctuations in fairness along several decades between the three systems:

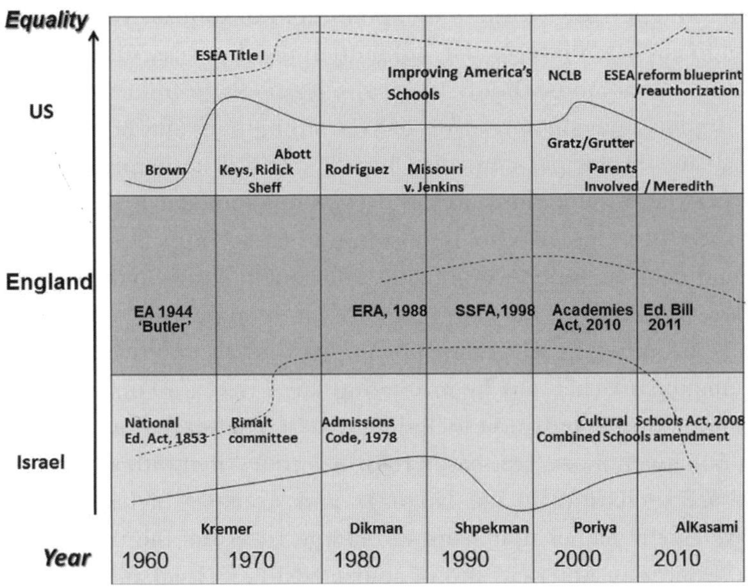

Figure 3.1: A social justice meter for law-based education reform

Among the three, a glance at Figure 3.1 shows the relative isolation of legislation in England, not balanced (but also not backed) by constitutional policymaking or policy-breaking case-law. In the American and Israeli cases, the courts stepped in to equalize or re-equalize the system when legislation became grossly unfair.

Another point that should be at the back of one's mind when making this type of comparison between these models, indeed between any national models of law-based reforms, is that the differences between them cannot be isolated in education legislation alone and are connected to much larger localized factors. These include factors within the legal system and the legal tradition and beyond them, into the system and structure of government and governance, of society, of politics, and of the history and demographics of each country. This is important when policy-borrowing becomes an epidemic (Ball, 2008b), as models are often borrowed and implemented with minimal regard for the unique local conditions in which they were developed. However, the three cases present the obvious. Even in light of the growing forces of globalization, the transnational forces are creolized, forged by the various local settings.

Typical issues of law-based reform in England, the US, and Israel are similar in some aspects. Laws in all three countries are struggling with a high-stakes standard-based framework that becomes more and more centralized while committed to decentralization, to schools, and to local autonomy. The three countries are messing with the local and municipal control of education – perhaps a matter more evident in England's education politics and policy. Local control is praised as a virtue but scorned as a practice, as a catalyst of inefficiency, of waste, of low standards, and often of corruption. There is a constant search in the three countries for a 'magic bullet' of a new or alternative form of non-political local control. This is an inherent contradiction in law-based reform. The solution in the three cases is alike. It consists of creating local autonomous schools, or groups of schools, or frameworks for schools to join and adopt in a way that preserves or even strengthens autonomy, but weakens local political and municipal control. Charter schools, academies, free schools, chains, networks, and federations are all part of this toolbox. It is a never-ending cycle. When these new types of schools or groups of schools appear in large numbers, gain power and respect, and use more and more public funds, public outcry, often backed by research and by ideology, calls for more supervision and regulation. Such outcry is magnified by alleged or proven accusations of 'cream-skimming', by using problematic curricula and by promoting ideas that are contrary to those of public education, insufficient audit including that of headteacher and staff training, segregation, and much more. Law-based reform is concerned with all of these.

There are similarities in the language and structure of legislation as well. The laws have catchy names that seem to emerge from the minds of copywriters, for example 'Educating America' and of course NCLB. In England this is apparent in the names of white papers; 'Higher Standards Better Schools for All', 'Every

Child Matters', and 'The Importance of Teaching' are the highlights. In Israel, the scarcity of legislation on reform has so far saved it from extravagant titles such as these. However, in line with the Talmudic proverb 'one cannot be exempt of it all', the 2005 committee on school reform whose title itself belongs to this series (the 'National Task Force on Education') came up with a report entitled 'Because Every Child Deserves More' – indeed matching up to the English and American drama in law-based reform. The 2008 legislation on 'Cultural Education Institutions' that camouflages the growing segregation and stratification of Israel's public education is also part of this phenomenon.

The laws in both England and the US are huge, and include hundreds and sometimes thousands of sections and articles. From a regulatory and governance perspective this has two important implications. The first implication is that issues and arrangements that were previously dealt with in secondary legislation (for instance regulation, circulars, and directives) are now increasingly 'upgraded' to the status of primary legislation. My theory is that this is part of the 'educational regime' model on which education policy is grounded. Primary legislation allows ministers more control over education and leaves much less discretion to local authorities, local politics, and communities. This centralized power is often achieved by authorizing and empowering statutory agencies to audit, supervise, commission, and deliver education services (Ball, 2007; Cohen *et al.*, 2007). This type of legislation also minimizes the power of civil servants and professionals who traditionally are, or were, involved in phrasing regulations and other secondary legislative instruments. The second implication of the volume of new legislation is that the size and numerous parts, sub-parts, sections, and articles create an opaque field that makes it extremely difficult for the implementers of policy to determine whether they have, or have not, reached the goals intended by the legislator. This places even more power in the hands of central/national education authorities to determine whether agency X (whether a municipality, a district, a community, or a school) has indeed reached the targets and complied or not. Such legislation creates a culture of constant insecurity that perhaps strengthens the initiators of the law, on the one hand, but also creates suspicion (if not cynicism and ridicule) among implementers and professionals, on the other hand. This is a double-edged sword that I believe has far-reaching implications for education policy and governance and for the validity and reliability of legislation as a policy and regulative tool. The nature of legislation in England and in the US produces a culture of consultancy and expertise in the interpretation and understanding of legislation that is far from traditional legal advice. In Israel, the opposite is the case: the scarce and outdated laws create a culture of anomie.

The three principles of education reform that were presented in Chapter 2 (namely that equality and choice cannot happen simultaneously; that micro-changes in schools can be influenced and controlled by macro legal, economic, and organizational processes; and that a neoclassic market can exist in education) are reflected in legislation in all three countries. All legislation declares commitment to equality. However, the sub-text is one that assumes choice, as a mainsail motif of reform, as a basic right for parents, and as an equalizing mechanism. In Israel, there is also reference to the right of choice of groups (mainly religious in nature) under multicultural or ideological entitlements. The second principle is discernible in the English and American legislation through the high-stakes system, the audit requirements, the links between improvement and public funds, and, again, by open enrolment. All these are construed to control, improve, and guide micro-processes within schools and classrooms (such as teaching and learning processes), through the legal, organizational, and financial arrangements. The sub-text here is that schools will compete with each other, and thus improve. In addition, legislation is favourable towards semi-public schools and 'messy' definitions of public education and school-finance, consequently encouraging the further spreading of these schools (charter schools and vouchers in the US, or academies and free schools in England, for example). Finally, all of the legislative provisions are under the 'cloud' of the concept of a neoclassic market – the third principle of reform. Responsibility for the success of the changes falls mainly on the public – the 'consumers' of education services (Harris, 1993). Without their informed choice and rational behaviour, legislation, as an equity tool, will not reach its targets in terms of equality and mobility. Given that the empirical validity of the three principles is low, it is perhaps upsetting to see how strongly they are part of law-based reform. Legislation is therefore full of inconsistencies and paradoxes. From a regulative point of view, Ogus's (2004) words resonate with the law-based reform in all three countries:

> ... the centralized pool of information on which rulers must rely for regulatory measures could never replicate the widely dispersed fragments of knowledge which individuals use in pursuance of their own ends and therefore could never be adequate to anticipate all the variety of circumstances to which specific regulation must be applied.
>
> (Ogus, 2004: 57)

He goes on:

> In a political context, the end result of the 'transaction' is normally legislation which has a general coercive effect, applying to, and often imposing costs on, those who did not vote for it or did not want it. From a normative perspective, it should be noted that unless a unanimity voting rule (allowing any potential cost-bearer to veto a proposal) is adopted, the collective choice may give rise to economic inefficiency ... But in the absence of constitutional constraints, collective decisions made on the basis of less-than-unanimity voting rules can be used to oppress minorities.
>
> (Ibid. 59)

Welner's 'third rail' theory can provide an answer to the falsity of equity through democratically-controlled legislation. The courts not only balance the power of those better off, but also 'incorporate the values and beliefs of non-judicial actors. This would logically include those who produce prominent social science research' (Welner, 2012: 20). The new legislation is a far cry from the hierarchical orthodox structure in which primary legislation is phrased in general terms and relatively short texts that leave an important role for local authorities, civil servants, and professional educators to expand into secondary legislative instruments. Such amendments and alterations can also add delicacy and finesse to the general arrangements, and correct flaws according to acquired experience. Ogus noticed back in 2004 that the minister's role in this type of regulation is 'diminishing' (ibid. 105). Remarkably enough, the huge volume of primary legislation does not necessarily come at the expense of secondary minister- or civil servant-controlled legislation. Perhaps on the contrary: the large and frequent primary laws are often followed by similarly large and complex secondary legislation, all making it very difficult both to comply and to govern. This over-legislative culture may highlight the fallacy of linear implementation and isolation and control of dependent variables. It seems that governments have a religious belief that if they just legislate a bit more, they can control everything and reach the intended outcomes. When this is part of a free-market decentralization managerial ideology, the result is sometimes peculiar and troubling.

This brief overview of three complex systems and three examples of law-based reform does yield some disturbing insights. Having been thwarted by, or disillusioned with, the outcomes of uniform, state, and provider-controlled education, the heavily regulated models of law-constructed decentralized systems do not promise relief either for citizens or policymakers in terms of fairness. The next part of the book attempts to understand how this happens, who the players in this field are, and how law-based reform is part of their professional lives.

Notes

[1] School Admissions Code, 2010; School Admissions Code, 2011; School Admission Appeals Code, 2012; The School Admissions (Admission Arrangements and Co-ordination of Admission Arrangements) (England) Regulations, 2012; The School Admissions (Appeals Arrangements) (England) Regulations, 2012.

[2] The Building Schools for the Future Programme 'Renewing the Secondary School Estate', report by the comptroller and auditor General HC135 session 2008–9, 12 February 2009.

[3] www.education.gov.uk/schools/pupilsupport/premium/a0076063/pupil-premium-what-you-need-to-know

[4] Brown v. Board of Education of Topeka, 347 US 483 (1954); Brown v. Board of Education of Topeka 349 U.S. 294 (Brown II)

[5] Swan v. Charlotte-Mecklenburg Board of Ed. 402 US 1 (1971); Keyes v. School District no. 1 413 US 189 (1973); Dayton Board of Ed. V. Brinkham 443 US 5266 (1979); Riddick v. School Board of City of Norfolk 627 F. Supp. 814 (1986); Board of Education of Oklahoma City Public Schools v. Dowell 498 US 237 (1991); Freeman v. Pitts 503 US 467 (1992).

[6] Missouri v. Jenkins 115 S. Ct. 2938 (1995).

[7] Abbott v. Burke, 575 A 2nd. 359 (NJ 1990).

[8] Parents involved in Community Schools, v. Seattle School District no. 1; Crystal D. Meredith, Custodial Parent And Next Friend of Joshua Ryan McDonald, v. Jefferson County Board of Education et al 416 F. 3d 513 (2007).

[9] Elementary and Secondary Education Act (ESEA), 1965 pl. 107–10.

[10] PUBLIC LAW 89-10-APR. 11, 1965, Sec. 201.

[11] Individuals with Deficiencies Education Act (IDEA), 1973, 1997, pl. 105–17; Goals 2000: Educate America Act, 1994, pl. 103–227; Improving America's Schools Act, 1994, pl. 103–328; No Child Left Behind (NCLB), 2001, pl. 107–10.

[12] **"SEC. 1502. DEMONSTRATIONS OF INNOVATIVE PRACTICES.** "(a) IN GENERAL. – From the funds appropriated for any fiscal year under section 1002(e)(1), the Secretary may award grants to State educational agencies, local educational agencies, other public agencies, nonprofit organizations, public or private partnerships involving business and industry organizations, and consortia of such entities to carry out demonstration projects that show the most promise of enabling children served under this title to meet challenging State academic content standards and challenging State student academic achievement standards. "(b) EVALUATION. – The Secretary shall evaluate the demonstration projects supported under this title, using rigorous methodological designs and techniques, including control groups and random assignment, to the extent feasible, to produce reliable evidence of effectiveness. **"SEC. 1503. ASSESSMENT EVALUATION.** "(a) IN GENERAL. – The Secretary shall conduct an independent study of assessments used for State accountability purposes and for making decisions about the promotion and graduation of students. Such research shall be conducted over a period not to exceed 5 years and shall address the components described in subsection (d). "(b) CONTRACT AUTHORIZED. – The Secretary is authorized to award a contract, through a peer review process, to an organization or entity capable of conducting rigorous, independent research. The Assistant Secretary of Educational Research and Improvement shall appoint peer reviewers to evaluate the applications for this contract. "(c) STUDY. – The study shall – "(1) synthesize and analyze existing research that meets standards of quality and scientific rigor; and "(2) evaluate academic assessment and accountability systems in State educational agencies, local educational agencies, and schools; and "(3) make recommendations to the Department and to the Committee on Education and the Workforce of the United States House of Representatives and the Committee on Health, 20 USC 6493. 20 USC 6492.

VerDate 11-MAY-2000 14:55 Mar 26, 2002 Jkt 099139 PO 00110 Frm 00173 Fmt 6580 Sfmt 6581 E:\PUBLAW\PUBL110 115 STAT. 1598 PUBLIC LAW 107–110 – JAN. 8, 2002 Education, Labor, and Pensions of the United States Senate, based on the findings of the study. "(d) COMPONENTS OF THE RESEARCH PROGRAM. – The study described in subsection (a) shall examine – "(1) the effect of the assessment and accountability systems described in section (c) on students, teachers, parents, families, schools, school districts, and States, including correlations between such systems and – "(A) student academic achievement, progress to the State-defined level of proficiency, and progress toward closing achievement gaps, based on independent measures; "(B) changes in course offerings, teaching practices, course content, and instructional material; "(C) changes in turnover rates among teachers, principals, and pupil-services personnel; "(D) changes in dropout, grade-retention, and graduation rates for students; and "(E) such other effects as may be appropriate; "(2) the effect of the academic assessments on students with disabilities; "(3) the effect of the academic assessments on low, middle, and high socioeconomic status students, limited and nonlimited English proficient students, racial and ethnic minority students, and nonracial or nonethnic minority students;

"(4) guidelines for assessing the validity, reliability, and consistency of those systems using nationally recognized professional and technical standards;

"(5) the relationship between accountability systems and the inclusion or exclusion of students from the assessment system; and

"(6) such other factors as the Secretary finds appropriate.

[13] 'The Legislature shall provide for the maintenance and support of a thorough and efficient system of free public schools for the instruction of all the children in the State between the ages of five and eighteen years.' [N.J. Const. art. VIII, § 4.].

[14] San Antonio Independent School District v. Rodriguez, 411 US (1973).

[15] See: The Center for Education Policy and Law, university of San-Diego (USD), founded 2007, www.sandiego.edu/soles/centers/cepal; and Education Law Center of Pennsylvania (ELC), founded in Pennsylvania in 1975, www.elc-pa.org/law/law_disabilities.html

[16] Robinson v, Cahill, 303 a.2d. 273 (N.J. 1973); 306 A.2d. 65 (N.J. 1973); 335 A.2d. 6 (N.J. 1975); 351 A.2d. 713 (N.J. 1975); 355 A.2d 129 (N.J. 1976); 358 A.2d. 457 (N.J. 1976); 360 A.2d. 400 (N.J. 1976).

Abbott v. Burke, 495 A. 2d 376 (N.J. 1985); 575 A 2nd. 359 (NJ 1990); 643 A.2d. 575 (N.J. 1994); 693 A2d 417 (N.J. 1997); 710 A. 2.2d. 450 (N.J. 1998); 748 A.2d. (N.J. 2000); 790 A.2d. 842 (N.J. 2002); 798 A.2d. (N.J. 2002); 832 A.2d. 891 (N.J. 2003); 832 A.2d. 906 (N.J. 2003); 181 N.J. 311 (2004); 182 N.J. 153 (2004); 889 A.2d. 1063 (N.J. 2005); 901 A.2d. 299 (N.J. 2006); WL 1388958 (N.J. 2006); WL 1518909 (N.J. 2007).

[17] National Task Force on Education, 2005, Appointed by Israel's government 2003, Chair: Shlomo Dovrat (NTF).

[18] HCJ 10296/02 The Union of Secondary Schools Teachers vs. The Minister of Education [2002[.

[19] Amendment section 11a. to the National Education Act, 1953, 2007.

[20] Amendment no. 10 to the National Education Act, 1953, 2007.

[21] HCJ 152/71 Mordechai Kremer vs. Jerusalem Municipality and the Ministry of Education [1971].

[22] HCJ 4363/00 the local committee of Poria-Elite *et al.* vs. the Minister of education *et al.* [2000] IsrDC (3) 3114.

[23] Tel-Aviv DC 35243-03-10 Al-Kasami and the parents association of Al-Kasami Secondary school vs. The Ministry of Education [2010].

Chapter 4

From social democracy to neoliberalism? From the Education and Inspections Act, 2006, to the Education Act, 2011 (they're not what you think)

The framework of the laws

Both the Education and Inspections Act 2006 (EIA 2006) and the Education Act, 2011 (EA 2011) are what is known as 'omnibus legislation' (DeMitchell and Fossey, 1997; Hill *et al.*, 1997). This type of law gathers together a mosaic of previous legislation, new legislation, regulations, circulars, policy initiatives, and more, all incorporated into one law. Omnibus laws require complex accommodations and adaptations to previous legislation and by-laws. When omnibus legislation is as frequent as it is in England, the task of accommodation and adaptation becomes much harder and the risks increase. One risk is that stitching together all the previous and parallel legislation will not be as precise as is necessary, and 'loose ends' can remain. The second and more eminent risk is that the final product will be cumbersome and therefore very difficult for practitioners to implement. This is not because of their lack of legal literacy but because of the sheer volume and complexity of information. Furthermore, the short periods between laws make it difficult to understand them quickly enough and notice all the subtleties of the new law; and there is also a temptation to read and implement superficially, knowing from years of experience and recurring incidents that a new complex piece of legislation is just around the corner anyway, so 'why bother?' The endless list of schedules (that amend, erase, and add clauses and text to previous legislation) minimizes the probability of any practitioner or policymaker ever grasping a full picture of the new law, thus rendering it as something between a text that is apposite exclusively for the apprehension of legal advisers, and a dead letter. These two major acts will be analysed with attention to politics and fairness – the main themes of this book.

The Education and Inspections Act, 2006

Just like any other major act, the Education and Inspections Act, 2006 (EIA 2006) was not enacted in a void. It came after several comprehensive and vastly prominent changes in England's school system, and also after the system became used to frequent legislation. First, one should draw an imaginary timeline from the ERA 1988, that peaked in terms of the main modifications and reforms under Prime Minister Thatcher (that is, open enrolment and schools choice, 'opting out' and gaining 'grant maintained' status, and adopting the National Curriculum). This was followed by Prime Minister Blair's panoptic reforms: the strengthening of Ofsted, introducing Education Action Zones and Excellence in Cities, establishing and operating numeracy and literacy strategies, founding the National College for School Leaders, introducing Key Stages, and encouraging the spread of specialist schools and academies (towards the end of his tenure), for example. In this sense the 2006 EIA is a summary of these reforms, a reaffirmation and perhaps in a way an effort to balance previous reforms. The 2006 EIA, it could be said, set the course for New Labour's education policy and future reform, as well as resolving certain dissymmetries that had emerged from previous legislation. The main imbalance was ostensibly between the weakening or changing role of LEAs and the appearance of trust schools in their various forms and shapes. Since the mid-1980s, different types of schools have been introduced in an evolutionary process: beginning with Grant Maintained Schools (renamed 'foundation' under New Labour); at about the same time, City Technology Colleges (CTCs); and later Specialist Schools and Academies – the most recent addition (from 2005 in substantial numbers).[1]

The act was the final stage in this series of acts under Prime Minister Blair, when the premiership was on the verge of being passed to Gordon Brown and the Brown–Balls administration of education policy. The act received serious attention in Harris's (2007) analysis, when it was a proposed bill. Now from the perspective and distance of six years, some new hindsight emerges, especially in light of the 2010–11 legislation. Although the act was criticized in 2006 and earlier in 2005 when its predecessor, the 'Higher Standards Better Schools for All' white paper, was presented, I think that in term of fairness it is less aggressive than later legislation and perhaps also than some of the earlier laws. I wonder when reading the act whether it was a hasty attempt to correct or weaken the supposed or real neoliberal stream of thought that was prevalent in England's education policy and reform in the 12 years of Blair's governments. Looking at the headings and titles of the various sections and articles shows that the act is strongly in favour of local democratic control of schooling – in other words, local authorities and elected bodies:

> **Part 1: Education functions of local authorities**
>
> Duties in relation to high standards and fulfilment of potential
>
> Duties in relation to diversity and choice
>
> Duty to consider parental representation
>
> Duty to identify children not receiving education
>
> School improvement partners
>
> Functions in respect of youth work, recreation, etc.
>
> **Part 2: Establishment, discontinuance or alteration of schools**
>
> Invitation for proposals for establishment of new schools
>
> Proposals under section 7 relating to community or community special schools
>
> 11 Publication of proposals to establish maintained schools: special cases (1)
>
> 12 Establishment of school as federated school
>
> 13 Schools established outside area of relevant LEA

The language of the act portrays an effort to push a finger into a (large) hole in the dyke that threatened to overwhelm England's education system with several waves of decentralization, 'flattening' the governance process (Ball, 2007) and structure, and allowing and encouraging businesses and the powers and bodies of a civil society to take a proactive and even dominant part in the control, commission, and provision of education, and in the establishment of schools and their organization into groups and authorities. The white paper itself opens with a thought-provoking perspective by the Prime Minister. Under the title 'The history since 1944' there is a short (positive) review of the Butler Act, ending with:

> … the system had two main weaknesses: grammar schools catered for the brightest students, but 80% of children had to go to secondary moderns which failed to challenge them and where many achieved few if any qualifications. Moreover, technical schools never really played a major part in the new system, denying opportunities for a vocational education.
>
> Pressure, initially from middle class parents angry with standards in secondary moderns, led to comprehensive schools and the conversion of grammars and secondary moderns in the 1960s and 1970s. But, their introduction was often accompanied by all-ability classes, which made

> setting by subject ability too rare. Many retained their old secondary modern intake, and failed to improve. There were simply not enough pressures in the system to raise standards.
>
> (*Higher Standards, Better Schools for All*, 2005: Foreword by the Prime Minister)

In these words Prime Minister Blair plants the seeds of contradiction that are also explained by Harris (2007). For what is the logical outcome or policy from this analysis? On the one hand, grammar schools, the temples of selection and segregation (perhaps disguised in meritocratic neutral terms – Levačić *et al.*, 2003), are criticized. On the other hand, the public (in the US 'Boydian' sense) modern secondary schools are blamed for other shortcomings of the system. Which is it? Grammar schools are too selective but mixed ability groups are too integrative? The solution is outlined, as summarized in the next paragraph, following two decades of reform:

> Lord Callaghan recognized this as Prime Minister in 1976 when he urged a National Curriculum. When it was introduced in the late eighties, it was accompanied by greater accountability through national testing and regular independent inspection. Schools were also encouraged to apply for grant-maintained status, where they had more freedom over their assets and staffing, though critics complained that they were unfairly funded compared with other schools, and that their admissions were unfair.
>
> (Ibid.)

And then:

> ... a process of reform that has accelerated since 1997.
>
> After 1997, this government extended such accountability, with literacy and numeracy reforms in primary schools, and targets to encourage improvements in all schools. Failing schools were expected to improve quickly. Under-performing schools were challenged.
>
> (Ibid.)

This declaration not only minimizes the role, and even the reality, of the massive reforms under Prime Ministers Thatcher and Major, but also distances the reforms made under the Blair administration from most of what predicated it. There is a passionate debate among researchers on the question of whether New Labour was truly a straightforward continuance of the Thatcher–Major reforms, which is the dominant view (Whitty, 2008). Blair's declaration was also substantiated by an attempt to reconcile a growing concern for diversity with a traditional commitment to equality, a reconciliation that was endeavoured to be made through a vast investment of public funds in many aspects of education. These aspects ranged from curricula, through to teacher preparation and professional development, careful headteacher selection and preparation, Education Maintenance Grants (EMGs) that boosted retention in the upper secondary level, and finally the ambitious 'Building Schools for the Future' (BSF) initiative that took it upon itself to rebuild many of England's schools with the aim of bringing them up to date as modern facilities for teaching and learning, as well as making them accessible for a diverse population of pupils. However, Whitty (2008: 171) cautions that, eventually 'Indeed, it seems to have gone further down the market route and much further down the privatization route, than the Conservatives ever achieved … '. This is corroborated by Harris (2007):

> The idea that what is needed is 'schools working with parents, children and local communities to drive reform' reflects a form of communitarian idealism …
>
> … it is still not clear why diversity of school providers holds the key to breaking cycles of underachievement and deprivation that the government says it is committed to tackling.
>
> (Ibid. 132)

A similar observation is delivered by Whitty, thus finalizing this conclusion both from a leading legal scholar, and a leading sociologist of education policy:

> … the evidence to support the case that diversity and choice are the key to higher standards for all remains weak and highly contested … overall, the evidence on the positive impact of diversity and choice is not sufficiently robust to justify New Labour's strong commitment to this approach.
>
> (Whitty, 2008: 176–7)

These solemn conclusions are troubling, mainly due to researchers' warnings that previous centralized 'controlled economy' models have yielded very few results in terms of equality (Ball, 2007; Levačić, 2002; Whitty, 2008). The conflicts between centralized education and decentralization, between mainstream dominant-culture education and multicultural education, and between selective, often SES-based, admissions policies and social cohesion, are scarcely harmonized. These conflicts stand out when reading the 2006 SIA. The language and structure of the act revolve around the LEA as the pivot of education policy, governance, commission and most of the delivery of education, education services, and education institutions:

> **Discontinuance of schools**
>
> 15 Proposals for discontinuance of schools maintained by a local education authority
>
> 16 Consultation in relation to proposals under section 15

17 Direction requiring discontinuance of community or foundation special school

Alterations to schools

18 Alterations that may be made under section 19

19 Publication of proposals for alteration of school

20 Restriction on power of governing body to publish foundation proposals

21 Proposals under section 19: procedure

22 Right of governing body to determine own foundation proposals

23 Rights of interested bodies in relation to proposals under section 21

24 Proposals under section 19: implementation

General

28 Restriction on establishment, alteration or discontinuance of schools

These large first and second parts of the law strengthen and reaffirm local authorities as the main bodies in charge of, and responsible for, both the commission and the delivery of schooling. In 2006 the EIA seemed like the apex of an era of law-based decentralization, and some would say deconstruction of local political planning and control over education. Now it almost seems like a mellow reaffirmation of this principle with the ostensibly requisite adjustments to a globalized economy run under neoliberal managerialist ideologies:

Part 3: Further provisions about maintained schools

Foundation, voluntary and foundation special schools

33A Requirements as to foundations

23B Powers of Secretary of State in relation to charity trustees of foundations

34 Parent councils for certain foundation or foundation special schools

35 Funding of voluntary aided schools: meaning of 'capital expenditure'

36 Disposals and changes of use of land

37 Staff at foundation or voluntary schools with religious character

38 General duties of governing body of maintained school

The following parts of the act again balance its denaturalized and deconstructive fundamentals, by referring to the admissions policy. Harris, who analysed the proposed EIA bill, cautioned that compliance with the admissions code might not be completely mandatory – which surely came true:[2]

School admissions

39 General restriction on selection by ability

40 Code for school admissions

(1) Section 84 of SSFA 1998 (code of practice) is amended in accordance with subsections (2) to (7).

(2) In subsection (1) –

(a) for 'a code of practice containing such practical guidance' substitute ' a code for school admissions containing such provision', and

(b) after paragraph (b) insert – '(ba) admission forums'.

(3) In subsection (2), for the words from 'include' to 'other matters' substitute 'impose requirements, and may include guidelines setting out aims, objectives and other matters'.

(4) In subsection (3), for 'to have regard to' substitute 'to act in accordance with'.

41 Role of admission forums

42 Support for parental preferences

43 Duty of governing body to implement decisions relating to admissions

44 Prohibition on interviews

45 Admission arrangements for schools with religious character: consultation and

Objections

46 Restrictions on alteration of admission arrangements

47 Objections to admission arrangements

48 Looked after children to whom section 87(2) of SSFA 1998 applies

50 Direction to admit looked after child to specified school

53 Schools with pre-1998 arrangements for selection by ability or aptitude

Although the act forbids interviews and selection by ability,[3] it is allowed for reasons of pupil banding, but as a general non-mandatory proviso later nicknamed 'soft banding':

> **54 Pupil banding**
>
> (1A) Subject to subsections (2) and (2A), the admission authority for a maintained school in England may make provision for selection by ability to the extent that the arrangements are designed to secure – (a) that in any year the pupils admitted to the school in any relevant age group are representative of all levels of ability among such one of the following groups as the admission arrangements may specify ('the reference group') –
>
> (i) children who are applicants for admission in that age group to any of two or more schools (including the school in question) in the area of the local education authority,
>
> (ii) children in that age group who live in the area of the local education authority, or
>
> (iii) children in that age group who live in England, …

LEAs are (re)given or (re)assured of their powers to intervene in failing schools, but no mention is made of trust schools or academies. The independence of academies and trust schools is being built gradually and, as will be seen, peaks in 2011:

> **Part 4: Schools causing concern: England**
>
> **Introduction**
>
> 59 Meaning of 'maintained school' and 'eligible for intervention'
>
> (1) In this Part 'maintained school' means any of the following schools in England –
>
> (a) a community, foundation or voluntary school,
>
> (b) a community or foundation special school, or
>
> (c) a maintained nursery school.
>
> **Schools that are eligible for intervention**
>
> 60 Warning notice by local education authority
>
> …
>
> (2) A local education authority may give a warning notice to the governing body of a maintained school where the authority are satisfied –

(a) that the standards of performance of pupils at the school are unacceptably low, and are likely to remain so unless the authority exercise their powers under this Part, or

(b) that there has been a serious breakdown in the way the school is managed or governed which is prejudicing, or likely to prejudice, such standards of performance, or

(c) that the safety of pupils or staff of the school is threatened (whether by a breakdown of discipline or otherwise).

61 School requiring significant improvement

62 School requiring special measures

Intervention by local education authority

63 Power of LEA to require governing body to enter into arrangements

64 Power of LEA etc. to appoint additional governors

This independence is highlighted in the definitions of schools, which create a distinct hierarchy between types of schools – creating 'tiers' in inspection, admissions, responsibility for allocation of placements in schools, and adjudication on appeals. The act does not declare this – it trickles into its various chapters, in the words of Ball creating 'social dislocation' (Ball, 2007: 186–7):

111 Meaning of 'maintained school' and 'relevant school' in Chapter 2

In this Chapter –

'maintained school' means –

(a) a community, foundation or voluntary school,

(b) a community or foundation special school, or

(c) a pupil referral unit;

'relevant school' means –

(a) a maintained school,

(b) an Academy,

(c) a city technology college, or

(d) a city college for the technology of the arts.

In terms of fairness and equitable instruments, the powers of inspection attached by the EIA are still substantial, and Ofsted's permissions of entrance are as wide as possible, and go back to the 1996 EA. This was combined with the Children Act 2004 and the Childcare Act 2006 that crystallized into a change in the name of the department and the change in Ofsted's title itself.[4] Consequently Ofsted became 'Office for Standards in Education, Children's Services and Skills' and title of 'Her Majesty's Chief Inspector of Education, Children's Services and Skills'.[5] Studying the role of the chief inspector shows that the EIA attaches an open-ended list of duties and responsibilities to this office:

> **Part 8: Inspections**
>
> (3) In performing its functions the Office must also have regard to such aspects of government policy as the Secretary of State may direct.
>
> ...
>
> **Functions: the Chief Inspector**
>
> 118 Functions of the Chief Inspector
>
> (1) The Chief Inspector has the general duty of keeping the Secretary of State informed
>
> about –
>
> (a) the quality of activities within the Chief Inspector's remit and (where appropriate) the standards achieved by those for whose benefit such activities are carried on,
>
> (b) improvements in the quality of such activities and in any such standards,
>
> (c) the extent to which such activities are being carried on as user-focused activities, and
>
> (d) the efficient and effective use of resources in the carrying on of such activities and services.
>
> (2) If requested to do so by the Secretary of State, the Chief Inspector must provide the Secretary of State with information or advice on such matters relating to activities within the Chief Inspector's remit as are specified in the request.
>
> (3) The Chief Inspector may at any time give advice to the Secretary of State on any matter connected with any activities within his remit, including advice relating to a particular establishment, institution or agency.
>
> (4) The Chief Inspector is to have such other functions in connection with activities within his remit as may be assigned to him by the Secretary of State.

(5) Subsection (6) applies where the Chief Inspector is requested under subsection (2) to provide the Secretary of State with information or advice on matters relating to activities within the Chief Inspector's remit.

(6) Any enactment by virtue of which –

(a) an inspection may be conducted by the Chief Inspector in relation to the activities in question (whether or not in pursuance of any duty), or

(b) any power of entry is exercisable by him in relation to those activities, is to have effect, with any necessary modifications, so as to enable him to conduct an inspection, or exercise any such power, for the purpose of complying with the request.

This extensive list is perhaps the most comprehensive range of obligations that was commissioned to the office in nearly a decade and a half of operation. A particularly specific and detailed part concerns inspections of LEAs. The power of HMCI and HMI are considerable, and the definition of 'schools' under the act is perhaps as wide as possible, referring to the EA 1996.[6] As the EIA was enacted in the post-2004 Children Act, the areas under inspection extend out to the Children and Family Court Advocacy and Support Service (CAFCAS). The act also adds to the responsibilities of the schools adjudicator. These include the freedom to look into complaints made by any persons (not just by parents) and an important power that allows advocacy (class action) to parents who feel uncomfortable with approaching authorities – often the case with disenfranchised groups – and to examine admissions arrangements in faith schools.[7] Further powers allow the adjudicator to look into the admission arrangements of a school, over and beyond a specific complaint,[8] and to request LEAs to present detailed reports of their admissions policies and appeals decisions:

121 Annual and other reports to Secretary of State

Chapter 4: Inspection and Review of Local Authorities in England

Functions to which this Chapter applies

135 Functions to which this Chapter applies and related activities

Inspections and annual reviews

136 Inspection of local authorities in England

(1) The Chief Inspector may inspect –

(a) the overall performance by any local authority in England of the functions to which this Chapter applies, or

(b) the performance by any such authority of any particular function or functions comprised in the functions to which this Chapter applies.

Chapter 5: Inspection of CAFCASS functions

Inspection of CAFCASS functions

143 Inspection of CAFCASS functions

160 Power of Chief Inspector to investigate complaints by parents about schools

163 Provision of advice by adjudicator

The course described in the EIA 2006 is analysed by Ball (2008b):

> ... an incremental process of breaking up established assumptions and modes of operation and taken for granted practices and replacing these with new 'freedoms', new players and new kinds of relationships and new forms of service delivery in many different parts of the education system, all propped up by a constant flow and reiteration of political rhetoric emanating from diverse sites and sources. ... Sometimes the progressive creep goes too far or too fast and is interrupted or compromised, most dramatically in the case of the 2006 Education and Inspections Act ... and not every policy move contributes directly to major or wholesale change.
>
> (Ibid. 195–6)

These inhibitions represent an eminent quality of the act.

The Education Act, 2011

Similarly to the description of the policy situation before 2005 by Prime Minister Blair, 'The Importance of Teaching' 2010 white paper that prefaces the Education Act 2011 presents a one-sided recent history of education policy. The new bill is depicted as a direct continuity of what happened up to 1997, pointing at the New Labour administration as responsible for 'severely constraining' the freedom of CTCs and academies (not mentioning that the latter were introduced by New Labour).[9] Everything that happened since 1997–2010 is described in unattractive terms, and vowed to be replaced swiftly. Some 23 years after the Education Reform Act that changed England's education for any foreseeable future, and finalizing a trajectory that began with a complete 360-degree circle, the Education Act 2011 (EA 2011) again is a dramatic addition to the lengthy list of England's legislation for education reform. Perhaps the most dramatic and climatically influential change in this law is hidden in one of the schedules. This clause is especially important because it communicates directly with the EIA 2006:

SCHEDULE 11 37 ESTABLISHMENT OF NEW SCHOOLS

Amendments to Part 2 of EIA 2006

1 Part 2 of EIA 2006 (establishment, discontinuance and alteration of schools) is amended as follows.

2 Before section 7 insert – **6A Requirement to seek proposals for establishment of new Academies**(1) If a local authority in England think a new school needs to be established in their area, they must seek proposals for the establishment of an Academy.

In practice, this clause determines that no new community (LEA) schools will be established, from now on. Together with some other sections and clauses that will be analysed further on in this chapter, this act may, or might, according to one's viewpoint – change England's education system in a manner that is second only to the ERA 1988 and in some ways more along the lines of quasi-privatization and privatization of England's public education, its regulation, its accountability to the public, and its consequences in terms of equity and equality. The following excerpt from the 2012 School Admissions Code pursues this policy:

3.22 **Secretary of State's power of direction (Academies)** – Where a local authority considers that an Academy will best meet the needs of any child, it can ask the Academy to admit that child but has no power to direct it to do so. The local authority and the Academy will usually come to an agreement, but if the Academy refuses to admit the child, the local authority can ask the Secretary of State to intervene. The Secretary of State has the power under an Academy's Funding Agreement to direct the Academy to admit a child, and can seek advice from the Adjudicator in reaching a decision.

The Admissions Code 2011, downsized by some 80 per cent from the 1998 version, is a natural companion for the reader and implementer of the EA 2011 and its predecessor, the Academies Act 2010. The code presents the spirit of the act and crystallizes the change that legislation and policy went through from the EIA 2006. In the legal foreword the code simplifies one of the vaguer aspects of the 2006 code:

11. The table below sets out the admission authority for each type of school in England.

Who is responsible for arranging/ providing for an appeal against refusal of a place at a school?	**Who deals with complaints about arrangements?**	**Who is the admission authority?**	**Type of School**
Academy Trust	Schools Adjudicator	Academy Trust	Academies
Local Authority	Schools Adjudicator	Local Authority	Community Schools
Governing body	Schools Adjudicator	Governing body	Foundation Schools
Governing body	Schools Adjudicator	Governing body	Voluntary aided schools
Local Authority	Schools Adjudicator	Local Authority	Voluntary controlled schools

Contrary to the non-specific language of the EIA 2006 and its 87-page Admissions Code, this straightforward 37-page document illustrates and mandates freedom from many of the inconsistencies and paradoxes that characterized the EIA 2006 and its by-law, the Schools Admissions Code. The 2006 legislation struggled with the status of academies and their admissions authority, positing in Section 1.15 that:

> **Admission arrangements for Academies**
>
> 1.15. Admission arrangements for Academies are approved by the Secretary of State as part of an Academy's funding agreement, which require compliance with admissions legislation and relevant Codes. An Academy is required to consult in the same way as other admission authorities do. Apart from increasing its admission number with local agreement following consultation, an Academy cannot alter its admission arrangements without the approval of the Secretary of State. Any objections to an Academy's admission arrangements will be considered by the Secretary of State.

However, the EA 2011 has gone the extra mile and freed academies of this secretarial control. Although in cases of during-the-year variations to the admissions codes it still says:

> 56. Section 88E of the SSFA 1998. Academies do not have to refer proposed variations to their admission arrangements to the Schools Adjudicator, but instead seek agreement with the Secretary of State. (footnote to Section 3.6)

Altogether, the EA 2011 has finalized the independence of non-LEA admissions authorities. This is a spectacular change with long-range effects on England's public schools system. The effects are, I believe, cultural, political, pedagogical, and moral.

The EA 2011 begins with the abolition of several QUANGOs (nicknamed by some interviewees in this book as 'QUANGOES' for this reason exactly), and changes to the status of some others. The main QUANGOs abolished are the General Teaching Council of England (GTCE – Section 7), the Training and Development Agency (TDA – Section 14), and the Qualifications and Curriculum Development Agency (QCDA – Section 25).

The Impact Assessment by the DfE and Explanatory Notes presented with the bill to parliament highlight the main points in the EA 2011:

> 3. The Education Bill is founded on the principles and proposals in the Department for Education November 2010 White Paper, *The Importance of Teaching* (CM-7980). ...
>
> 4. The Bill will remove duties on schools and local authorities to give them greater freedom to decide how to fulfil their functions. The Academies programme will be extended, with Academies for 16 to 19 year olds and alternative provision Academies.
>
> 5. The Bill will change school accountability, with more focused Ofsted inspections and wider powers to intervene in under-performing schools. OfQUAL, the independent qualifications regulator, will be required to secure that the standards of English qualifications are comparable with qualifications awarded outside the UK. The Bill will abolish five arm's length bodies, with many of their functions ending and those which are to continue being discharged by the Secretary of State, who will be directly accountable to Parliament for them. ...
>
> This Part repeals certain duties on the governing bodies of maintained schools in England and repeals the duty on local authorities to appoint a school improvement partner in each maintained school.
>
> 19. It also makes changes to the duties of local authorities in relation to school admissions. In addition, the schools adjudicator will no longer be able to make modification to a school's admissions arrangements in response to a complaint or a referral.

> 21. This Part also makes changes to the arrangements for the establishment of new schools by introducing a presumption that when local authorities set up new schools they will be Academies (including free schools).

The act puts a final lid on the role of LEAs as providers and commissioners of education, by redefining admissions authorities and breaking the connection between schools and LEAs. At the same time, while diminishing LEA powers, further far-reaching responsibilities are mandated to LEAs:

> EARLY YEARS PROVISION
>
> **1 Free of charge early years provision**
>
> (1) Part 1 of the Childcare Act 2006 (functions of local authorities in England in relation to childcare) is amended as set out in subsections (2) and (3).
>
> (2) For section 7 (duty to secure prescribed early years provision free of charge) substitute –
>
> **7 Duty to secure early years provision free of charge in accordance with regulations**
>
> (1) An English local authority must secure that early years provision of such description as may be prescribed is available free of charge, in accordance with any regulations under this subsection, for each young child in their area who –
>
> (a) is under compulsory school age, and
>
> (b) is of such description as may be prescribed.

The regulatory role, responsibilities, and authority of the Secretary of State, the DfE, and Ofsted are apparently strengthened under the EA 2011, although they are narrowed and focused, allowing schools, as the White Paper states – in the Prime Minister's words – to 'devolve as much power as possible to the front line', and – in the Secretary of State's words – 'granting greater autonomy for the front line' and 'having freed schools from external controls'.[10] But these powers are at odds with the influence of the attempt to free schools of control and fortify academies, perhaps at the expense, or instead, of LEAs:

> **PART 4**
>
> QUALIFICATIONS AND THE CURRICULUM
>
> *International comparison surveys*
>
> **20 Requirement for schools to participate in international surveys**

538A Power to direct participation in international surveys

The Secretary of State may direct the governing body of a community, foundation or voluntary school in England to secure that the school participates in such international education surveys as may be specified in the direction.

OfQUAL

21 The Chief Regulator of Qualifications and Examinations

23 Enforcement powers

Abolition of the Qualifications and Curriculum Development Agency

25 Abolition of the Qualifications and Curriculum Development Agency

Repeal of the diploma entitlement

30 Repeal of diploma entitlement for 16 to 18 year olds

31 Repeal of diploma entitlement for fourth key stage

41 School inspections: matters to be covered in Chief Inspector's report

(5A) The Chief Inspector's report under subsection (5) must in particular cover –

(a) the achievement of pupils at the school;

(b) the quality of teaching in the school;

(c) the quality of the leadership in and management of the school;

(d) the behaviour and safety of pupils at the school.

(5B) In reporting under subsection (5), the Chief Inspector must consider –

(a) the spiritual, moral, social and cultural development of pupils at the school;

(b) the extent to which the education provided at the school meets the needs of the range of pupils at the school, and in particular the needs of –

(i) pupils who have a disability for the purposes of the Equality Act 2010, and

(ii) pupils who have special educational needs.

44 Schools causing concern: powers of Secretary of State

45 Complaints: repeal of power to complain to Local Commissioner

PART 6

ACADEMIES

Academy arrangements

52 Academies: removal of requirement to have specialism

53 Academy arrangements: post-16 education and alternative provision

(1) Section 1 of AA 2010 (Academy arrangements) is amended as set out in subsections (2) to (6).

(2) For subsection (5) substitute –

"(5) The undertakings are –

(a) to establish and maintain an educational institution in England which meets the requirements of any of the following –

(i) section 1A (Academy schools);

(ii) section 1B (16 to 19 Academies);

(iii) section 1C (alternative provision Academies);..."

54 Consequential amendments: 16 to 19 Academies and alternative provision

Academies

Academy orders

55 Academy orders: involvement of religious bodies etc

56 Academies: consultation on conversion

59 Transfer of property, rights and liabilities to Academies

(1) Section 8 of AA 2010 (transfer of other property) is amended as follows.

(2) For subsection (2) substitute –

"(2) The Secretary of State may make a scheme (a 'transfer scheme') in relation to –

(a) property used or held for the purposes of the school by a local authority or the school's governing body, and

(b) rights and liabilities (including rights and liabilities in relation to staff) of the local authority or the governing body which were acquired or incurred for the purposes of the school..."

The schools adjudicator's powers have been weakened accordingly. While the act still allows 'any person' to make complaints (Section 36 (2)), it strips the adjudicator of the previous power to enquire into the admissions policies of a school once a complaint has been made (Sections 34 (4)),[11] but formally allows complaints regarding academies (Section 64):

> 3.23 **Local authority reports** – Local authorities **must** produce an annual report on admissions for all the schools in their area for which they co-ordinate admissions, to be published locally and sent to the Adjudicator by **30 June** following the admissions round. The report **must** cover as a minimum:
>
> a) information about how admission arrangements in the area of the local authority serve the interests of looked after children and previously looked after children, children with disabilities and children with special educational needs, including any details of where problems have arisen;
>
> b) an assessment of the effectiveness of Fair Access Protocols and co-ordination in their area, including how many children were admitted to each school under them;
>
> c) the number and percentage of lodged and upheld parental appeals; and
>
> d) any other issues the local authority may wish to include. (School Admission code, 2012)

These reports are a relic from the adjudicator's previous authority, but the grievances that may be referred to here have been limited,[12] and some were obliterated altogether:

> **Objections that may not be referred to the adjudicator**
>
> **21.** – (1) For the purposes of section 88H(2)(**b**) the description of objections that may not be referred under section 88H(2)(b) is –
>
> (a) an objection which in substance seeks an alteration to admission arrangements for a grammar school, which by virtue of section 104(4) may only be made in accordance with sections 105(**c**) to 109(**d**) (altering the school's admission arrangements so that it no longer has selective admission arrangements);
>
> (b) an objection which in substance seeks an alteration to admission arrangements for a selective Academy so as to remove selection, which by virtue of its Academy arrangements may only be made in accordance with those Academy arrangements;

(c) an objection that the admission number has not been changed or has been increased for –

(i) any school whose admission authority are not the local authority; or

(ii) an Academy;

To regard the call by the secretary of state to envision the EA 2011 as a direct protraction or descendant of the policies and legislation that ended in 1997 is tempting. But I believe that seeing the EA 2011 solely as a reaction to what happened in 13 years of New Labour governments is a bit simplistic. This is not only because some important parts of the New Labour legislation were adopted forthwith, as they are admittedly relevant to the Conservatives' ideals, but also because the EA 2011 builds on the continuity of both the Thatcher–Major era and also the Blair–Brown era, as I will explain later in the book.

Comparison and afterthoughts

The analysis of the Education and Inspections Act 2006 and the Education Act 2011 offers insights that can only emerge with the benefit of socio-political – not just legal – hindsight. Thus we can look at the EIA 2006 from a distance, but not so the EA 2011, which means, on the one hand, that one should express caution, for I am not sure how this act will be seen after several years. On the other hand, looking back at the ERA 1988 (Whitty *et al.*, 1998; Whitty, 2008) reveals that a substantial part of what was deducted at the time is valid now as well.

Ron Glatter (2002) defines and analyses a model of governance in education that comprises four approaches. The first approach, 'competitive market' or CM (ibid. 229), depicts the market as the main regulatory force, through open enrolment and choice, with the role of audit and inspection being to inform the consumer. The school, in this approach, is envisaged as a 'small business' and its form of accountability as 'contractual'. The second approach, 'school empowerment' (SE) emphasizes just that, and describes audit as a tool for school management. Both the CM and the SE approaches are focused on the end-units – the schools. The third approach is Local Empowerment (LE) which is characterized by a political perspective and devolves power to a 'family of local schools', typically, perhaps, within an LEA. The fourth and final approach is 'quality control' (QC) which accentuates a mandatory curriculum and centralized assessment, with accelerated guidance from government. The QC approach sees the school as a 'point of delivery' and emphasizes 'central or other state bodies' as the focus of the system. Legislation has a central role in each of these four approaches. In the CE approach its role is to define market rules, including perhaps privatization of schools or entrepreneurship, and to free central government from the responsibility of both commission and delivery of education services. In this approach, Glatter explains, the role of the middle tier is 'minimal'. In the SE approach legislation can empower headteachers and schools and possibly define legal models of school incorporation. In the LE approach the law would, ideally, define modes of devolution to a local authority. In the QC approach the law would establish and empower strong regulatory bodies and define their responsibilities. Glatter points at the tensions between the four approaches, each of which is hardly ever implemented in its pure form, but is often combined with factors or principles from the other three. These contradictions, often the result of political struggles or shortcomings in the political system, pose a challenge to law makers. Previously, in my 2004 study *Legalized Leadership* (Gibton, 2004b), I used this detailed model to dichotomize the Conservatives' 1988 legislation as typical CM, and New Labour's post-2002 legislation as primarily QC. In 2012, again, I believe there is a serious attempt by government to implement the CM approach as strictly as possible. Between, say, the mid-1990s and 2010, things were more complicated and messy (Hill, 2003). The EIA 2006 leaned strongly toward the QC approach. On the one hand, the centralized controlling policies of New Labour's legislation that aspired to micro-manage teaching and learning with frequent assessment and audits were accompanied by a further distribution of academies and trust schools. On the other hand, the EA 2011 offers enhanced CM features, but retains noteworthy regulatory measures. Also the LE approach that envisioned the LEA as the main force of this political control model may require updating, for the concept of a 'family of schools' means different things in 2012, for example chains and federations of academies and trusts that own and control more than one school. This means the scene has become considerably more complicated and burdened by new structures and players, just as Ball predicted in 2007. The EA 2011 is, in this sense, more coherent and cohesive than the EIA 2006. This is consistent with the debate on New Labour's legislation (Ball, 2007; Green, 2005; Manzer, 2003; Whitty, *et al.*, 1998) that is ridden with conflict and contradiction, and attests to the ambitions of New Labour to embrace what may have been seen as the benefits of a decentralized high-stakes system with some (and critics say more than some) neoliberal currents, and the 'Old Labour' controlled-economy egalitarianism.

A second useful model is by Bottery and Wright (2000). This model likens education policy to a boat going down a river, and offers three approaches. The first, Social Democracy, is portrayed as 'steering and rowing'; the second, the 'New Right', is portrayed as 'no steering no rowing'; and the third is labelled 'New Modernizers' – that is, New Labour, portrayed as 'steering, limited rowing'. Once more, as with Glatter's model, this model further attempts to explain the ideological and practical policy discrepancies that differ between the three approaches. The Social Democracy and New Right approaches are more consistent than the others, regardless, at this point in the critique, of their equity, equality, and social justice. The New Modernizers (that is, those who follow the 'third way'), who attempt to combine the better of two dichotomous worlds, are full of inconsistencies and contradictions, as the EIA 2006 clearly shows. I believe the reason for tensions in this model lies with the instrumentalist approach to markets, which is implemented while setting aside the cultural implications on schools and schooling. Instrumentalism goes well with legislation's basic impervious linear theme. The declarations on LEAs and the encouragements of non-LEA schools are the key example. The EA 2011 is freed from such indecisiveness and is more ingenuous. This is especially evident when reading the by-laws that offer a clear structure of the system and its norms.[13] Although, as Bottery found, both New Right and 'third way' leaders recognized the public concern to turn education from a provider-controlled to a consumer-controlled system, the mechanisms for reaching this are fundamentally different. While the New Right sees market forces as the foremost, if not exclusive, path to consumer control over education, the 'third way' sees central government as an agent for tightening citizens' control over education, by proxy. Again these models are hardly dichotomous but are more like phases along a continuum.

Nevertheless, when analysing the two laws in terms of fairness – the main theme of this book – the afterthoughts are melancholy. Both laws finalize the de-democratization of England's school system by decentralizing not just schools, but especially enrolment (admissions) policy. Figure 4.1 shows how various charter-type schools are becoming, gradually but steadily, alternative admission authorities – somewhat patchily at first across England's public education system, but eventually, in 2012 and prospectively in the coming years, evolving from a patchwork to a more uniform cover over, and beyond, democratically elected LEAs. Findings point at two 'independent school trajectories' intimated and established through legislation.

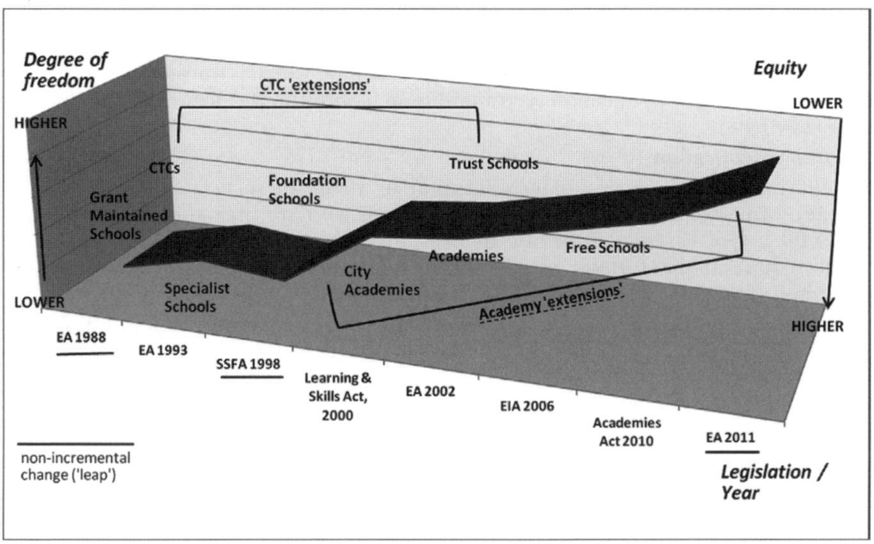

Figure 4.1: The evolving freedom of government-initiated schools

The first trajectory is that of CTCs, which were extended into specialist schools, then into trust schools, thereby exacerbating the distribution of academies and then free schools. The EIA 2006 marks the end of the CTC trajectory, and, capitalizing upon this, permeates the second trajectory of trust schools and their evolution into academies. The two partly-concurrent law-based trajectories are cornerstones in England's law-based reform that jeopardizes fairness, at first hesitantly (the EIA 2006) and then indefatigably (the EA 2011). The two trajectories merge reforms along two decades of law-based reforms into one route, thus creating a continuance of the two types of schools presented in Figure 4.1. Ultimately, to quote Ball (2008b: 196), the 'progressive creep' was 'compromised' only temporarily by the EIA 2006, perhaps to be set back to the expected course by the EA 2011.

Notes

[1] Academies have their legal base under section 482 of the EA 1996, but were not named as such. In the EA 2002, section 65 they were part of the City Colleges. In 2005 their numbers grew when the Department of Academies and Trust schools was set in the Department of Education. In the EIA 2006 their status was expanded and strengthened, and their title was changed from city academies to Academies (EIA 2006 schedule 3, section 8 'In section 332B of EA 1996 (resolution of disputes), in subsection (8)(c), for 'a city academy' substitute 'an Academy')

[2] Section 40 (4).

[3] Sections 44 and 53.

[4] Department for Education (DfE); Department for Education and Employment (DfEE); Department for Education and Skills (DfES); Department for Children, Schools, and Families (DCSF); and more recently Department for Education (DfE) once again.

[5] Section 8 (6).

[6] EA 1996 , sections 4–6 'Educational institutions':

4 Schools: general

(1) In this Act 'school' means an educational institution which is outside the further education sector and the higher education sector and is an institution for providing any one or more of the following –

(a) primary education,

(b) education which is secondary education by virtue of section 2(2)(a), or (c) full-time education suitable to the requirements of persons who are over compulsory school age but under the age of 19, whether or not the institution also provides part-time education suitable to the requirements of junior pupils, further education or secondary education not within paragraph (b).

(2) For the purposes of this Act an educational institution that would fall within subsection (1) but for the fact that it provides part-time rather than full-time education shall nevertheless be treated as a school if that part-time education is provided under arrangements made under section 19(1) (pupil referral units).

(3) For the purposes of this Act an institution is outside the further education sector if it is not –

(a) an institution conducted by a further education corporation established under section 15 or 16 of the Further and Higher Education Act 1992, or (b) a designated institution for the purposes of Part I of that Act (defined in section 28(4) of that Act); and references to institutions within that sector shall be construed accordingly.

(4) For the purposes of this Act an institution is outside the higher education sector if it is not –

(a) a university receiving financial support under section 65 of that Act …

4 Education Act 1996 (c. 56)

Part I – General

Chapter I – The statutory system of education Document Printed: 2010-09-10 Status: This is the original version (as it was originally enacted).

(b) an institution conducted by a higher education corporation within the meaning of that Act, or

(c) a designated institution for the purposes of Part II of that Act (defined in section 72(3) of that Act); and references to institutions within that sector shall be construed accordingly.

5 Primary schools, secondary schools and middle schools

(1) In this Act 'primary school' means (subject to regulations under subsection (4)) a school for providing primary education, whether or not it also provides part-time education suitable to the requirements of junior pupils or further education.

(2) In this Act 'secondary school' means (subject to regulations under subsection (4)) a school for providing secondary education, whether or not it also provides further education.

(3) In this Act 'middle school' means a school in respect of which proposals authorized by section 49, 198(6) or 291 are implemented (that is, a school providing full-time education suitable to the requirements of pupils who have attained a specified age below 10 years and six months and are under a specified age above 12 years).

(4) The Secretary of State shall make regulations for determining, or enabling him to determine, whether a middle school is to be treated for the purposes of this Act and the other enactments relating to education as a primary school or as a secondary school.

(5) The powers conferred by sections 49, 198(6) and 291 and subsection (4) above are exercisable –

(a) notwithstanding anything in this Act (and in particular section 1); but

(b) without prejudice to the exercise of any other power conferred by this Act.

6 Nursery schools and special schools

(1) A primary school is a nursery school if it is used mainly for the purpose of providing education for children who have attained the age of two but are under the age of five.

(2) A school is a special school if it is specially organized, and for the time being approved, as mentioned in section 337(1).'

[7] Sections 23, 23 (4–5).

[8] See Sections 46–47.

[9] The Importance of Teaching 20210 white paper, executive summary, p.8.

[10] See: 'The Importance of Teaching, the Schools White Paper 2010' the Prime Minister's foreword p.3, the Secretary of State's foreword p.6, and the executive summary, p.8.

[11] And see also Section 21 of the EA 2011.

[12] In 2012 the Chief Schools Adjudicator is Dr Elizabeth Passmore OBE. Up to 2011 the Chief Schools Adjudicator was Dr Ian Craig.

[13] See: the Schools Admissions Code, 2012; the School Admission Appeals Code 2012; the School Admissions (Appeals Arrangements) (England) Regulations 2012; and the School Admissions (Admission Arrangements and Co-ordination of Admission Arrangements) (England) Regulations 2012).

Part 2

Who is involved in England's law-based education reform, and how?

Chapter 5

The map of prominent figures in law-based reform, their views, and the roles they play

Introduction

'The common aim of such studies is to understand how law and legal institutions work in practice, how law is experienced by officials and the public, and how it influences their behaviour' (Galligan, 2010). This chapter first maps the key figures and bodies that influence, are involved in, and are affected by, legislation for education reform in England, between 2000 and 2011; and then portrays their accounts of law-based education reform. Appendix A presents the study that provided the data base for this book. Legislation is part of the everyday life, thoughts, and feelings of educators in England. This is perhaps not surprising given that the system is, as I demonstrated in previous chapters, over-legislated. Legislation has an imperative part to play in the culture of educators and academics. It has deep meaning for the participants in this study, who effortlessly responded to my invitation to talk on the subject. As will be shown in Chapter 9, the anticipation for new legislation, the guessing-game regarding what it will include, the looking for 'well connected' individuals who have had a glimpse of a draft or have an inkling of its content, are all part of a kind of ritual among policymakers and educators. Getting used to new laws is almost a constant for them, as they go through their professional lives in an unstable limbo *between* laws, incessantly resituating themselves as legislation is renewed and reintroduced.

Methodologically, this chapter draws upon the 'social network' theory and method (Wasserman and Faust, 1994) in empirical legal-policy studies (Deleon, 2006; Galligan, 2010; Partington, 2010). As early as 1998 Victor Kuo, a (then) doctoral student at Stanford University, used the social network approach to uncover political influence networks in a dispute over a high-profile court case on public school finance in Kentucky. Tichy *et al.* (1979: 508) presented 12 'network properties' that can be borrowed for this study. The properties that are most relevant to this study are: 'nature of the links' (that is, strength of links, clarity of expectations, and links to multiple relations); and 'structural characteristics' – the most important of which are 'changes in the network over time' and individuals who gain 'star' or 'bridge' status ('an individual who is a member of multiple clusters in the network') and therefore become 'linking pins' or 'gatekeepers' ('a star who also links the social unit with external domains'). (All terms are taken from Tichy *et al.*, 1979: 508.)

The reason for relying on network analysis is that the interviewees in this study are part of a network. It is a social network, partly, and an organizational network – as one can view the education system as a loosely-coupled (Orton and Weick, 1990) organization. Later, Stephen Ball (2007; 2012) describes social networks in his maps of power relating to a national and global analysis of education policy. Again, although the subject of this study is not an organization, the UK education and government system can be seen, I believe, as a loosely coupled (Orton and Weick, 1990) one. This is how Tichy *et al.*'s model becomes useful, as will be shown at the end of this chapter. Deleon (2006) explains that modern public policy studies:

> ... tend to examine issue networks, including governmental units on the ... state and municipal levels; these are constantly seen to be interacting with important non-profit organizations ... on both the national and the local levels, and various representations from the private sector as well.
>
> (Deleon, 2006: 50)

The term 'issue network' provides the most accurate description of the cohort of participants who took part in this study.

Pierre Bourdieu (1987; Hacker, 2008), in his work on the juridical field, offers one of the most exciting socio-legal viewpoints on the law as a social construct. His work was originally limited to the adversarial characteristic of a trial and was not applied to legislation. Hacker, in turn, expanded Bourdieu's model to a broader field:

> ... a deep and complex understanding of a specific legal field ... can be achieved through an empirical application of Bourdieu's concept of law as a social field, but without making a priori assumptions regarding the field's boundaries, positions, prizes or logic.
>
> (Ibid. 5)

Together with theories such as that of Galligan (2010), this chapter will map the figures involved in England's law-based reforms, present and analyse their views, and show, in the following chapters, how they are all interconnected within one field.

The leading figures in law-based reform

Twelve groups of influential figures emerged for the sampling process in this study. Not surprisingly, perhaps, there is some overlap with the groups or people in these groups with some recent policy studies in England (Ball, 2007; 2012; Bangs *et al.*, 2010). But these studies have done more in terms of pointing out individuals, and perhaps less in pointing out groups of policymakers, although there are references to some groups or organizations. This study focuses on education law and law-based reform. Of important assistance to this study is the evolving concept of policy as discourse (Ball, 1994; Deleon, 2006). Findings here can be validated through these studies. Following is a description of the people and organizations that form the field of education legislation in England. Some suggest it, plan it, and phrase it. Some advise as to what it should include. Some are the enforcers, deliverers, and evaluators of its implementation and outcomes. Some are the recipients, whose professional lives are governed by it.

Senior DfE officials

The first trivial place to look for people who shape and determine legislation is the huge ministry known (as of now – the title has changed five times in two decades)[1] as the Department for Education, or DfE. Civil servants from the DfE comprise this first group of the cohort, which includes senior heads of departments in charge of educational reform, legislation, and planning. On the one hand, they are experts on school reform in England. On the other, they are, in a way, victims of educational regimes' attempts to circumvent officials, bureaucrats, and professionals. The members of this group show all the signs of crises that characterize the civil service in general (Foster, 2005), not specifically in education policy. In light of England's tradition of a professional and impartial civil service, and the gradual but definite change in their status and role, learning about their role and their views on legislation is crucial to the subject of this study. Meanwhile, the change in the civil service is a secondary theme of this study, but an important one. What happened to the civil service has a direct bearing on law-based reform. Three phenomena came up in the findings, each worthy of a separate piece of research. The first phenomenon is civil servants' role in what Foster calls 'conviction politics' (ibid. 211–12), in other words, the role of civil servants vis-à-vis the political goals of the politicians who run the department. The second phenomenon is the gradual movement of civil servants into the private or quasi-private areas of education policymaking. In 2011 it was fascinating to re-encounter some of the individuals I had interviewed in 2001 and 2005, away from the government and now working in privately financed foundations that establish and own schools, train teachers and headteachers, and consult LEAs and other education organizations – all part of what Ball (2007) refers to as the 'education business' and the 'education service industry' (ibid. 39). The third phenomenon is the gradual recruitment of political appointments into the civil service, whether as consultants, as heads of ad hoc short- or long-term projects, or as full members of the service and heads of departments within the DfE. I believe all three phenomena have an influence on the views and work of the 'traditional' or 'career' civil servants (I use inverted commas because even this strict definition is hazy), both from the perspective of the competition and challenge posed by these groups of individuals, and from the point of view of offering them new insights into their role, their work, and law-based reform.

DfE political appointments

Following on from the changes in the DfE civil service described in the previous part, this title refers to educational professionals who, at some stage of their career, became affiliated to the party (formerly New Labour, now Conservative–Liberal-Democrats) and administration. This affiliation may have developed through local government or through think tanks. In the past they were school principals – perhaps superheads or supervisors or officials in Local Educational Authorities (LEAs/LAs), or ex-ministry civil servants that were subsequently offered a new post. This relatively new group is not always appreciated by the old guard of civil servants. Overall they are passionate representatives of government policy and reform, and sometimes see the career civil servants as a reform-preventing factor.

Teachers' and headteachers' associations' officials and heads

Two central forces in education policy, with direct interest in legislation, are teachers' and headteachers' unions. The two are not united in their views on law-based reform. While teachers' unions have been weakened by reforms, headteachers' organizations have gained strength. Their voice, amplified by managerial practices that see them as carriers of change, have become important. The older National Association of Headteachers (NAHT) is being challenged by the more recent Association of College and School Leaders (ACSL), formerly the SHA. The two largest teachers' unions are also somewhat opposed: the traditional, and larger, National Union of Teachers (NUT) and the Association of Teachers and Leaders (ATL). Headteachers, as will be presented in detail in Chapter 7, are central to education reform and some also move on to higher posts within the 'issue network' of law-based reform. Unlike teachers, their involvement in law-based reform is not just by proxy of their unions but mainly personally, as I will explain.

Consultants

As reform and marketization speed up, consultants play a significantly growing role. Some are ex-government officials, ex-headteachers, ex-HMIs, academics or ex-academics, and perhaps early retirees. Some are people from the financial, business, and media world who have acquired expertise and knowledge in school reform. As much of law-based reform is implemented through non-government firms and agencies (popularly known as QUANGOs or ALBs), consultants are a group worth listening to. They are involved in policymaking at all levels of this study (Ball, 2007), from parliamentary select committees, through the DfE, onwards to LEAs, and down to school level. Consultants advise and supervise operations for QUANGOs, NGOs, ALBs, think tanks, training agencies, and other bodies and organizations that influence, or are influenced by, law-based reform.

LEA/LA directors and officials

Needless to say, LEAs, despite growing criticism of their role in educational reform, are still the backbone of England's system, organizationally as well as politically, and are the carriers, implementers, and popular punch-bags for every problem, sometimes seen either as catalysts or as obstructers of change. They are also at the heart of controversy and debate regarding regulation that is handled through legislation. Directors of education for LEAs come from diverse backgrounds. Some are educators, for example ex-headteachers. Some are local political figures. Some come from the business world, ran NGOs/QUANGOs, were senior academics, or worked for the civil service. Some are a mix of all or several of these.

'Superheads'

Superheads are headteachers, a few in primary but more in secondary schools, who have acquired fame as leaders in their schools and communities, as well as in the media (Earley and Weindling, 2004). Their status can be attributed to within-school educational reform, to success in government assessment, and sometimes to success in advancing weak populations. New Labour governments began collaborating heavily with some of them, and involving them in national decision-making. They were invited to take part in consulting groups, to sit on public committees, and to apply for senior posts, whether in the ministry, in government regional offices, in Local Educational Authorities, or in outsourced government organizations and educational projects, and to share ideas informally. Several are also connected to a political party (more so to New Labour, now Labour), sometimes informally. Such leading headteachers, to whom Chapter 7 is dedicated, comprise several distinct sub-groups. The two leading and significant groups are the heads of large LEA comprehensive secondary schools and the heads of academies. The first group has borne the brunt of secondary education in England for the last three decades and is therefore habitually at the heart of public and government concern and critique for failing or insufficient results, retention rates, SES- or ethnically-based gaps, violence, and other major ailments of the system. They are also, or at least according to some findings (see Chapter 7 and also Bangs *et al.*, 2010), the leading adversaries of charter-type schooling and of quasi-privatization developments in the public school system. An authoritative sub-group among the comprehensive school heads, certainly between 2000 and 2006, is that pertaining to the heads of specialist schools (Taylor and Ryan, 2005). These pre-historic predecessors of academy heads (some of them would sternly disagree with this label) were considered the 'cutting edge' of headship during New Labour administrations and the focus of public interest, as a solution for many of the problems of secondary schooling. Heads of academies represent the 'future', or the future of secondary schools, in England. They are usually ex-heads of comprehensive schools, yielding views that are enormously valuable to this study. For the last six years, and now more than ever before, they are the focal point of inspection, assessment, and criticism, as they represent the hopes of governments and perhaps the parents, and the fears of the guardians of comprehensive maintained LEA-owned-and-run schools.

Senior Ofsted personnel

The powerful audit mechanism Office for Standards in Education (Ofsted) grew rapidly both in size and especially in influence in the early to mid-1990s, and since then has maintained a steady and central role in education policy and law-based reform. Ofsted is headed by Her Majesty's Chief Inspector of Schools (HMCI), who is allocated formal statutory power (under the EA 1992, the SIA 1996, and many other by-laws), and there is a specific section in nearly every piece of legislation authorizing HMCI and Ofsted to evaluate and assess parts of the new mandatory conduct of schools. Ofsted officials hold vast basic information on law-based reform and its impact on schools. In addition, they have synoptic views of education policy as well as in-depth close acquaintance with schools, headteachers, teachers, teaching and learning methods, governance, and programmes of all sorts. Due to the immense broadening and diversifying of Ofsted's responsibilities in the last decade – and especially after the 2004 Children Act and the 2006 Childcare Act that brought many new services under the responsibility of education departments, and after placing pre-schools under inspection – Ofsted officials acquired even more important knowledge and insights into legislation, regulation, and governance in new fields, making them valuable participants of this study.

Legal advisers

Legal advisers deal directly with legal issues with the ministry, teachers' associations, and trusts. They are some of the most prominent experts on law-based reform and also carry historic knowledge on the intricacies of change in legislation.

MPs, heads of the parliamentary select committee on education

This dominant and senior committee is responsible for debating and passing educational legislation, and often clashes with the government in the process of transforming white papers into laws. The committee is an arena for discussions on current high-profile issues of education policy as well as for regular and ongoing deliberation of education policy, nearly always with legislative implications. Many of the participants in this study appear before the committee, whether as experts or to give evidence. While at the beginning of the New Labour era the committee was sympathetic and supportive of law-based reform, it grew quite critical towards the end of New Labour's term. Under the Conservative–Liberal-Democrat administration the committee is an important engine for promoting white papers and bills.

Advisers and heads of government units

These powerful figures have had considerable influence over educational legislation and school reform, especially since 1997. The delivery and standards unit's heads and various advisory posts to the Prime Minister and the secretaries of state often hold the key to law-based reform, whether initiating and leading policy, or behind the scenes.

Leaders and CEOs of NGOs, QUANGOs, and ALBs

All of these are part of a growing force of civil society and have parallel influence on education policy and legislation. The terms 'QUANGO', 'NGO', and 'ALB' represent a maze of organizations with various forms, structures, intentions, levels of engagement; roles within, beside, and with government, LEAs, or schools; and modus operandi. They include advocacy groups of parents and educators, civil rights groups, religious groups, teacher and headteacher training agencies, charities, and many others. All have substantial impact on policy.

Senior academics

These are often involved in law-based reform in various stages. Some have political ties and have become consultants, heads of ministry departments, and heads of, or senior figures in, LEAs. Some run large intervention and change initiatives. Many serve on committees, parliamentary or royal, that investigate education policy issues or form and suggest reforms. This is not an exclusively English phenomenon (Levin, 2005). Their multiple viewpoints, both as researchers and as policymakers and implementers, make them useful for this study.

Private finance initiatives (PFIs) and think tanks

For quite some years PFIs and think tanks have had a growing influence on policy. One can add to these, international consultancy firms (although the latter were not included in this study). Their main role used to be in lobbying and promoting policy agendas and programmes. Lately, however, their involvement in education policy has moved from the advisory and agenda-setting role to a more proactive role with two separate types of participation. The first is providing specific functions for the government especially in training and recruiting, and most lately in establishing new schools; the second function is assessment and evaluation, both nationally and internationally.

Figure 5.1 maps the figures who participated in the study according to two denominators. The first denominator is hierarchical: top to bottom, from the government or the national level through the local level to the schools level. The second denominator is conceptual, organizational, economic, and legal-regulatory. It runs the gamut from the public dimension to the private dimension, again with the quasi-private mid-range level along the way.

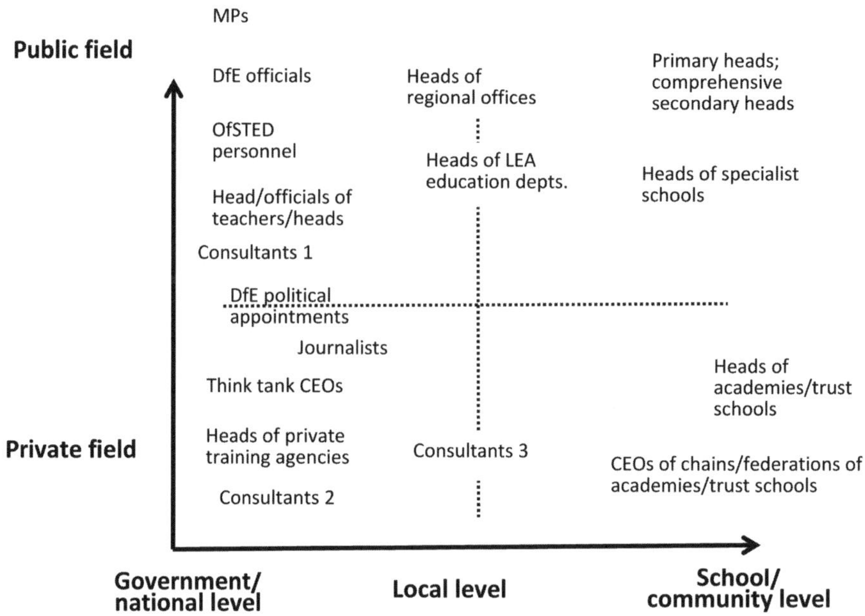

Figure 5.1: Figures in law-based reform: Place and connections – mapping the field

Figure 5.1 shows that while the national and school levels are still quite distinct, the public–private range is becoming quite complicated and the boundaries are unclear. This is similar to other findings (Ball, 2007; Bangs *et al.,* 2010).

The next sections of this chapter will present the views of the participants on law-based reform. First, in this chapter, their compiled views are introduced; and in the next chapters, the views of separate groups and individuals among them will be analysed, including in respective periods.

Legislation is necessary for policy

The interviewees are very well aware of the role and importance of legislation for education policy:

> Where legislation is most needed is about maps of control and Ofsted, Number 10, and the delivery unit. And the coupling and reforming of Ofsted powers. This is very time-consuming and we tend to [have] an awful lot of time wasted on [these power games].
>
> (Senior education adviser 1)

> All governments use legislation to bring about shifts in behaviour and push change in the system. All administrations are interested in improvement. The system is constantly adapting to that and politically both the previous Labour and the current [Conservative–Liberal-Democrat] administrations

> have a strong commitment to addressing social mobility, improving access and so on, and there was some continuity and some discontinuity in their policy. This government has a strong commitment to slimming down the prescribed curriculum. On the other hand the EBacc is a new performance measure. They [the current government] are committed to reducing bureaucracies in schools. The bill will include measures on schools not having to do this [follow a prescribed curriculum]. Secondary schools achieving 5 A to C [grades in GCSEs] will have some levers changed [i.e. they will be granted more autonomy in return for improved performance].
>
> (Ofsted officials 1 and 2)

> The Conservative party, for good or for ill, they want to free the schools of reins, if standards fall. These guys are politicians. We do try to address imbalances. That's where legislation comes in, there is the academies bill, [which] has tried a light-touch approach. Some will say that it's a conspiracy to undermine the state system, but the state system has to stand on its own two feet. If you take a school from local authorities they lose the 10 per cent and they might say 'we [only] have 40 per cent [left so] it's not worth while any more [continuing to maintain control of schools]. Preschools shouldn't be under an Ofsted inspector who closes it – it should be the parents but in a rural area you need choice. You can't allow the schools to shut down, there isn't enough money in the pot. There are social issues you have to address and you can only do this with law.
>
> (Think tank CEO 1)

> These days in modern politics the main weapon most political parties use is the law. If you go back to Michael Oakeshott's 'between civil association and enterprise association what's happening is the civil societies', in the enterprise association the government is the manager and it uses whatever means it has – law – as legitimate compulsion. Government agencies use public funds according to legal mandates.
>
> (Think tank CEO 2)

Interviewees agree that legislation is necessary for achieving three main targets. The first target is translating political and ideological goals into education policy. The main tool politicians have is legislation. This aspect will be explored in the next chapter. The second target is regulation of a decentralized system. Regulation is necessary as more and more powers are devolved to schools, as the system is constantly reorganized while powers are shifted from one level to another, and new bodies and organizations (including schools and groups of schools) are established. It is apparent that in a decentralized system major changes can be achieved *only* through mandatory regulation. If schools belong to the state, or strictly to LEAs in a uniform model, with heads and teachers working for the public ownership, whether national or local (a model of commission and delivery), then reform can be administered through administrative tools, and legislation is not required. But in a decentralized system in which the government assumes a regulatory position, legislation is the key to reform. The modifications include issues of governance and provision, and pedagogical change. This, of course, does not justify or explain the frequency or volume of legislation, but that is another matter. This target of legislation can therefore be concluded as being twofold: regulation of a decentralized, multi-commissioned, and multi-delivered system; and mandating pedagogical programmes and administering teaching and learning methods, standards, and assessment.

The third function of legislation is equity – that is, to ensure, or at least to improve, equality and fairness, protect weak, disenfranchised groups, and promote multiculturalism and diversity, thus preventing mainstreaming and supremacy by a dominant culture. This role can only be achieved through legislation because market forces alone naturally work for the benefit of stronger groups. There is supposedly a paradox because it is the strong groups that also influence legislation. But somehow on a national level, social struggles, protest, political necessities, civil unrest, and the media, sometimes allow a balancing force, even for a short while, that serves as an 'equity window'. When such a window opens, legislation can create conditions that will balance market forces and improve the situation for those worse off. Once such legislation is accepted, it is not easy for governments, acting upon incidental or simply short-term political whims, to change legislation and weaken social rights. Notwithstanding, England's political and legal system, having strong, one- (or at the most, rarely, two-) party governments that are around for long periods and several terms in a row, with minimal constitutional intervention by supreme courts, does accommodate government's infringements on hard-won rights in education:

> You had in the 2006 legislation various things that are being repealed now, and in the 1998 legislation as well, things that introduced fairness like the schools adjudicators whose powers are lessened now and admissions guidance that became the admissions code, and we had discussion on foundation schools that worried the LAs will punish them for choosing GM status so we had an independent adjudicator. So these mechanisms were quite important in ensuring fairness but also that this fairness will not be unfair to certain schools. In the 1998 and 2006 legislation there were three things you need on admission, if you have choice it's important this is not only for middle class parents. So three mechanisms, one was that transport was given to schools LAs saw as preferred, and they had three close schools, and the second point was … the admissions code which became legislation that schools have an admissions policy based either on banding or on a lottery, so you don't give preference to people living really

close. The third aspect was the concept of choice adviser, which wasn't really introduced but the idea was that people who lived on estates will get help to choose a school. So when you had arguments from back bencher MPs, and we had more safeguards, such as giving LAs the right to propose new schools, we wanted them to become commissioners, in regard of new schools in today's bill this was introduced, but we couldn't do this to them. NL always introduced safeguards to allow desegregation although whether this has the greatest impact is objective. Multicultural issues were on the table but the things that had the greatest impacts are academies themselves and literacy and numeracy strategies.

(Senior adviser to the government)

We have 4,000 schools that are their own admissions authorities and 6,500 CE and RC schools the dioceses are working hard to pull there, and retain their status. My worry is that this current government is going back with these constraints and abolishing admissions forums where all admission authorities come together. It's not the LA any more, we need a new coordination group. This government says we don't want this anymore. We already didn't do a compliance exercise this year so the only way to check is the annual report and the new bill (clause 34 and sec 88j of the 2011 act that stops us from changing admissions arrangements). We had a Muslim school in the autumn where they had one issue and we found 26 other illegal things other than what was referred and now this power has been abolished, there are crap schools and manipulative governors and heads. The regulative free market is being eased so the question is, how much more of this will be eased? The new Conservative government is led by dogma, it's not thought-through, it's free market policy, by simplifying the procedures and weakening the admissions authority's power

(Senior DfE official)

Admissions is not an answer to anything at all although of course it shouldn't be discriminatory. We did a big piece of research about segregation and how segregated the system would be if pupils went to the nearest school. And we found the overall effect of segregation was nearly zero. Like Catholic schools have other patterns of admissions, but that people think that admissions policy will crack segregation issues is untrue. It's more about practice issues – how it's done and organized is important, who can go to which schools, but if you want to shift that it's not just admissions.

(Senior DfE official)

These last quotes demonstrate the seed of what is perhaps the deepest controversy regarding legislation's regulatory role. One question is whether legislation should have a clear mission of fairness and serve as the leading equity instrument and social equalizer. A second question is whether, while regulating the forces of the free market, legislation should ensure that gross injustices – especially those created by the education system itself and not necessarily outside of it – are avoided or controlled. This argument will be explored further, in this chapter and elsewhere in the book.

Having established the roles of legislation and its necessity, the interviewees are generally critical towards the main phenomenon analysed in this study.

'A sledgehammer to crack walnuts': The dangers and hardships in using law for education policy

A lot of the interviewees thought that legislation is overused and therefore abused, and that the system in England is overregulated, even when the government wishes to free it of constraints:

> There is something that isn't there about legislation: it is a very crude tool. It's the only tool that politicians have. You use sledgehammers to crack walnuts. Politicians are used to using legislation like this. One watches with fear when the minister goes to some foreign country – you say they will come back with this new idea, it could be systems or process or national curriculum. And when they go there they always see the best schools, and just a few of course, then they return and in a short while there's a bill that implements what they've seen all over the country. How do you ensure the schools that are failing receive assistance, and how do you address that and trusting the rest to do a good job without treating all of them with suspicion?
>
> (Superhead 3)

And this is not said at the receiving end of legislation alone:

> The draft legislation for what was to become the January 2012 inspection framework was there and we had to think how we should develop this into an inspection framework and guidance. So we set up a small project group of people and as they work on the draft framework and guidance there is a process of interaction and consultation, and we offer a perspective. Usually we arrange some trial inspections and discuss the results with professional associations, headteachers and focus groups.
>
> (Senior Ofsted official, 2012)

> The first thing is that law is not on its own when it comes to equality and social justice. Changing the law doesn't impact on these things. What makes a difference is the practice in schools and local areas and the law can only influence that with a strong implementation policy. … What changes

> outcomes is law deployed carefully and skilfully – a tool in the toolkit. If you look at things, tools have to be successful with poorer children so trying to effect that dealing through the law alone is ineffective. You have to consider each issue on its merits. If you don't have to change the law it's better. It saves 18 months. Changing the law is not sufficient, it's effective with a broader programme of change implementation of the NC, LMS, Ofsted, academies – these have a big impact in the system, the thing they have in common is that just changing the law is far from enough. EAZs were wrong as an implementation programme. There's no doubt that some of it was fundamental for reform. There have been occasions for an opportunity to legislate like EAZs, or for academies – you need an arrangement that will allow schools to convert. But there have been examples that came with a fanfare and didn't go anywhere. Lasting reforms had a legal component and a serious implementation, resourcing, and persuasion component.
>
> (Senior DfE civil servant 1)

This quote presents an authoritative framework for the role, the content, and the structure of legislation and its place in an all-encompassing panorama of policymaking, agenda-setting, and regulation. This senior DfE civil servant sees the law as essential for changing the fundamental, basic, components of the education system: a tool in a toolkit that is often used for the wrong reasons or issues. This creates a culture of cynicism towards new education law. Many of the interviewees in this study reacted with an opening deep sigh when asked about legislation, as if a bit embarrassed by this phenomenon. Sometimes, though, legislation allows for interpretation by those who inspect, assess and regulate:

> A lot of what Ofsted does has to do with legislation that doesn't specify how we do it but that we have to inspect it and report on certain key areas. Legislation specifies a duty but not usually anything around methodology, or how we go about the task. … We then issue a draft document that proposes how we see the inspection side of the law. However, legislation does tend to define how often we should inspect a type of provision, but not – for example – how long an inspection should last. However, in some types of work, such as independent school inspections, there are set regulations for the providers that we must inspect against.
>
> (Senior Ofsted personnel 1)

Despite the volume, frequency, and details of law, the regulation through Ofsted is open-ended. On the one hand, this is good news because it leaves important regulatory decision-making to the members of the professional audit mechanism who are well experienced in auditing and have hands-on, intimate acquaintance with, and knowledge of, what goes on in schools.

But on the other hand a lot of room is left for interpretation, as one LEA head said:

> It's not enough that you have so much legislation that we have to read, master, and act upon. Thing is that Ofsted has its own interpretation that finds its way into countless forms and inspection tools. So there's one 'letter of the law' and one 'letter of Ofsted' and often they are quite distinct from each other. Ofsted language is more detailed and often more user-friendly, I admit that, it's clear whoever puts these forms together knows a lot about lives in schools, but still they are two separate cultures that overburden our work, and reading the law does not necessarily allow preparation for the upcoming inspection policy because of the gap between them.
>
> (LEA headteacher 3)

This statement also points to the power struggle in which LEAs are constantly involved and, at least during the last decade and a half, ever more so. Crushed between the ministry and government on one side, and the schools and heads who strive for autonomy on the other side, they fight for justification of their role in the system and of course for their own control over schools that has gone through decades of decline – an issue that will be explored further in Chapters 7 and 8.

Many members of the cohort referred to the declarative quality of legislation that all too often is accompanied by insufficient funds – left to LEAs (but even more critically, and often – because the responsibility is on them directly and as their budget is more limited – to schools and headteachers) to finance through their LMS autonomy. When mandated reforms amass one on top of the other, encumbrance is considerable. Finances aside, say the participants, legislation is often not even followed by the required reorganization, training, or pedagogical outlines and methods. Sometimes these arrive a long time after the policy was mandated in law, or on a timetable that is unreasonable for schools to follow or fit to their yearly cycle and their obligations towards teachers' work-days, work-weeks, breaks and holidays. The following account by a headteacher depicts these problems vividly:

> The DfEE just announced a policy on 'anger management'. A circular was sent to all heads requiring us to set aside a special room [now sometimes referred-to as 'sin bins'], preferably with carpets, soft music, and a teacher or staff member trained for this specific role. I don't have a spare room in my school and not enough staff or staff-hours to man it. The person who runs the room needs special training but no university or college has offered a training programme yet, and we're talking probably 25,000 such teachers not to mention that large comprehensives like this one need more than one. And then, who will finance and organize this? So there's a directive but the problem is ours. It lands in our lap, usually during the

> summer, or close to the end of school year. Immediately there's an item in the *Telegraph* and parents knock on my door asking for the new programme or service while our clock ticks at a different pace.
>
> (Comprehensive superhead 3)

This vignette points at the practical side of legislation implementation by the recipients of policy and law. Law serves politicians and officials for declarative purposes, and perhaps they have an unaware schema of law as (1) linear and positivistic; and (2) a concept according to which its actual enactment generates a secret and covert process of instantaneous change in educational reality. By writing 'positivistic' I refer to the Cartesian rule that allows the isolation of one denominator or variable and the measurement of its exact effect or size on the dependent variable. This is a type of schema that can be defined as 'once it's in the letter of the law, it's done', while what *should* be is that legislation is just the 'end of the beginning', to quote a famous Englishman's words. Those who hold to this schema believe that the fact that each law is followed by another so quickly adds an incentive to see legislation as the *end* of the policy process. This is, of course, not completely true but there is such a trend, and certainly that is the experience of practitioners. Such feelings in turn feed mistrust, create a light-hearted stance towards legislation, and probably generate evasive survival techniques that allow the recipients of policy to 'talk the talk' without really 'walking the walk'. In other words, as each festive act of a new law is quickly replaced by another, one should go through motions of acceptance and implementation, while deep change becomes a rare luxury.

Who wins? Who loses?

Whom does legislation serve? Many interviewees think that it represents the stronger groups in society and rarely succeeds in benefiting 'the many not the few'. As I reported earlier in this chapter, there is deep and ceaseless debate on whether, and how, legislation should be devoted to this goal:

> I do think I have strong views on the impact of policy on the most disadvantaged. My belief is still that there's a level of dishonesty around the notion that raising attainment narrows gaps. My experience over the last 15 years is that we take the easy option, that if we keep pushing standards up and blaming schools, gaps will narrow – but that's not the case. Our class system is too big to take on.
>
> (Secondary comprehensive superhead 5)

> The only thing we have is this notion of one culture. The curriculum offers biblical Hebrew but not Bengali as an advanced language in the new the English Baccalaureate.[2] The articulate middle classes will always keep ahead of us, they will always manage, I don't genuinely think that it

> doesn't drive me but history tells us that anytime we tried to address this issue they kept ahead.
>
> (Secondary comprehensive superhead 1)

> There was increasing recognition that attainment gaps between social groups have become greater. There are still variations between schools in different areas, and these necessarily influence good practice. Gaps have not narrowed sufficiently. It may have to do with prescription and targets that are a part of knowledge, and provide a toolbox that raises the bar for schools that have to improve significantly and constantly but there is more to be done to consistently challenge the impact of poverty on the lives of children. Whatever government is in power they would have to act. There's no standing still, you have to improve all the time.
>
> (Senior Ofsted official 1)

> We can't have social mobility, it is a huge lie that all are born free, it's the lie, and the US had the lowest idea of social mobility that gives promise to the vast majority. This government expanded accessibility to Higher Ed but it's still the case that the poorest students, they won't go to university. This is a big lie of this government as well. If you take away the possibility of LAs to provide speech therapy and Sure Start this is the support schools can give. This government says it has genuine concern on poor people and then they cut public spending, they have a nonsense idea of Pupil Premiums.
>
> (Senior teacher organization official 2)

Finally, the last effect of over-legislating the system is that educators in the field believe that everything is in the law, even when it is not:

> I talked to 400 headteachers and I asked 'how many of you were using the SEFs?' All said they did, and they didn't know it's not mandatory. So much [for] speaking about the law [as a policy tool]. They had an imaginary paper on compliance and subversion, and a head said they [must] comply, as they see it to be a mandate and their legal requirement, [so] ignoring it would mean subversion – flying below the radar – and that's much more challenging.
>
> (Senior academic involved in policymaking 3)

The place of law-based reform in changing the system

As I mentioned earlier in this chapter, a major, natural, and expected role of legislation is in introducing long-term structural and pedagogical transformations in England's education system. Many comments touched on this central purpose. Some comments were about the swift abolition of policies that were extremely demanding for schools and heads and that suddenly disappeared, only to be replaced with new ones, equally demanding on the time, resources and culture of schools:

> The national strategies were sucked away by the department and will become a thing of the past, but the question is: who will hold them accountable? The challenge is autonomy, yes, but who will hold them accountable?
>
> (Superhead/CEO of privately-financed foundation)

> We assess LAs and some are doing very well. Many have a good reputation in securing education but others do not, and the government supports a steady move of power to schools. Faith schools, foundation schools, community schools, and now a further development – academies and free schools.
>
> (Senior Ofsted official 1)

> This government is doing things as if it's not around for a long time. I don't know if there is another government that's electable, and at least they're doing things that we didn't dare do; my deputy is about improving practice and I'm glad he's doing it, because if Labour came back it wouldn't be spending that much anyway any more. They would keep the EBacc. I think academies will be more under control. I'm not sure free schools would remain – perhaps, but not grow in numbers, and in a few years they would be called something else and perhaps controlled by LEAs. Ordinary Liberals, and what was the Lib Dems, won't be there long, they can't stomach that much of it. There might be people on the streets, if something awful happens like it rains in the royal wedding. Things this country counts on, it will change. So as they do not seem to be around for too long they are doing things as if they are going.
>
> (Secondary comprehensive superhead 3)

> What happens if a group of people set up a school and after ten years they are not here? There could be a degree of volatility that people don't like, and you're dealing with kids' education. In Sweden the parents put a kid in another school [but] they don't do that here … the odd parent might do that. They learn it's not the schools – it's something else.
>
> (Think tank CEO 1)

> It's cyclical. We seem to come back to introducing new types of schools, obsessed with finding the magic bullet or wand, we keep looking for these. Assessment for learning is a good strategy. Structures do matter but we keep looking for things to minimize gaps. If you had a rule that if someone

> applies there's a waiting list and you have to take them. If we have this system now that academies kicked out kids and other schools have to take them, the school should be made responsible for the kid whatever happens. You could take them out of the classroom and into a special unit. At the moment you are not allowed to ask whether a parent helped out in events in the previous schools. There are plenty of examples of schools that do this, and other ways to get around it if you really want to – it's not difficult. We know that with the right attitude you can do a good job. It's not as though we haven't tried to let LAs take care of failing kids, but they [the LAs] failed.
>
> (Think tank CEO 2)

These last comments point to some of the more problematic aspects of law-based reform. First, the power of the law allows pivotal change to be administered in schools from one day to another. Political change is, of course, the main catalyst for some of these reforms but others occur within the reign of a single administration, perhaps when the government feels results are not sufficient. It is important to be attentive to results but some types of change that have absorbed massive resources both from government and from LEAs, and from within schools, wither away precipitately. This is not only about financial resources. Such change places a heavy burden on the organizational structure of schools and on the roles of teachers and heads and other personnel, and demands swift developments in school culture – something that usually takes a long time. It is as if legislation and legislators had an imaginary vision of what a school is, a vision that is much closer to that of a financial enterprise or IT firm than of an academic, human-service institution. This concept, regardless of how strongly it is embedded in the minds of legislators, does not come to life simply due to the agenda of law alone. Second, the concern that a change that just happened will not sustain itself after a few years, perhaps just when it is finally sinking in and beginning to bear fruit, is another problem.

Conclusion: A legislation network?

> Occasionally people ask me questions that are based on the supposition that I or someone else is the CEO of an organization called UK schools, a centralized system in which we manage schools, and we don't at all. In all sorts of ways we have less ability to do that than we ever had. People who think that the law is massive in centralization, or on how people teach, and that all is determined from here … this is the wrong end of the stick. It's absolutely nothing like that. We are very much more engaged in questions such as 'what's in the curricula and processes of teaching and learning?' than thirty year ago, when it was a matter for teachers. We have a view the

> system is sometimes more dependent on what we believe, sometimes the system believes we influence it more than we do.
>
> (Senior DfE official 1)

It is this viewpoint that creates severe misunderstandings and perhaps misconceptions between practitioners, policymakers and politicians. These misconceptions and misunderstandings are full of contradictions. On the one hand, legislation is seen as overly and overtly interfering, while on the other hand, in important areas of the education debate such as admissions policy, equity, and equality, it is not aggressive and far-reaching enough. These contradictions and viewpoints will be explored further and analysed in the next three chapters of Part 2.

Despite, or perhaps beside, the contradictions, a definite 'issue network' (Deleon, 2006) emerges from the analysis. Many of the interviewees mentioned each other, often by name, not just by title, and with obvious close and personal ties. Drawing upon Tichy *et al.*'s (1979) model, there are emerging network patterns that change constantly but with a relatively stable cohort. Chapter 10 of this book will show how the members of the legislation issue network not only interact, but share careers and exchange places and points of influence. A main finding is that leading headteachers – superheads – act as 'bridges' (Tichy *et al.*, 1979: 508) as they move from headship to government posts, to senior posts in LEA education departments, and lately into PFIs, and are involved in headteacher and teacher recruitment and training, and in networks of schools. A second interesting group includes 'stars' or conceivably 'star gatekeepers' (ibid. 508). These are a small group of individuals who have had a fundamental role in legislation, in its structure, character, and role. These include certain senior ministry officials, advisers to the Prime Minister and/or the Secretary of State and a few academics who took it upon themselves to get involved in legislation.

Notes

[1] Department for Education (DfE); from 1995: Department for Education and Employment (DfEE); from 2001: Department for Education and Skills (DfES); from 2007: Department for Children and Schools (DfCS); and from 2010 Department for Education (DfE) once again.

[2] EBacc: Following in the footsteps of an emerging international standard of matriculation exams known as the International Baccalaureate and the European Baccalaureate, which were first administered in an EU network of schools and are gradually gaining a foothold in many countries, perhaps as a template for local versions, the Conservative–Liberal-Democrat government announced the EBacc in 2010.

See: www.ibo.org and see sections 4.21–4 of the 2010 white paper, The Importance of Teaching. However, it is still not part of legislation.

Chapter 6

Ideology and politics, past and present, in law-based reform

Introduction: The method of this chapter

This chapter maps the views and roles of the different groups of interviewees, according to several variables. One important aspect that I wish to explore is how their views and alliances changed over time. Another aspect is an attempt to understand how the two parties that controlled the Ministry of Education (Conservatives and New Labour), and were responsible for legislation on education reform, legislated, and hence how the differences in approach were translated into the volume, frequency, content, and targets of legislation.

As detailed in Chapter 2, Ronald Manzer's theory is that:

> Educational regimes are focused on a primary problem of political economy, hold a recognizable core of organizing ideas, and have a distinctive set of policies for the provision and governance of education.
>
> (Manzer, 2003: 26)

In his work Manzer (ibid. 19, 55) differentiates between 'communitarian conservatives' and 'liberal conservatives'. The first are opposed to any 'penetration of capitalist markets' while liberal conservatives are 'proponents of the market as a key sector in the ideal political economy' (ibid. 20). As explained in the second chapter of this book, legislation is a key factor in the process of allowing (or inviting) the free market into the organization and governance of education. It is often understood – and not in England alone – as a remedy for some of the most profound problems of public education as a state-commissioned and delivered service, supposedly free from political influence, and desegregated, as Boyd (2003) describes in his somewhat utopian account. Utopian, because as Ball (2007: 187) himself wrote, 'there is no going back to the past' because 'there was no such past'.

> The law is premised on the notion that local education politics are fundamentally broken, and that only strong external pressure on school systems, focused on student achievement, will produce a political dynamic that leads to school improvement. ... Frustrated by the tepid results wrought by decades of school reform, policymakers decided that high standards, meaningful sanctions, and federal leadership were essential ... Ultimately NCLB was intended to provide political cover to superintendents and

> school board members to encourage them to take controversial and difficult steps to root out mediocre teachers and administrators, shift resources to poorer schools, challenge collective bargaining provisions regulating teacher transfer and inhibiting efforts to link pay to teacher quality, and overhaul central office processes.
>
> (Hess and Petrilli, 2006: 23)

In order to canvas, break down, and differentiate between the ideological agendas of the participants in this study, I chose four streams of thought, or forms of government, that emerge from the literature (Ball, 2007; Bottery, 2000; Diamond and Giddens, 2005; Harvey, 2005; Manzer, 2003; Whitty *et al.*, 1998). The four streams are democratic socialism (Manzer, 2003), social democracy (Bottery, 2000; Manzer, 2003), third way (Bottery, 2000; Diamond and Giddens, 2005), and neoliberalism (Ball, 2007; Bottery, 2000; Harvey, 2005). Manzer describes democratic socialism as a form of government that is centred roughly on the state but can be attained through a democratic process rather than a forceful revolution. Social democracy involves some 'detrimental' (Bottery, 2000: 30–1) views on markets, and envisions an education system in which both commission and delivery of education services are under the legal power of the state or some equivalent public–political power (for example, LAs). Third way individuals, or 'new modernizers' as Bottery labels them, see education governance as one in which the government provides a framework for commission, while delivery can be done by a 'mixed' (Bottery, 2000: 31) assortment of suppliers. A neoliberal, that is, New Right (Ball, 2007; Bottery, 2000; Whitty, *et al.*, 1998), system relies to a high degree on market forces and privatization. However, as Ball notes, third way and neoliberalism are 'the same and different' (2007: 21).

The ideological shifts in law-based reform and its protagonists

Figure 6.1 presents the distribution of the interviewees among the four forms of government, as it was documented in 2000–1.

Figure 6.1 is divided into four quarters. In the democratic socialist bottom left-hand quarter there were very few individuals. This quarter includes representatives associated with Old Labour. The upper left – the social democratic quarter – included a massive presence of field- and school-based educators. It is no surprise that teachers' unions senior personnel were to be found in this quarter as well. At the time of the 2000–1 interviews, so were the ministry civil servants, but they leaned towards the third way, in the upper right-hand quarter.

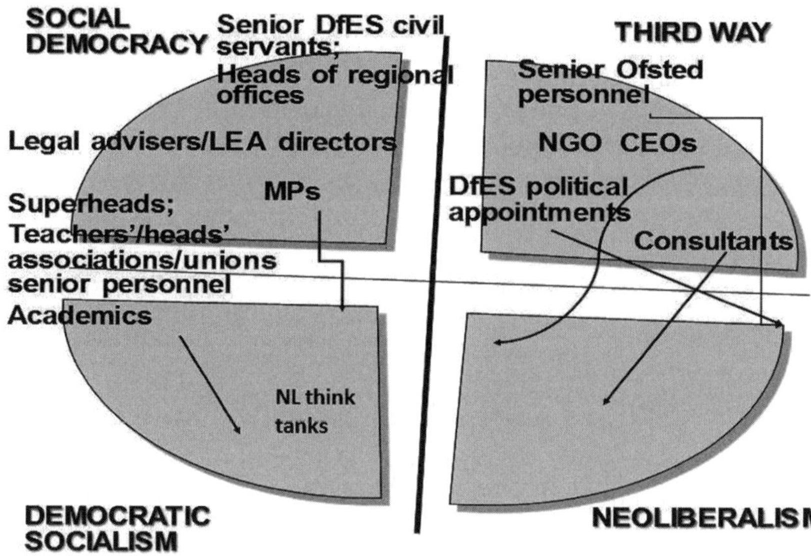

Figure 6.1: Ideology and political tendencies of interviewees 2000–1

> There's something almost clichéd about democratic unity and about accountability. Some academies are a person selling carpets making a network of schools. It's fascinating, when I started teaching education wasn't political – parties defined themselves by foreign policy and finance policy, now it's health and education.
>
> (Superhead, 2005)

> Callaghan said education was a secret garden, and he started the great debate in 1981 [recte 1976]. 'Til then, the sec[retary of state for education] didn't even sit in cabinet; education has become a top political priority and Blair's mantra 'education, education, education' set the pace for everyone. There is an agreement that we have to do [it] not for the few, it's not altruism, it's an economic imperative; the education scene has changed a lot and schools are better now although there's a long way to go. There are figures to prove that social mobility has improved. Some say it hasn't changed for 50 years; I say the system has opened up and the consensus is that this can be done by giving headteachers more freedom and giving them more accountability through inspection and audit.
>
> (Academy head, 2010)

The upper-right 'third way' quarter includes, in uniform contrast to the upper-left quarter, government officials, including those from Ofsted, from the DfES, heads of NGOs, and consultants. This can be explained, as the managerialist practices of the New Labour government were accepted as more favourable among these groups of participants. Very few, though, present neoliberal views. This is still perhaps the 'euphoric' period (Bangs *et al.*, 2010) combined with a strong feeling that New Labour had 'corrected', or was on its way to correcting, a lot of the Conservatives' policy flaws – mainly going too far on the path to marketization – without a reactionary swing that would upset the important assets of the Conservatives' policies (freeing up schools and empowering communities, for instance). It is interesting to see that the headteachers, still deeply situated within the upper left-hand quarter, are not charmed, and retain quite a lot of the Old Labour controlled-economy flavour. The 1998 SSFA is therefore described in remedial terms, while post-2000 legislation, especially the performance-related pay policy, was treated with overall resistance by staffs in schools and in LEAs, as a policy entirely conflicting with the caring and community-focused personality of education:

> The unions were the closest, the insiders of the insiders, so where are we? We had huge influence on legislation, we wrote regulations, teaching standards, working agreements, routinely asked before things went out, consulted about anything related to the workforce, a whole range on teachers' and headteachers' pay and reward issues. You'd be amazed at what we were consulted about in all the green papers, white papers, regular meetings; certainly there was massive control. We were notified this week that the government will change the regulations on performance management, but this government says 'we are going to inform you'. Go through the statutory process and then do it.
>
> (Teachers' union senior official, 2010)

The reader can see that the lower-right quadrant is quite empty in 2000–1. In 2005–6 the mood swings, but not in one direction, as can be seen in Figure 6.2 (p. 104).

By this time, a whole series of laws has been accepted, and the heavy toll of the change in legal constraints on schools is there. The unions were fiercely opposed to policy change and especially to the use of legislation in what they saw as constant, covert, and formal attempt to weaken unions. While they were grateful for the large amounts of money that had been invested in schools, a lot of this was in the form of assistants to help teachers lessen their workload – a move that worried them for it was feared as a threat to teacher professionalism and to their exclusive status in the classroom. This was followed by a strengthening of government-established QUANGOs that offered support and contested with unions, such as the TDA, and allowing headteachers to 'buy-in' teaching from non-unionized sources. These changes, together with the appearance of larger numbers of academies and trust schools, caused anxiety both among unions and also LEA officials. The accounts by the participants in this study regarding the 'remodelling of the workforce' are backed by other research as well (Bang *et al.,* 2010; Gunter, 2008). Headteachers, in turn, also

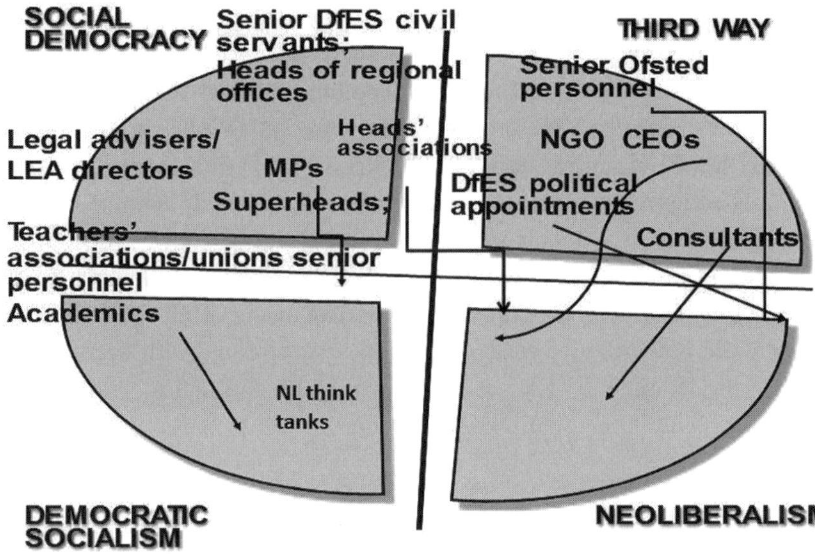

Figure 6.2: Ideology and political tendencies of interviewees 2005–6

still in the upper right-hand quarter of Figure 6.2, as they were in 2000–1, saw these latest changes as an attack, first from the outside, on the ideology and structure of comprehensive schooling, and second, from inside schools, as a further narrowing of their autonomy through prescribed mandated policies, especially the numeracy and literacy strategies. The 2006 EIA was seen by the participants in the upper left-hand quarter as a welcome, though perhaps not entirely satisfactory, rectification of some problems and a bit of a return to some Old Labour policies – but again with a fear that this precluded further prescription and pedagogical control, as the semi-Old Labour Brown–Balls administration seemed to be much more reluctant to allow schools the same freedoms they had had under Prime Minister Blair.

However, not all the reactions to legislation and the policies it carried in this period were negative, as can be seen in the upper right-hand and lower right-hand quarters of the figure. A trickle of headteachers, non-existent in 2000–1, together with some DfES personnel, and certainly consultants and CEOs of NGOs, welcomed – sometimes warily, sometimes enthusiastically – the structural changes that included a gradual movement of delivery from LEAs to new types of schools. A new breed of entrepreneur–educators (Ball, 2007; Gunter, 2008) was part of the puzzle, seeing the change as an opportunity. Then again, the 2006 EIA is seen by these 'prehistoric' neoliberals as a threat and a return to bad habits.

This period, underscored by the 2005–6 interviews and characterized by the forbearance of the Brown–Balls government to continue Blair's policies, marked the end of New Labour governments. This was a time of anxiety, in which legislation materialized past, present, and future distress regarding what was to come, combined with impatience and disillusionment towards what *was*. All of this was combined with a gradual acceptance of a new culture of education management and governance.

This last period of uncertainly was replaced, in 2010–11 by a clearer picture, for better or for worse, according to the participants in this study. Figure 6.3 shows the shifts in opinion in this more recent period.

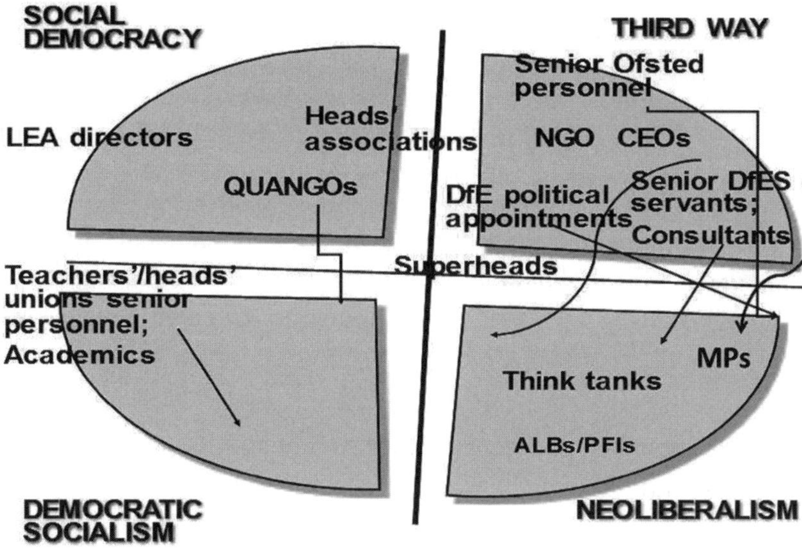

Figure 6.3: Ideology and political tendencies of interviewees 2011

This period can be summed up as one of extremities, with some groups of participants moving into the neoliberal fourth lower right-hand quarter, and a general shift of views from the left-hand side of Figure 6.3 to the right-hand side, while others return to the first lower left-hand quarter. By now, many headteachers are much less deterred by the idea of running an academy, joining a trust, or having an academy side-by-side with their comprehensive school. This will be explored in Chapter 8. Quite a few see a second career opportunity in a PFI or ALB that trains teachers and leaders, or establishes and supports new types of schools. The DfE officials are also much more relaxed, if not supportive, of government legislation, and acknowledge the problems of over-prescription that characterized the 2006 EIA. The 2010 Academies Act is criticized by many as being hasty, but the 2011 EA is accepted as more balanced and having a clear vision. In a way, this is a repetition of some of the feelings that were expressed in 2000–1, perhaps with some caution, as the 2010–11 interviewees have matured in this age of frequent legislation and policy change. There is a feeling of freshness and anticipation among those in the bottom right-hand side of the figure. However, as I have explained, there is also a large group of educators, academics, and especially members of two significant groups, namely the unions and the LEAs, who describe these two laws as apocalyptic. They view them as an inescapable path that leads inevitably to the complete privatization of England's education and the abandonment of public responsibility and commitment to equitable measures and equity in education.

The great debate: Sequaciousness or juxtaposition between parties?

The second finding I wish to explore in this chapter is the great debate on the differences between the Conservatives and New Labour in their treatment of education law:

> In the Blair early years there was a perception that if you got GCSEs going up that's all you had to do. We will not let these grades slip, but you should look at things beyond grades – what were the loopholes? In maths and English GCSEs there hasn't been such a strong improvement – a lot of the improvement is because of other subjects. This government isn't as obsessed with the overall grades but is looking at learning core subjects.
>
> (Think tank CEO, 2011)

> New Labour talked to academia and LAs and Mr Gove talks to the Tory elite and it's a one-size-fits-all solution, too much influence of business people. There's a fallacy of organizations like Capita who will make a profit – it is a lot like what is going on in health. It happened with LMS but there was a balancing hand that could look at a basket-case school that wants to use half a million on travelling abroad. I'm all for getting rid of fat but they want to get rid of skin and bones as well. Who will look at a head who pays too much, flies the kite, and the school goes bankrupt? At the moment we won't let that happen. This is a much more dogmatic government than before.
>
> (LEA Chief education officer, 2010)

These two views represent a clear distinction between New Labour legislation and the Conservatives'. Whether criticizing or praising one party or the other, these two views represent the clear-cut approach, namely that New Labour represented a controlled-economy balanced policy as opposed to the fierce privatizing, ideologically-based, deconstructive thrust of the Conservatives. This being the criticism, the praise goes in the opposite direction. New Labour represented, according to this second view, a confused attempt to attain a let-us-appease-all controlled-economy policy with some important initiatives that could just as well be part of Conservative policy, and some figures that could easily 'walk across the floor' from New Labour to Conservative, both in their analysis of the problems and in their ideas for possible solutions:

> The new Conservative government is led by dogma, it's not thought through. It's free market policy, by simplifying the procedures and weakening the admissions authority's power.
>
> (DfE official)

> There was a time that was a real force in the Labour party, when the Labour party had an alternative economic model. The co-op, the producer cooperative, the welfare system was mainly to be mutual aid and not state [aid]. We wanted to write in a way that would appeal to people in the Left. And the Tories in opposition picked up on that. We did try and use arguments on the health service, that the really important thing was that everybody should have access to health care. There's always conversations going on. We were arguing that it was important to make sure everybody got their chance, and the state system wasn't doing that. And we said any organization that can support itself should be allowed [to,] and the business motive and the profit-maximizing motive are not necessarily a bad thing. When there's a producer co-op the people can be replaced by the consumers, the charity model where the trustees can't receive any profit, or a provident association that is a hybrid for people who can be self-supportive but not totally.
>
> (Think tank CEO)

A main point that appeared in many interviews was the contradiction between New Labour's pragmatic approach, and the Conservatives' dogmatic one. According to these views, previous ideologically-centred Labour ideas were replaced by a 'what works' (or what is thought to work) culture that resulted in a mixed, often incoherent and contradicting, set of policies (Bottery, 2000; Bangs *et al.*, 2010; Riley, 1998). Except for the 1998 SSFA, New Labour's legislation is therefore seen as a reaction rather than a proactive approach to education. Some interviewees see this positively, as a quality of sensitivity to current affairs and crises. Social cohesion policy and national strategies are appreciated as examples. Others see such attempts as hasty, and often contradicting each other, thus shifting the problem of sorting out the alternatives and settling the contradictions to LEAs, headteachers, and schools:

> New Labour didn't get the credit they should have for investing hugely in education. Anecdotally, I always send the whole staff a Christmas card and there are now as many support staff as there are teachers. This is New Labour's doing and it changed things dramatically for schools like ours. I am worried this might disappear now.
>
> (Superhead)

> ... it could have been Tony Blair speaking when Gove was speaking but there still are differences: most legislation that involves social rights is

> in Labour times. It's a big change – kids with disabilities were bussed to distant schools and laughed at, now they enrich our society.
>
> (Superhead)

> We're not normally used by governments to evaluate other agencies and bodies specifically, although we *do* do reports on particular policies or strategies. This government's ideology is based on giving schools greater freedom and autonomy, and that diversification would lead to more improvement. There's always a tension between how much freedom you may need, and accountability. How much freedom you want to give society. To balance autonomy there is a need to ensure accountability, and inspection is one way of providing the checks and balances needed.
>
> (Senior Ofsted official, 2012)

One thing that is agreed is that when each party came to power, legislation was better planned and thought through, mainly because of a long period of deliberation while being in opposition. Think tanks and academics had the time for careful forethought and phrasing. Unfortunately as the cadence of a government progressed these qualities weakened:

> Before the 1997 election we had a lot of things prepared. Our think tank did the legwork and we produced policy documents on teacher training, a detailed policy, and Blunkett was keen on this and in the first white paper we knew … what we wanted to say. David Blunkett had discussions for eight months but something we did was the Standards and Effectiveness unit under Michael Barber because the civil servants were OK on drafting but had a bit of a weak spot on delivery. Since 1988 the power of LAs was eroded and you needed your own delivery from the centre; we had partnerships and it worked on single issues rather than running the whole school system.
>
> (Senior adviser to the PM)

> Labour was a bit more towards the enterprise end; they had concluded that LAs were the obstacle and they tried to create schools that were free but most of the Labour party were against that so the law looks likes that is the intention but it gets altered all the time, in the 2006 act. They did try to move to a reduction of public centre and a less centralized system. The whole thrust of the New Labour government was to be a chief executive and use whatever compulsory power it had in its power. This government renounced that approach in the notion of the big society. They are moving towards a civil association … This coalition is ambiguous but they are more towards a civil association, they think the important things should happen in pluralistic private arrangements. Because there isn't an obvious solution

> there isn't necessarily one answer. It's a coalition. They are looking for a pluralistic liberal society. You can caricature this as a profit motive and private greed, but it's a religious argument.
>
> (Think tank CEO)

> I came from a Conservative authority, we've never seen more legislation than in the last ten years, it's come out of our ears and been focused on the rights of people, children, and parents within the system but at the same time there's brainwork that might be quite the opposite going on right now.
>
> (DfE official)

One important aspect of legislation under the two parties is the sequential feature that is often disregarded by the interviewees. Most of their views treat legislation under New Labour and under the Conservatives as two separate processes or sets of outcomes and then compare them, either concluding that they are alike, or not. A few of the interviewees are aware that legislation is developing from each administration to the next and is not just influenced or underlain by the current administration's ideology or plans for change. What I mean by sequential is that each era creates conditions for change that sometimes do not exist at a given time but are planted and then are ready to reap later. Such ripening occurs, perhaps, when a new administration comes to power, freed of its predecessor's constraints, whether ideological or political. Such was the case with the 1998 SSFA that allowed a certain degree of rebalance of the marketized policies established first by the 1988 ERA and later especially by the 1992, 1993, and 1996 EAs. New Labour enjoyed the power to retain some of the Conservatives' main ideas, due, perhaps, to a certain ingenuousness on the part of the public, without being blamed because, in comparison, the free market aspects were weakened and New Labour enjoyed initial trust in contrast to the mistrust felt towards the intentions of the Conservatives. This happened again within the New Labour period, when the 2006 EIA made some moves that were criticized but also welcomed as Old Labour. Yet again in 2011, the Conservative government consolidated many changes that were either introduced or enhanced by New Labour (such as academies and trust schools, and a weakening of LEAs) to allow their legislation to go ahead, above and beyond the New Labour laws but without the possible public and professional outcry:

> One difference between them, it's hard to talk about New Labour – I voted for New Labour in 2005 and didn't vote for them in 2010. Gordon Brown and Ed Balls believed they could mandate social justice through education and mandated processes – this is how you get resentment rather than 'we will measure you and you will figure out a way to get to it'. This government moves from a prescription of processes to a process of outcomes. This is

easier said than done, but free schools is the example. 'We will ask you questions if that is not done.' No government has brought back things about admissions. They have not changed admissions or faith schools, or their admissions policy, which is interesting. There are many similarities.

(Superhead, 2010)

I think under the previous New Labour government there was a coming-of-age about rebalancing what we had under the Conservative rule, shifting the agenda from a minority profit-making nation to social stability, and redress of funding to poorer communities; there was lip-service towards pacifying the headteacher and teacher unions, they redressed that. I think their focus on targeting money towards initiatives was important. However, it became a heavy hand – if you were on the receiving end of money and in the cold light of day if you looked at all the money and grants for gifted and talented, the actual increase made schools a bit more complacent and leaving the authority to someone else such as LAs or authorities in charge of the project, although in an area of deprivation such as this it made us an attractive employer and high-resourced, and got on the agenda as never before and it made it better for us to have a Labour-controlled government and borough. The Blair–Adonis administration wanted to get failing schools going again. Gove could have really driven that policy if he had done it right and consulted with LAs and said 'give us your worst-performing schools', but he consulted with sixth formers. You will get benefit for few, creating a two-tier system, [so] that some schools will take the top 10 per cent.

(Superhead, 2011)

At the beginning, New Labour was very focused on equality and social justice but they lost their way. They had too much legislation. The power of the LA to say 'this legislation is a mockery' – there was very little power to say that. The coalition is taking an absolute hatchet [to that approach] because [in their view] everyone is equal, and that is dangerous – ignorant of the social context that some groups [find it] very difficult to take care of themselves. The 'big society' will be blown out of the water.

(LEA chief education officer, 2011)

New Labour relates to Tony Blair and his influence on New Labour. He was common [practical] about it, and I wish he'd been more fundamental [and stuck to Blair's basic principles of decentralization and empowerment]. When they came to power, people thought 'they will swing back the clock' – which they didn't. When Tony Blair got control of the party, he became much more market-oriented. They were shocked that the government uses

> private firms to do what LAs had once done. Why? Because it sticks in the gullet that you hand over the mid-tier jobs to someone making a profit – any company is required by law to benefit the stockholders. By 1988 LEAs, which before were asked [to decide] what happened about the curriculum in the beginning of the 1980s, then lost their power to schools through LMS – that was the precursor for GM schools, they were the first step. All this reduced the power of the local educational authority. The civil service has shifted during the Thatcher years and through New Labour, from a civil service into an administration – they are advocates. The academies will end in tears. Blair was a very good Prime Minister. Politicians operate within the civil service and have enormous influence. They have no sense of history. The role of NGOs and QUANGOs has increased; the school is increasingly controlled by the QUANGOs or by the government itself and there is a growing sense of compliance. Ofsted had become a feared activity. When they came to our city I had advisers and psychologists say good things about each other. We know more about school improvement and teaching and learning than we ever did, but the downside is that the behaviour problems are a part of that because you labelled the child and it stuck in your head.
>
> (Senior adviser to LEAs, 2006)

One aspect that is common to both administrations is, as described before, the anticipation and anxiety, the constant guessing-game, before each new piece of legislation is introduced – often, as explained, without a significant period of time allowed for understanding, let alone implementing and absorbing the previous one(s). Entangled in this process is the attempt to understand what will happen following the declarations in a white paper and the actual law, both often being mixed up by the bewildered interviewees:

> Generally, I guess the obvious thing is this aspect of not relying on targeted budgets to get things done. Ring-fenced grants are redirected. It's a shame that New Labour had the model of central control by having a set of top-down targets but they never had the confidence to free up that. In 2006 you had to do what you had to do, and suddenly all this is freed up for the whole council. Now the whole framework for inspection is gone and we're a 4-star authority, we don't want to see that it has all gone down a road of massive bureaucracy. There were a lot of people happy with feeding that giant beast and knew how to make it work. As a school, we had a couple of solutions, but now, with all the non-civil servants working with government, we had all the known civil servants who sent two different messages and that was the downside and a massive bureaucracy. To make it all work, you had a framework, what to do to make it work; the thing that

> is coming home to roost is that a lot of people think what will happen with Ofsted, it will change; whereas schools were used to constant raising of the bar, the LAs were quite upset with that, they didn't know how to do it. My colleagues in other LAs are upset we actually perform better than we did last year, the bar is going up, it's the new algorithm, we did better but went down from four stars to three, and I tell my colleagues 'that's how you raise standards in schools'. The fact that whether someone may have directed Ofsted to find what they found in Haringey,[1] it was doing badly but we were totally horrified that this was political need. So Ofsted has done no favours to itself, for doing what it did, and it brought a blame culture rather than accountability.
>
> (LEA head of education, 2011)

> Trying to justify this with the LEA is difficult. We have to be very specific in our programmes. The press have misinterpreted the white paper, as they often do. The government is going to face serious opposition in the next elections for the first time so there is a populist approach, talking about parent power. There is a parent council. The idea of trust schools is *so* Tony Blair; when he talks about trusts being independent from LEAs, it's foolish. The accountability will simply be shifted away.
>
> (Superhead, 2006)

> Free schools and academies are free from the LA because it's central government-approved and free from national prescription. One of the intents of this government is to pass less legislation. New Labour passed bill after bill after bill, endlessly changing things and now we may have less prescription. They are all about less system control. If you look at what New Labour were saying about education before '97 it was much more specific and the Tory stuff was more about systemic change. This government is the most radical the Conservatives ever had.
>
> (LEA head of schools, 2011)

> A big intended difference is that this government intends to be a lot more transparent, and holds itself accountable. This is a big change, like the Freedom of Information Act, it will have many consequences. The FoI has massive influence on education. It's the media and political opponents that will be using this a lot more. This will make a huge difference.
>
> (CEO, school's trust)

Legislation allowed the New Labour governments to change things quickly, often involving various figures such as senior academics and think tanks. My findings show that it is yet unclear how the current administration will act on this issue. However, it is already evident that the ministry is much more involved in legislation compared to outsiders, and also that, within government, the secretary of state enjoys more control and autonomy, with less participation by the Prime Minister's office through the delivery unit.[2] This development has not gone unnoticed by educators, who generally welcome it:

> Consultants were thriving under Blair, so much money came into the system, so many people came out from the woodwork, visionary education experts who hadn't been in education for years, headteachers who were kicked out; there's a list of approved consultants and they don't kick people off, and it's a licence to print money. Private businesses know about success and are happy to challenge existing practice in a way bureaucracies often can't. They've done their share and the next stage would be for-profit schools.
>
> (Superhead, 2011)

> The PM, both of the Labour PMs, took interest in education. They had a high-powered policy unit. Andrew [Lord Adonis] and Michael [Professor Sir Michael Barber] and David [Professor David Hopkins] were very engaged. My insight is that it wasn't like the wider world, though it was because partly Number 10 liked to spin things this way and it was a convenient story to tell that they were coming in and imposing the things on us. The PM had strong ideas, and things emanated from the policy unit, but it's very hard to think of an example where there was a straight arrow – is it policy 'A' and policy 'B', or an example where policy had happened without serious debate. Things that came from here [the DfE] and were discussed with Number 10 and vice versa and there was a productive dialogue and better ideas on implementation There were competitions but the account that there are some things that were Number 10's ideas and got done, and the other way around, is not accurate, as things were more complicated. Number 10 didn't have technical expertise or knowledge, it's a factual question if you need to change the law or not.
>
> (Senior adviser to the PM, 2011)

> Blair got 300–400 academies but Balls said you couldn't get an academy without the LA's consent; there were things you could do to pressurize the BSF grants, now there's no question this will be a Conservative local authority. These flagship policies are about quality not quantity and New Labour lost that case too, and being judged by national results didn't help much, it's a high-profile electoral issue. It has advantages – you get a lot more money and attention and the best people in the civil service to work in education, but the downside is political impatience. The thing

> that happened over the last three years with Balls dismantling the national accountability system, with KS3 being abolished, you don't have those measures to look at having a national benchmark to give you an indicative progress. They want Ofsted to be more proportionate to success.
>
> (Superhead, 2010)

> I don't see much difference in the two governments. They both use legislation as a means to achieve what they want to achieve in terms of the overarching structures of education. One thing that will be critical is if the government decides to tackle teacher paying conditions. We have a legislative framework for teacher pay. Forty or 50 years of brokering to have a uniform and transparent way of pay, and breaking that down will break down the power of the unions. It will make things much more difficult to have the unions to [agree to].
>
> (Union consultant, 2005)

Perhaps the most interesting view is that of the ministry officials who both hold all the professional and political data, and also are required to translate ideas into legislation, and then legislation into policy and work plans. I found this group to be very well-read in educational policy research, representing a responsible, solemn, though not reactionary, view of change. However, they are some of the most critical voices, calling for a downsizing in the frequency and volume of legislation, regardless of its content, as they see the organizational and pedagogical outcomes in their daily work and often bear the brunt of the headteachers' and LEA personnel's discontent:

> Just last week we determined to allow teachers to move up the pay scale. The Labour government [proposed this] at the time but it didn't go on. But that was decided nationally. But if this will change now there will be local unions [for example, of staff in chains and/or federations of academies] and also issues of how much holiday they have or how many hours they teach. That's the big worry for the teachers, and that will determine whether the unions do a valuable job or are destructive. It will be brave of the current government to take it on to that extent. But if you think that certain aspects of teachers' pay have to be changed, I don't know of any other profession that has 13 weeks of holiday and full pay. The unions are valuable in protecting the vulnerable, but teachers are better valued than they are now. There was a strange situation of teachers having industrial unions but wanting to be a profession. There should be professional maturity.
>
> (DfEE senior civil servant, 2005)

> Opening the headlines 'silly policies being pursued', as Ken Baker said in 1988, which introduced the ERA that said what children should learn

> followed by LMS and schools having the answers. Callaghan, Baker, Thatcher, then Blair – when his first government was spent on throwing money, often badly spent, EAZs: Excellence in Cities, New Deal Schools, a whole range of policies, and the national strategies sucked out a lot of good people [by over-prescription] who didn't have influence on the classroom. The new white paper called 'improving teaching' means that we have money, but it has to go to the right places. The public realized that good teaching is important. I'm a great supporter of the current secretary of state for freeing up schools.
>
> (Superhead, 2011)

> I say the Conservatives' admin also talked to headteachers but only those who agree with them, people who bolt into their policy, they are having cold feet [and then] they revert to 'we know what's good for you'. In '97 the message was 'this is what we are going to do, you may not agree but don't worry about it, we know what to do' and this alienated people enormously; and then they understood they should talk to professionals, (though professionals are not always right). But now they are going [and the Conservatives are saying] 'but' to [a new version of] 'we know what's right. Blair was putting his neck on the line but we know what's best for you'.
>
> (Superhead, 2010)

> My feeling is that while I supported the Labour government, I think they don't see that a lot of the defining reforms were done by the Tories and the rest they have been playing around with. The Labour government has been interested in the nature of teaching and learning and pedagogy. All the money put in EIC, changes in LMS and Ofsted are not that different. Specialist schools have been good for creating networks, for teaching and learning, but it's not ground-breaking change, I'm not sure the NCSL had been such a great success but a lot of thought and money has been put into training, and management has improved, using data, technology. Schools have become more streamlined but the ground-breaking changes have not been made by them.
>
> (Superhead, 2011)

This is summed up in the following statement, that also has corroborations in my findings:

> The rhetoric of partnerships is part of New Labour's denial of binaries which make possible the treatment of radically different terms as equivalent. Partnerships constantly recur in New Labour discourse and policies; almost any relationship between organizations or social agents is a

> partnership. They are a classic 'third way' trope which dissolves important differences between public sector, private sector, and voluntary sector modes of working, and obscure the role of financial relationships and power imbalances between 'partners'.
>
> (Ball, 2007: 116)

Ball (2007) points at the personal, or perhaps bipartisan, aspect of sequaciousness, by explaining that some of the prominent members of New Labour's policy network are 'survivors or carry-overs' (ibid. 126) from the Conservative period. Ball sees this also in the marketized policy known as 'new localism' which was at the forefront of New Labour's docket in education. However, following Ball's observation that new types of schools and organizational initiates such as EAZs are 'new, bold different thinking – more of the dynamic rhetoric of New Labour' (ibid. 172), several of the participants in this study accentuate that this novelty and boldness come from a basic ideology of government control, not from a deeply-rooted belief in free-market or consumerist responsibility for the education system. According to these interviewees, who come from all subgroups represented in my cohort, the free-market aspects are just a tool to achieve success – not to say control – through government initiative and regulation. It is in the light of this controversy between those participants who see New Labour as a direct continuity from the Conservative period, and those that see an imperative difference, that Whitty *et al.*'s (1998) now-classic analysis of 'devolution and choice' is worth revisiting. Situated at the critical intersection between the Conservatives and their replacement by New Labour, and the acceptance in Parliament of the 1998 SSFA, Whitty and his colleagues analyse the situation with hardly any reference to either Labour, New Labour, or Conservatives. Whitty *et al.* see both eras and policies from one synoptic critical perspective. They see legislation and policies as an effort, on the one hand, to secure legitimacy and confront a legitimacy crisis, and on the other hand, through devolution, to accomplish a 'complete abdication of responsibility by the state … making educational decision-making the responsibility of individual institutions [that is, schools] and families' (ibid. 45). Both sets of administrations also emphasize the dialectic contradiction between opening new progressive types of schools that break the old system down, while at the same time returning to 'basics' and re-canonizing knowledge taught in schools. This last paradox is reaffirmed by the policies of the current Conservative–Liberal-Democrat administration as well. Whitty reaffirms the 1998 viewpoint and findings in 2008, but also strengthens the views presented by my findings, that New Labour had a genuine distinct agenda that nevertheless executed consumerist policies introduced by the Conservatives. Both understand that these are useful and form policy accordingly – an observation made by Lawton (2005) as well – but also that returning back to a system that results from a controlled economy would, first, ignore the multicultural diversity aspects necessary for post-2000 school reform, and, second, be 'politically unthinkable' (Whitty, 2008: 179).

Finally, appearances, fashions, and branding play a role as well, emphasizing the declarative role of legislation as a cultural tool:

> I don't think there's a huge amount of difference but Brown, God bless him, he was Old Labour, he gave more money through local democracy although they haven't delivered good education for years. The Conservatives believe in opening up the system and New Labour didn't fundamentally believe in that. Blair was a pink Labour. The Conservatives are going for free schools breaking the mould even more so, and parents can set up their own schools to set up even more competition in the system. The government will allow people to set up a new school, in an old hospital or factory, so there's a real opportunity as the current system is no good. New Labour thinks that this will allow white middle class families to choose their schools and through the back door bring in selection. But selection is here now anyway.
>
> (MP, 2010)

> Labour is sexier than Conservative – they pledge to change while being in charge, it is much less frightening than an open-ended plan to free the system.
>
> (LEA CEO of education)

> Cameron is new and different and young, a lot will depend on the economy, if they get in they have a problem whether to vote for the new reforms Labour are offering; the Tories have given a bad press, I'm not sure the Tory party would have done anything different. The Tories might bring back selection – there's more of a continuance. New Labour brought things to the centre. Anyway, they might play with LMS, no one will get rid of Ofsted, no one will get rid of the notion of comparing schools to each other, it is embedded in the system. The balance of power (which has shifted to their heads) will remain because local responsibility is the thing.
>
> (Superhead, 2010)

The summary of this enquiry is not completely conclusive, and it is certainly complex. Attempting to bring the controversies together yields the following explanation. There are, I think, undercurrents and 'overcurrents'. Looking at the two parties' policies and addressing of education reform legislation shows that there are some similarities or ongoing trends that cut across the two parties. The globalized (Baker, 2009; Ball, 2012) forces in education policy and neoliberal superstructure, both ideological and economic, pledge both parties to managerialist policies that materialize in decentralisation and in the introduction of quasi-market and quasi-privatized assemblies and practices and a high-stakes standardized curriculum, separating between provision and delivery, and separating both from the state. But there is agreement among the interviewees in this study that, at the undercurrent level, there are important differences between New Labour's policy and hence legislation, and the Conservatives' policy and law. One significant difference is that New Labour is committed in the deepest way to an egalitarian ethic, even though their implementation methods are, as explained before, not profoundly different from those of the Conservatives, whose commitment to these methods is ideological, not pragmatic. The second difference, derived from the previous one, is the overtly pragmatic approach of New Labour compared to the overtly ideological approach of the Conservatives. In light of these similarities, mixed with distinctions that are, I think, part of the clarification of the differences in the character of legislation between the two parties, some patterns emerge. Hence, the big, pivotal changes in education laws were carried out (in the ERA 1988 and in the EA 2011) by Conservatives. New Labour's legislation is more incremental and less dramatic. The 1998 SSFA and the 2006 EIA are attempts at comprehensive change but they show more commitment to the past and more caution than the two dramatic acts by Conservative governments. This can be explained both by the ideological undercurrent of Conservative legislation and their drive for deconstructing the notion of public education.

Notes

[1] The Haringay 'Baby P' case involved, between 2007 and 2010, an investigation by Ofsted following the death of an at-risk child who was well known to the local child services but eventually died before being removed from his home in Haringay. The investigation and public outcry that followed led to the termination of office of the local director of child services and an eventual denial of her appeal for compensation by the court, in 2010. The case reintroduced the debate on the efficiency of LEA services and supervision in England. See: www.bbc.co.uk/news/uk-11626806 (accessed 15 February 2012).

[2] This was abolished in 2010 and some of its responsibilities were retained by the Efficiency and Reform Group.

Chapter 7

Tinker, tailor, soldier, spy:[1] Four cases and four figures in law-based reform

Introduction: The method of this chapter

In this chapter four figures involved in law-based reform will be presented. The figures do not represent actual individual participants in this study, as for ethical reasons a whole portrait of any one interviewee cannot be detailed here. Both ethically and methodologically, the technique I have chosen is based on the work of Goldring and Rallis (1993). In their study Ellen Goldring and Sharon Rallis built an imaginary character of a headteacher, based on empirical data that they uncovered from numerous sources: questionnaires, interviews, observations, and in-depth case studies, using an array of qualitative and quantitative methods and tools. Likewise, four figures are presented here: the 'tinker' – head of education for an LEA;[2] the 'tailor' – CEO of a think tank; the 'soldier' – a senior DfE civil servant; and the 'spy' – entrepreneur and CEO of a chain of academies or trust schools. My reason for choosing these four is that they – together with headteachers, as presented in Chapter 8 – represent the essence of law-based education reform, and perhaps the four polarities of what legislation and its policy have done to England's education system.

The tinker: Between forces, falling apart at the seams

Situated in a modern, open-plan office, perhaps an unintended miniature version of the DfE design that one can find in so many public offices in England, the chief education officer of a large urban LEA explains:

> Our achievements were set against nationally recognized facts that deprivation is overwhelming in areas like [our LA] but it gave us much more voice and opportunity. Not to say that some of it was not used widely and duplicated and spent on overheads. The hoops they set up in 'schools for the future' to jump through were impossible and we needed 5 million pounds to get 16 [the total required by BSF] and if you gave that cheque to a local authority ... they would procure it for much less money.

It is an accepted truth that the big losers in the realm of legislation, and of education policy and reform, are LEAs and local government as a whole. Gradually, with distinctive 'drops' on the way down, their status has weakened and declined, beginning with the GM schools and 'opting-out' in the 1980s, and settling since then into a steady downward incline. The various types of schools that were established since the mid-1980s (see Figure 4.1) from the GM schools and onwards to academies and free schools in 2012, and their formalization in legislation, strengthened and re-strengthened this process. This legislation first established these schools and then added more and more autonomy, powers, and independence, up to a point where they are now organized in chains and federations that finalize the separation from LEAs and the creation of an alternative middle-tier in education, commission, and delivery:

> I think previously there was a monitoring power [reserved] for Ofsted and HMIs. Ofsted needs to change its remit, it's obsessed with ticking boxes and not teaching, it's a bad trajectory of value-added. They need less power and a much-reduced role. Regional offices didn't deliver. But now there will be even more power for consultants and from private groups; the new legislation is clear that any new schools will go to the market and the LA will have nothing to do with it – it is so skewed, I think heads and their unions will have much more power. We don't manage schools, never have done. We have a watching brief on schools in trouble and intervention powers which we will not have any more unless it's on special measures.

The fictional chief education officer in this chapter believes in two principles. The first principle is that the LEA can provide a unique and indispensable service to education, to the organization of education, and to the fulfilment and guarantee of the placement of every child in a school, and can provide professional support for schools and school staff, including crisis management. The second principle is that LEA control over education is the crystallization of an important factor of a democratic society – that is, the communitarian aspect of education can only be provided by a democratically-elected local authority. School governing bodies, on the one hand, and the organization of new types of schools into business-type chains, on the other, even under the auspices of charities and trusts, cannot provide this. In Ball's (2007) terms, legislation that strips LEAs of their role in education is a true manifestation of the social dislocation process. This will be discussed further in Chapter 10.

Our head of education is still recovering from the shock of the 2004–6 legislation that, suddenly and contrary to the ceaseless decline in LEA powers, introduced a radical increase in the powers of LEAs in both depth and scope. This change was abolished a few years later, long before it could be understood, embedded in LEA culture, and implemented – leaving LEA heads, as well as headteachers, quite speechless:

> In 2006 I don't think putting social care in the same department was a good idea. We have a balanced agenda and social care is a big part of that

> – it's the child's journey, [and] when they get out of the other end it gives a cohesive approach if you're all under one department, although we're looking on someone to secure the job. Do we want a people's directory? Will it change when the government takes schools out [from] under our control – which is very loose in [any] case[, as] we don't manage schools? I have strong allegiance for the borough, I'm not a distant person coming in, I live and breathe the job, and I have strong connections with councillors; an ALB will not do the same. I'm not against change, but not after four and a half years, we're not a basket case, we take good care of our children, working with everybody involved with children in [our LA] not just schools but voluntary and third sector groups, but maybe that's what they want. The community wants a local body to look at 58,000 children. If I were a parent would I trust the government to do that for me?
>
> Power moved to the centre, the middle bit lost power to schools and the centre. If I'm paid by an LA I'll promote it and defend it through thick and thin. If I look at my role as a chief education officer in … or deputy in … local authority, I was in no doubt that we had the most influence as an LEA. We had a teacher training college, we were regulating their numbers, we had FE colleges that were ripped away, we controlled a lot that went on in the schools. Some LAs allocated money to the schools to decide for themselves, some wanted nothing other than getting a good headteacher. I was pioneering the idea of school improvement. The difference is between securing and providing.

The LEA's head of education can be blamed, as often happens, for the major problems of England's education. Often the LEA is perceived as outdated, over-bureaucratic, politicized, and even corrupt. Logically, as LEAs have had control over the commission and the delivery of education for four decades, they might be responsible for the results, academically and socially. However, the current structure does not provide an answer for local democratic representation in education. While LEAs themselves do not provide the best of answers to local representation (sometimes due to size or to separation from local councils), all the changes in the last two decades have failed to provide an alternative for this linchpin of public education. In addition, LEAs have, according to many interviewees, amassed considerable knowledge and experience in monitoring, supervising, and coordinating two particularly important aspects of education. The first aspect is admissions, and the second is guiding schools on pedagogical matters. Parts of these, especially the latter, can perhaps be provided by new types of organizations. But as of yet, it seems, there is still a growing void between school level and ministry level in terms of pedagogical and other professional scaffolding for schools. It remains to be seen, empirically, whether this void is a source of anxiety for schools or an emancipatory power.

Our head of education vows to return to power, stating that 'there will be a role for LAs in opposition-recycling and things change quickly'. Judging by the consistent developments of the last two decades, most participants in this study think this view is disproportionate, even exaggerated.

The tailor: Head of a think tank

Invictus[3] – the imaginary think tank that was constructed through the views of think tank CEOs I have interviewed – is located in an old, renovated building, in Westminster, or perhaps on Kingsway, or the City, or the South Bank. It is close to the centres of power, perhaps a walking distance from Portcullis House. On its website its mission statement declares it is 'Moulding the policymaking schedule and social future for the public, communities, and citizens.'

Like other think tanks it is closely involved not only in drafting policy initiatives, planning programmes for intervention, and new legal arrangements, but also (through liaison and through sister-organizations and subsidiaries) in instigating change in education, recently through a new group of schools and a focused intervention in a poor municipal LEA in a big city. It also takes part in promoting change outside of England, in one Asian and one African country. Its CEO reflects:

> This is the great debate and the debate is really of increasing autonomy to schools. If you have a charter system that has high bars, if they are not exclusive in their admissions, [then the other schools remain behind]. I think that one of the things that has not been expressed is the nuance of the debate. There is a way of doing this. The government isn't implementing the Swedish model, it's the American charter system. The debate is much more basic. We have a different system and history, grammars are still a scar, the Right believes in selection – I don't – and the Left think that if you get the admissions right you don't have to worry about the schools, there is no such thing as a good school or a bad school but just schools with the right intake. Our job, as I see it, is to think outside of these two paradigms and offer viable alternatives, based on research, and on sustainable solutions that can work in the field but that can also be crafted and implemented politically and publicly.

In line with Kingdon's triangle of policy windows, our CEO states that 'the role of our organization is to bring together ideas, solutions, and political feasibility.' He continues:

> Over the course of the last four to five years, developing the new education policy was in a think tank. In a Labour government there was more clear water to paddle big ideas like academies; now it's not up to us to come up with the next big idea, we should be a critical friend, look at being on the back burner, make sure things don't fall through the cracks. Most

> of the agencies that did that for New Labour will be rolled up or folded into the department. There will be different numbers of people in these agencies, the system will be less on legality and checking, and LAs will have to become more sophisticated in how they manage the system. The recession, while it would have been better if it wasn't here in some ways, it facilitates this idea of autonomy and responsibility, one silver lining is perhaps that.
>
> We drafted the education bill quite a while before the general election. One of the things I've been slightly shocked by [is that] laws are rushed and badly drafted. Legislation doesn't mean what it should ... it's true to all our governments, and it certainly affects education.
>
> Essentially what the academies bill is doing is a huge overlap with GM schools and CTCs; they are not inventing something brand new, they would agree with Adonis that the free schools are a new concept. The academies are allowed to bring in sponsors, the free schools are allowed to bring in parents. Academies will need to look at new ways for management, and chains could be a way to do that.
>
> Of course there are forces [that influence the power to change], but it always matters what brings forward the human capacity to override events. Another criterion [for our reform plans] was the epic or millennial view on the human condition. We aim to revolutionize reform and change [to see] if we can remove any obstacle for an alienated society. And the other human condition is our lack of ability to disillusion ourselves. A lot of people in the Left are socially deterministic. Gove is about personal responsibility in all circumstances even when you have no control. It's the human condition to side with one of these extremes. I see our role as one of breaking down these unseen walls and offering models, solutions. We were told 'you don't want to waste your time with politicians of the day but with people from newspapers, intellectuals, reach all political parties'.

Sometimes the think tank attempts to actually implement its ideas on its own, and not through the government. The results are often a sober awakening:

> We became involved in an experiment to set up a new type of school. It was a private school, charging the lowest possible fee and getting away with it. So that was an early free school without the option to receive the taxpayers' funds for it. We also tried a type of 'Sunday school'. Some children are not taught properly in primary schools, they can't read, so we set up Sunday schools – we have several of these, all over, and allow children to catch up. But that depends on the parents bringing them in – they were not

> supportive, it doesn't happen, so we set up a booster school but closed it after a year, because we couldn't find anyone we could depend on, and a foreign bank has given a lot of money for that, some headteachers resented that but some don't. … The LAs put up all kinds of difficulties, traffic problems and so on.

Think tanks represent the 'flattening' of governance (Ball, 2007). As time progresses they become more influential. Even though their views vary, from Right to Left, as a phenomenon they represent neoliberal regimes. Their essence is one of entrepreneurship and managerialism, a quasi-privatization of decision-making, regardless of their agenda. Their influence is evident in all tiers of government – national and local – and their interest in legislation and law-based reform is stronger than ever before. A deeper analysis of their role can be found in Chapter 10.

The soldier: Crafting legislation against policy logic

Perhaps the most commonly-found group of participants in **law**-based reform are the civil servants – those charged with crafting and drafting legislation, and the ones responsible for translating policy initiatives into law. I have interviewed quite a few at middle and senior levels of the DfE in all three periods of this study. Their openness and frank approach are, I think, an ideology of transparency and democracy. They all have strong beliefs in the right of the public to receive up-to-date information on education policy, through research and academic publications. They are all well-informed in the field, not only through UK studies but also regarding what is reported in the US, Canada, Australia, and New Zealand, as well as in the EU in general. Their role, as they see it, runs the gamut from seeing themselves as guardians of non-political professionalism (often disturbed by 'politics'), to serving as politicians' apostles in achieving their political goals through education policy. And their posture is somewhat sombre and aloof, in respect of the changing times and the changes in their roles that are brought about as a result.

> One thing you would have worked out by now, is that it's a centralized country and our politicians have enormous power. Department lawyers may draft it [the legislation] but it's heavily influenced with politicians and political aides. The government has power to do things very fast and politicians are extremely important. That said, we have very few political appointments, the secretary of state doesn't have the appointment power.

> I see my job as one of responsibility to provide policy, structures and procedures that can work, in order to fulfil the political goals or visions of the politicians.

> Legislation is utilized hugely in policy in this country because of the set-up we have with LAs in their responsibility to education. If government wants

> people to do something it either legislates or gives money for employment and benefits. There isn't a local role.
>
> This organization is a bloody sight less corrupt and more efficient than some LAs and not less efficient than others. It's always about stopping the worst [rather] than freeing up the best.

Picking up on the last quotes by our senior civil servant, he sees his main job, through the law, as preventing and containing catastrophes and, as the announcement on London Underground declares, maintaining a 'good service':

> We've created more demand, with less difference, making the system more rational while you have county councils and then inner London boroughs and the metropolitan boroughs, now there are 150-plus LEAs. Now some are unitary and some are two tiers. The best of them do things really well, much better than we can do from here, and others are absolutely shocking and others are good at some things and not so good at others. A lot are incredibly parochial so the people are incredibly dissatisfied.

Making the government's ideas work is another main target for the civil servant:

> For instance this government is always going to promote academies, people in this building [Sanctuary Buildings, the DfE headquarters] say 'this is your job, these are the implications'; some comes from court decisions, some from experience that things are not working, some from the Lords, from public opinion. The fashionable current think tank is always influential.

When structural change and power shifts are required, legislation is almost invariably the exclusive instrument:

> When we say we can't do x, y, z the next thing we say is we have to legislate for it, we don't have the administrative tool because of LAs. One minister is about choice, and wants Ofsted to inspect, so if you want that you need to legislate. LAs would say it has taken a lot of their power. We had an inspectorate before we had a ministry of education, and when Ofsted was set up the joke was that schools were inspected once every 60 years, and LAs inspected but without any power.

A close connection emerges between the change in data-gathering and legislation. The tremendous amount, diverse types, and immediate response of data-gathering and analysing systems make legislation much more effective and adept at intervention in more fine-spun topics:

> The system didn't have any data so there was no real accountability. Some teachers were always more accountable – if you had exam groups, you always were more accountable. A primary school teacher has less data, they had some, but this has changed a lot. We now have a high-stakes system based on the understanding that schools make a huge difference for individual children, [so] if anyone thinks that taking most of their waking time between 5 and 16 – [that] that doesn't really make a difference for their lives – they are wrong.
>
> There's a huge research-based evidence, and my experience is [too that] what you actually legislate for people, and ideas that come from inside this building [Sanctuary Buildings – home of the DfE], think tanks, academics, heads, visitors from abroad, all of these influence policy, the process from getting to people level – there's data that these have been a tremendous influence with real outcomes. What we legislate to is about what is a conversation between officials and ministers for any number of reasons: one is because it's technical things, and if we want the impact we want to know what the options here are – the technicalities you can't have a conference about. The second point is that despite all the broader pressures and trade-offs, the people who decide are the ministers. If given, this is the policy, so what do we need to legislate about and for?

The civil servant speaks freely on issues of governance and social engineering that are quite above the responsibility of the ministry, and reach to the fundamentals of democratic structure and control in England:

> I was once more powerless, but I don't know if this is if you do a power-cake [a pie chart] the department is responsible for more than before. And of course it's possible now to have a relationship with 20,000 schools. We are really schizophrenic about whether we want local government or local administration. A lot of things are done locally but they don't have to be local government. My friend, the chair of governors in a very good LA, and the deputy and head were in hospital at the same time, with very little impact, so clearly it's easy to have someone in [xyz LA] … even 50 miles away, but is this local government? So there's a difference between an LEA that represents a community and one that does not.

An interesting role is placed, informally as well as formally, in the hands of Ofsted officials, who have a unique role in the planning and implementation of law:

> We're not a primary legislator, but we have a role in monitoring the implementation of policy that is outlined in, or through, legislation.

> A lot of what Ofsted does has to do with legislation that doesn't specify how we do it but that we have to inspect it. Legislation specifies a duty but nothing around methodology, or how we go about the task. For instance on the issue of … the draft legislation was there and we had to think how we go about this and what we should do. So we set up a small group of people working on an idea and as they work on the draft guidance, there is a process of interaction, and we offer a perspective, we then concentrate on how we inspect it and what we expect schools to do. We were keen on scales and dimensions. We then issue a draft document that proposes how we see the inspection side of the law.

A special type of civil servant is appointed to the ministry after a long career in education, sometimes with strong party ties or experience in a politically-disposed think tank. This relatively new type of civil servant is a hybrid between the classic civil servant and the education entrepreneur. Often such appointments are made to serve a specific target or type of change, as in the case of EAZs and the first academies. It is not clear why these officials are brought into the department. The participants in this study offer some possible accounts. One reason could be, as one said, to circumvent 'Sir Humphreys' within the department.[4] Another reason, perhaps more positive, is because the specific figure had already led or initiated the proposed change on a smaller scale, perhaps as a headteacher or as a chief education officer for an LEA. Sometimes this type of civil servant may head a group of employees who are hired on a limited-time contract, often with strong ties to the business, banking, and media worlds. One such civil servant explained the need to operate academies:

> GCSE results are, on the whole, positive. One school that got 6 per cent now gets 30 per cent. This does not reflect on the staff – when a school has been struggling for so long it is difficult to believe they will succeed. The sponsors have a record of success, especially the private ones; and businesses, they are very good at setting goals and do not accept no for an answer. When someone says 'this does not work' they say 'great, let's see why and make it work'. It's a different way of looking at problems. Schools have a new headteacher or a new building, there needs to be a huge injection to persuade they can do better but it's even more difficult to make the county believe they can. It's sponsor-building, staff development, the corporate [level] and individuals get to share courses that their corporate staff would share.
>
> There's legislation compliance but legislation changes when the mood changes, and then the landscape. So 70 per cent will be independent state schools and then you can intervene with the others. So you can see we freed the whole bloody system. I think this is the direction but the question

> is if this will raise standards. Standards can plateau and slightly dip. But this will change if you can grow a substantial sector. That's an absolute opposite to micro-management. The legal power of a converted academy.
>
> Legislation is necessary to have the powers to change the system. But it's not enough ... Without legislation we do have schools that have a dominant minority group. We still need a committed department to manage and make sure this happens. The heads will know how to circumvent the rules, play the game even more effectively in terms of selection. We're not managing these schools every day. But in a way, yes, intervention is bureaucratic – beware what you wish for.

Crossing the lines back and forth from a local authority to a think tank, then to a political appointment and then into the civil service, gives our politically- or professionally-appointed civil servant a unique point of view on the department:

> You can't work here at a senior level without being aware of the politics – it's politics with a small 'p' – and ignoring this will be a problem. I came here as an adviser. There was an explosion of advisers – the standards unit was the spearhead of policy and then every policy team had its own adviser or group of advisers, and this group became very difficult to monitor and receive value for money [for their services], so they are being culled.

Finally, our senior civil servant provides a historic overview of legislation's role in policymaking, especially as a balancing power between contradicting and competing forces:

> Over time there were some profound shifts – as recently as the late 1970s or early 1980s this department could fairly be seen as totally outside most of the main professional debates on teaching and learning, or curriculum; they were preoccupied with numbers of teachers and buildings. Managing a capital programme and leading education committees, and the NUT were the dominant professionals. In the 1980s the legislation became highly centralized – Baker decided by to get the National Curriculum. Ofsted became very influential on the behaviour of every school in the country, with a high level of transparency and publication of reports. Those who argue that the LA's powers were diminished are completely correct. Schools are very powerful. Schools and the centre [the ministry]. The power of the NUT is much less than what it was. They are still very influential, they are listened to, we want to know what they think about what is do-able and implantable, but they had a practical veto power [before] and in the last governments they were influential in the tripartite partnership in which

> the teachers' associations had an important role. Some professional or public committees ran the system by large [to a large extent].
>
> This government does not believe in using legislation to make statements, it wants to de-clutter the law. This is an important difference from the previous governments. The Academies Act is intensely practical, it does something you needed to change the law to do and it is fundamentally enabling. About conversation that is a fundamental part of policy but it doesn't do anything. It's pretty simple, it doesn't prescribe about process – for instance GM schools had ballots among staff and parents, that too was enabling. We don't know that there is a new piece of legislation coming but the general trend is no clutter and no prescription.

In these words, and the previous statement on not being the CEO of UK schools, and the omnipotent character of the 'centre', our civil servant points at the change that legislation has brought to the ministry. Yes, it is a gradual process of friendly takeover, justified by international competition, the right to education for children, constant disappointment with the quality of management and outputs by local government, and the need to appease the clash between political and pedagogical timescales. Powerful data-mining tools combined with public demand for change, critical media, and semi-privatized think tanks that offer detailed reform – all these make our civil servant a noteworthy contestant in the game of law-based reform. The need for a highly ethical base for the service is ever-present and greater than ever before.

The spy: Moulding an organizational and educational vision into legislation

In 2005 I was a member of a committee that offered school reform in Israel.[5] During that time there were many public debates on a particular report, its agenda and its consequences. A short while after its publication, I took part in a symposium on the report, and on the panel was the CEO of a large food company in Israel. In my presentation, I pointed at some of the shortcomings as well the attributes of our work on the committee. The next day, the CEO from the panel called the chair of our reform committee (himself the chair of a large Israeli IT firm) to say that he was shocked to hear I had made reference to certain problems, and did not say that *everything* about the committee was great. 'It's a brand,' he explained – 'you never say anything negative about your brand in public.' This account taught me a valuable lesson on the viewpoint of managerialism and the business world, and how it often clashes with that of a professional civil service or of academic research.

An elegant London private club is the venue for my meeting with my fourth imaginary figure: the entrepreneur, founder, and operator of a chain of new schools. These schools, as explained in Chapter 4, have appeared in large numbers since the early 1990s in England. They have taken on various titles and structures, as well as several forms and models of governance and ownership. In general I see them as a type of charter school, English-style, perhaps combined with the tradition of independent grammar schools. They represent a force in the system that peaked in 2010–11 under the Academies Act 2010 and the Education Act 2011. Education entrepreneurs understand government and legislation, and try to harness the processes and qualities to their advantage. Their role is one of lobbyists, looking for opportunities to expand and formalize their initiative:

> I think things happen in public services because essentially the skills and ability drive of ministers, that is the driving force. Personalities are much more important – you have to have the statutory tools but they [the ministers] follow the initiatives. The 1988 act was much more important; we now have a de facto voucher, a school voucher, at the school level.
>
> When I think of the role of sponsors in schools, none of that is legislated. The prime movers were the PMs and secretaries of state. We would never get ... schools spread without David Blunkett and the PM and Andrew Adonis as chief adviser. People driven by belief and commitment to raising standards.
>
> Stealth is important. We now have XXX YYY school because people just woke up and said 'well, we can'.

A main belief and slogan of our spy is: 'what cannot be measured cannot be improved'. He or she believes that the role of legislation is to free the system as much as possible, not only by granting autonomy to existing schools, school leaders, and bodies, but – perhaps because of being disappointed by the prevalent cohort of education managers – also by allowing swift entrance into the managing echelons of the system to an entirely new type of education manager (after: Ball, 2007 and the Education Service Industry and its new entrepreneurs). The spy, or perhaps secret agent, moves with stealth, but is also well connected politically to any ruling education regime (Manzer, 2003). Influencing emerging legislation is important for the spy, no less than influencing new financial legislation or corporate legislation is important for a banker. Meanwhile the spy has invaluable insights into the education system, and quickly masters education policy research and data. His or her critical view of education should not be brushed aside simply as a neoliberal onslaught on public education and equality. Ball (2007), after 186 pages of well-founded criticism of privatization and marketization of education, reminds his readers that 'acceptance of some kinds of private sector participation are more defensible than others and that some public sector "work" is not as defensible as all that' (Ball, 2007: 187).

> A big difference was made by the enormous focus on data, and the department should be congratulated for producing data on schools so schools can't hide any more from the data produced on them. We know at

> what level children are entering – what their level is when they entered – and how they perform after a number of years, and it has allowed schools to track and monitor individual pupils. So ability, or uniform, or structure wouldn't be enough to get appointed [as headteachers]. Independence to schools is the key. There's general recognition that stand-alone schools don't succeed; our job is to bring schools together. Any principal who said 'I don't believe in setting rather than mixed ability' is not accepted. An LEA has 150 schools and most of its money is taken away and they don't have the expertise. And being head of schools for an LEA is not seen as a prestigious job any more, being head of a school is seen as prestigious. Small groups of schools supporting each other are the future. LEAs will not be involved in school improvement, and perhaps imposing a fair admissions process is a residual responsibility.
>
> I think they're in the terms of the Academies Act. It's the implementation [that] will be interesting – the ability to deliver is far less than the aspiration. It's interesting. In terms of policy, the demand is [that] the white paper brings in a lot of the funding end, school improvement will be stripped out of LAs, and schools with no funding will want to become an academy because they don't have funding but they won't go through the system … the extent to which this kind of QUANGOcracy is dismantled. All those support services that in some cases were not high quality but received huge funds. Having schools doing school-to-school support and not having a national force of advisers telling schools what to do; but if they get dismantled quickly how will schools pick up the slack? But I'm quite optimistic. This is where legislation can do a big job.

The whole agenda of the spy is one of enabling: how can legislation create a framework, a landscape for administering a different agenda? At this point the spy sees legislation as the ultimate tool for setting the stage for his or her entrance and allowing them to become meaningful players. To do this, what is needed is swift change and then stability that can allow careful planning, building trust among communities, parents, and staff, and specifically financial development of an idea. This is one of the points on which the spy is most critical towards the frequent legislative changes:

> Targets were moved by NL continuously and the same thing is happening now. How can one play when the goal posts have been shifted so often? Now somebody has picked up the picture. The game has become crooked. As a multi-academy sponsor I had to appear before him [the secretary of state] every year to sit in front of … and a bunch of civil servants. They went over our schools rigorously, asking 'this is the legislation, what are

> you going to do about it?' But I said 'wait a minute – last year there was another bill.'
>
> I listened to Michael Gove, and the way he introduced himself [it seemed] there were two Michael Goves – one the libertarian ('it's teachers who know best, politicians don't know') and then there's Gove the Stalinist who says 'you will do this and that; teach this, teach that'. If you are a champion of freedom and take the initiative, you are then bolted down with these big pieces of legislation. We are spending huge amounts of public money, around £80 million a year, we should be accountable. It's like when there's a game of football and it turns into rugby and the goalposts are moving all the time. Academy sponsors allow schools to break away from local government control but not from central government control.

Bottery, in his book on the ethics of education leadership (1992), predicts a system that does exactly that, a football game with several referees, each one deciding according to a different set of rules, changing unendingly, with goalposts and scores changing and moving around as well.

The spy looks for ability, but also for innovation through legislation – innovation that will allow the new types of schools and their ownerships to flourish and become sustainable for a long period. This requires new definitions and new types of regulatory bodies and measures:

> It will be much easier to open a school in an industrial facility but it's still not as fast as this government would like, although six months before the elections they thought of profit-making entities but the *Guardian* got hold of the story, and the government backed down and they said we can't make money from schools but we can make money from training, curriculum, HR, and many others. Someone said 'Everyone is making a fortune out of schools, shouldn't we make some money out of them?' Put some money back into schools. Our organization came about because I said to ... 'you need more organizations that commission academies.' But there was a problem. Organizations are very small because of localism – what they want is to do something fabulous in education, that's what you need for academies but they have to put so much effort into getting funds and [thinking about] their next year and [they] cannot run a large secondary school. So we set up an organization that will help these to come up [become stronger]. A community with the social capital for people, essentially if it's left for such natural selection, it's middle class communities creating quasi-independent schools for middle class kids. In an attempt to win them [communities, parents] over we mentioned we talked to 750 families asking if they wanted to send their children to a secondary free

> school. So there's a disconnection between MPs and the communities they serve. That's the biggest con. Unless we see a bunch of organizations that do community education reorganization.

As I have shown in the second chapter of this book, the neoliberal powers of education regimes can well be criticized. However, what can be learned from the character of the spy are two things. One is that this new tier, culture, or group of educators are here to stay, not only in England. As Ball points out, ridding the system of them is not reasonable as of now. New ways of thought and new structures are prerequisite. Secondly, some important things can be learned from the sharp analysis offered by some of these education entrepreneurs, and the debate on equity and fairness cannot ignore their point of view any longer:

> As a trust school you don't get the same freedom as an academy. These schools will be bound by the NC, by teacher paying conditions, so whether this will be attractive enough for businesses ... the Left argument is 'don't bring in business at all', [while] the Right says these schools should be freed. The change is dependent on a commissioner–provider split that has diversity of ethos and approach that underpins choice. This has to go hand-in-hand with school improvement. Admissions is such a big issue, the choice is between a good and a bad school; we want to create a system that offers choice between good schools but with a different ethos. The challenge has always been how much dynamism you want without having the system completely fragmented. We haven't gone that far. The 'building schools for the future' programme is still much more controlled – we want a level of accountability that brings up standards. This might not work in practice. We can do things in the bill, we can define the relationships between LAs and schools, but we can't foster dynamism [or] champion parent – this is a lot about culture.

Notes

[1] Le-Carré, J. (1974) *Tinker, Tailor, Soldier, Spy*. London: Hodder & Stoughton.

[2] Tinker: 1) A mender of pots, kettles, pans, etc.; 2) An unskilful or clumsy worker; 3) A jack of all trades (*Random House College Dictionary*).

[3] Latin for unconquered or unvanquished.

[4] The classic civil servant permanent secretary portrayed by Nigel Hawthorne in the British television comedy series *Yes, Minister* and *Yes, Prime Minister*. The series focused on how the permanent staff never allowed politically elected superiors to actually influence policy. Broadcast on the BBC (1980–4 and 1986–8) and written by Antony Jay and Jonathan Lynn.

[5] The National Task Force on Education, known as the 'Dovrat' committee after its chair, Shlomo Dovrat.

Chapter 8

The unique driving force of 'superheads' in law-based reform

Each time our secretary of state visits a foreign country and is invited into the one successful school – we cower in fear and prepare for the worst.

(Secondary school principal – 'superhead', London, 2011)

They take on our worst performing schools in deprived areas with some of the toughest pupils in the capital and turn these so-called 'unteachable' kids into stars. Superheads they call them, and although they're handsomely rewarded with salaries typically in excess of £120,000, they put in ferociously long hours and punch well above their weight when it comes to ramping up results. Superheads are regarded by the Government as the key saviours of inner-city state comprehensives, often parachuted-in to save failing schools, and if education secretary Michael Gove had his way, he would bottle their wisdom and franchise it. So who are they? And what makes them worth their pay packets?

(David Cohen, *London Evening Standard*, 31 January 2011[1])

'Superhead' ... defends plans to convert school to academy
Concerns raised over 'lack of transparency' surrounding pay, but ... cites flexibility and freedom as advantages.

(Jeevan Vasagar, *The Guardian*, 9 September 2010[2])

£200,000 superheads: Best leaders will take on chains of poor schools – with rich rewards
Heads of successful state schools could earn close to £200,000 a year if they help under-achieving neighbours. Schools Secretary Ed Balls wants schools to work together in 'chains'. High-performing state establishments would merge with struggling ones. Any that refused would be marked down in Ofsted ratings.

(Laura Clarke, *Mail Online*, 29 June 2009[3])

Gove to double the number of 'superheads'
An army of 'superheads' will scour the country spreading their educational prowess to struggling state schools, under plans announced by the Education Secretary, Michael Gove. He said the number of heads helping to tackle under-performance will be more than doubled. At present, 393

> heads rated as 'outstanding' or 'good' by Ofsted have taken part and this will rise to 1,000 by 2014. Under the plans, the best heads will be given a national role in turning schools around. 'Good' heads will be sent into neighbouring schools where inspectors have identified weakness. Mr Gove said: 'There are many superb heads in our state system doing a wonderful job. But there are also many schools which are not giving children the start they deserve.'
>
> (Richard Garner, *The Independent*, 17 November 2010)

Introduction: conceptualizing headship and law-based reform

The opening statement by a London 'superhead' points at the extent to which senior headteachers see themselves both as involved in, and also influenced directly by, government policy and legislation. The media headlines that follow show that superheads are an important interest group in England's education debate and education policy, with growing public awareness as to their role. In a way this is the doing of two decades of successive governments' rhetoric and policy that strengthened schools and placed headteachers on a pedestal as both the champions of education's success, and the bearers of shame when it failed. Although the role of headteachers in education (Leithwood *et al.*, 1999; Oplatka, 2010; Stoll and Stobart, 2005; Rallis and Goldring, 2000) and national policy issues is becoming more important in general terms, England in particular is a leading country in this development (Earley and Weindling, 2004; Earley *et al.*, 2002). Superheads are a distinct group of headteachers, usually of large secondary schools – but also some primaries – who have been earmarked as outstandingly successful. The criteria for being labelled as a superhead are vague and fluid, often temporary, fashionable, and political. Success at standards-based accountability measures and advancing their school in tests and league tables is an important benchmark, especially when attainment is measured as value-added and can be correlated to promoting attainment among weak populations. Initiating and implementing internal school reform and acquiring funds and donations are other criteria. Having a voice on national policy issues, political links – locally and/or nationally – and serving on committees is probably a second stage that follows the initial pedagogical and organizational results. Superheads can be rogue (Earley and Weindling, 2004) and revolutionary, or reactionary and compliant. From my study, after talking to many of them, I can determine they are powerful and passionate. They have pizzazz and panache. They give headship a flare that was previously more characteristic of political leaders or charismatic business CEOs. A thorough search has not yielded any results as to the origins of this title. In the US the terms 'leading principal' or 'outstanding principal' are common. But the difference is not just in the term. As extreme as England's educational legislation is, in both scope and frequency, a generation of superheads has emerged that has consistent influence on education policy and law. Considering that on a national level each headteacher is one of many thousands, it is interesting to reflect on the role and voice of these superheads. The appearance of this type of influential leader did not happen in a void, and from a socio-political critical point of view it is part of larger neoliberal streams in education policy. Many researchers (Ball, 2007, 2012; Bangs *et al.*, 2010; Bottery, 2000; Darling-Hammond, 2010; Gunter, 2005; MacBeath *et al.*, 2007) see the strengthening of school leaders and the growing interest in leadership as a promising cure-all for the problems of education systems as a downright manifestation of the neoliberal ideology in the form of managerial practices seeping into the public sector:

> To the extent that these new responsibilities are taken seriously, the social, political, and economic goals of the state are reproduced within the commitments, choices and obligations – the conduct that is – of individual actors within public sector institutions. These 'new' professionals act prudentially and innovatively to protect and further the interests of their organization – to achieve targets, to maximize income and to compete effectively with other providers within the new market-like mechanisms which are inserted into public sector schooling ... Enterprise is the trope that holds all of this together.
>
> (Ball, 2012: 35)

Ball describes the school as a miniature version of the neoliberal state, and in it the qualities of a private firm are duplicated. The characters of quasi-markets and quasi-privatization, including tangible privatization, require that the headteachers of quasi-privatized schools 'go with the (market-competition) flow', as fierce decentralization of the system introduces new demands for headteachers. Levin and Fullan (2008) present the cycle of managerialism. This cycle has probably changed the role of headteachers:

- In order for schools to compete, individual schools would require much more autonomy.
- Parents would need to be able to choose the schools their children attended.
- In order to choose, parents and the public would require comparable measures of student achievement and education quality for all schools, based on a single national curriculum.

(Levin and Fullan, 2008: 289–90)

These principles outline the framework in which headteachers operate, and have been operating, since about the mid-1980s and certainly, from a legislative standpoint, since the enactment of the 1988 ERA. When New Labour came to power in 1997, a feeling of euphoria (Bangs *et al.*, 2010: 11) swept over many headteachers in England, for many of them opposed the aggressive decentralization and quasi-privatization under the Thatcher–Major administrations (Gibton, 2004a). They nevertheless welcomed LMS and, to an extent, the GM experience as well – seeing them as an opportunity to empower headteachers and stimulate leadership in schools (Gibton, 2004a). Later on this euphoric feeling was replaced by growing criticism of the over-prescribed policy, of the growing involvement – the meddling, according to some – of government in teaching and learning methods (by establishing numeracy and literacy strategies and by attempting to tightly control the structure of lessons), and the performance-management scheme. These policies not only posed serious threats to the recently-acquired autonomy of headteachers, but also severely hurt the financial autonomy of schools, because the government forced them to allocate fixed sums of money to administer and manage the structured modifications, or allocated new money exclusively for these. However, as the spread of charter-type schools grew, headteachers, especially in the secondary sector, became more powerful than ever before. Their personal status improved, too, as their salaries rose imposingly. The relationship between headteacher and their staff has also changed:

> Transformational leadership is endemic in the English field, and is based on a separation of leaders from followers, hence leadership is based on what role incumbents have as skills and attributes that enable them to be inspirational, to appeal to individual and groups of followers, to influence their thinking and to build an emotional commitment to the organization. The elevation of the role incumbent as a leader who does leadership from those who do other work has been based on the redefining of management (and indeed teaching) as lower level activity that is technical and about getting the job done. ... What is problematic is the separation of the headteacher as leader from others, except as a linear causal impact on those others.
>
> (Gunter, 2005: 175)

> It has been observed, however ... that these increased demands for administration, planning and reporting upwards may unintentionally diminish school leaders' capacity to attend to more strategic matters of educational leadership within the school. This may reduce rather than enhance the quality of education.
>
> (Goldspink, 2007: 29)

A most significant change in the work of headteachers seems to have materialized in outer circles, between headteachers and their environment: the school governing body, the LEA, Ofsted, the ministry, and other external QUANGOs and ALBs. This change, has, in practice, transformed headteachers into school CEOs, especially in the secondary sector. This conversion in the nature of relationships between the school and its surroundings is dominated by the notion of consumerism (Harris,

1993; Bottery, 2005), perhaps another result of neoliberalism's ideological drive into education, that is translated, as explained before, into managerialist structures and practices:

> The mention of the word 'consumer' in educational circles is likely to generate four different reactions. A first is the reaction of educational entrepreneurs, who welcome the use of the term, and are totally at ease within a conceptual universe of business and markets. ... A second reaction is that of educational pragmatists who believe that, for good or ill, consumerism belongs to a conceptual universe that accurately reflects the world in which they live. ... They accept that this is how governments see their function, and that this is how, driven by financial steers, they increasingly need to see parents and children. ... A third reaction is that of the public sector advocate who, despite recognizing such governmental steers and assumptions, is still concerned with the use of the term 'consumer' in public sector practice. One reason is the fact that concepts like payment, profit and consumerism imply a set of values which is fundamentally at odds with the public-sector values by which they may have lived their entire professional life ... They are likely therefore to believe that the term over-simplifies the educational relationship between professional and client. The final reaction is that of welfare state advocates, who subscribe to all the concerns of the public sector advocate, but who ... also see education as being defined by the role it plays within the welfare state project.
>
> (Bottery, 2005: 270–1)

Ranson (2011) cautions on the deterioration of school governance (also: Balarin *et al.*, 2008; Earley and Creese, 2003; James *et al.*, 2011), and calls for the strengthening of 'community governance' (ibid. 409–10). As power within a system seems to me to be a finite resource, perhaps not unlike energy, the accumulation or attribution of power to one figure or tier is unavoidably at the expense of others, as no new powers are introduced. Headteachers have undoubtedly absorbed many new powers along the last two decades, at the expense of governing bodies, LEAs, and their own staff. They have also become much more accountable, on a personal level, because they now operate in an environment in which the stakes are much higher. But whether this strengthening of headteachers has undeniably improved educational outcomes is still at the centre of a huge debate among researchers. Without immersing ourselves into this debate here, I can only point at findings that show that the correlation between leadership and educational outcomes is, as yet, vague, mainly due to the difficulties of isolating this variable from others, and the non-direct influence of headteachers on students as they are removed from them several times over. Levačić and Dawnes (2004) explain that such studies still present a serious challenge to researchers, although some development is noted (Levačić *et al.*, 2003). Darling-Hammond (2010) explains how this controversy is tied to educational accountability:

> In the currently prevailing paradigm in the United States, accountability has been defined primarily as the administration of tests and the attachment of sanctions to low test scores. Yet, from the perspective of children and parents, this approach does not ensure high quality teaching each year, nor does it ensure that students have the courses, books, materials, support services, and other resources they need to learn. In this paradigm, two-way accountability does not exist: although the child and the school are accountable to the state for test performance, the state is not accountable to the child or school for providing adequate educational resources. Furthermore we have seen test-based accountability schemes have sometimes undermined education for the most vulnerable students, by narrowing curriculum and by creating incentives to exclude low-income students in order to boost scores.
>
> (Darling-Hammond, 2010: 301)

> If education is actually to improve and the system is to be accountable to students, accountability should be focused on ensuring the competence of teachers and leaders, the quality of instruction and the adequacy of resources, as well as the capacity of the system to trigger improvement.
>
> (Ibid. 301)

Accountability measures and the involvement of Ofsted in the life of headteachers have had a substantial impact on their work and on perceptions of their job. My findings show that headteachers have grown accustomed to high-stakes inspection. When I interviewed them in 2000–1 the presence of Ofsted was much more ominous than in 2005–6 or in 2010–11. In 2000–1 there was certainly fear of the school's closure or of being put on special measures, although the powers to do so evolved gradually in legislation,[4] and the numbers of schools placed on special measures are, to this day, exceptionally negligible.[5] Consequently, in 2005–6 and in 2010–11 there was a gradual acceptance of, and even support for, the audit culture, as will be presented in the next part of this chapter.

Along similar lines to Chapter 7, this part will evolve around six 'superheads'. In this case it is easier to conceal identities so I will provide a bit more detail on the careers and work of the six individuals. I believe their story is typical of what is happening with the involvement of headteachers in policymaking and law-based reform. Here is a short introduction of the six heads:

- Headteacher 1, large comprehensive, south London, working class area, predominantly black intake. Male, late 60s in 2011.

- Headteacher 2, large comprehensive specialist school, affluent suburban-rural area north of London. Female, late 60s, head for 12 years.
- Headteacher 3, large comprehensive, east London estates and immigrants, predominantly Bangladeshi/Bengali Muslim/some white intake. Male, early 50s, head for ten years in 2011.
- Headteacher 4, large comprehensive, affluent north London area. Male, early 50s in 2011, head for six years.
- Headteacher 5, large, well-known academy in an urban poor area. Male, mid-50s.
- Headteacher 6, large comprehensive urban secondary school, mainly Bangladeshi/Bengali Muslim/some white intake. Female, mid-40s.

In 2000–1 they used to think ...:[6] Understanding and anxiety

> On the one hand, the law makes education the absolute theme of central government. It's an important statement. But sometimes I feel that some has not been planned, just sending endless lists of initiatives that have not been thought about. There is a serious issue of teacher recruitment that central government is ignoring ... In the sense that there has been a shift of responsibility to heads and their performance and part of me is with that, but I want a government that is sympathetic and doesn't just expect improvement year-by-year. I mean I was shouting into [the DfEE] like crazy on bureaucracy but getting asked to hoof it – government is not enough into structures. They hint what they want but don't go all the way. They talk on integration but keep grammar schools because there is more money in them.
>
> (Superhead 4, 2000)

> Law certainly focuses the mind and it very quickly gets the whole school going when you know that a government initiative is legally binding. Since 1988, legislation has been used as a policy tool, and we are very well used to the time that the Secretary of State uses this power [to legislate] to change policy. In many ways in our school, people get to accept that, while in the past, they tried to subvert it. Now they try to shape it. There's much less resistance.
>
> (Superhead 1, 2001)

The heads who matured, professionally and personally, in a period when, as one interviewee said, 'secretaries of state's only power was to demolish air-raid shelters', are growing accustomed to a culture of intervention and policymaking, strongly rooted in party socio-political ideology and agendas. This is the education regime (Manzer, 2003) in its initiation process. The observations on the growing utilization of legislation by the political sphere are followed by growing anxiety regarding issues such as the autonomy of the school and its head, and the audit culture:

> The accountability is huge in terms of who you are accountable to, you know we have a budget of five million pounds and are responsible for the well-being of young people, so I'm accountable to parents, governing bodies, LEA, countless government agencies. My immediate boss, well … I guess I have to be accountable to the governors but I have to say the relationship we have with the LEA is a real partnership.
>
> (Superhead 3, 2001)

Slowly an understanding seeps in, that legislation is not just a tool for intervention – the extent and justification of which can be argued but empathized with – but also a steadily-increasing process of passing on responsibility from government to LEAs and schools. As one head, perhaps an aspiring superhead, of a primary school in the east of England said in an unforgettable quote in 2001: 'once the government provided education – now it provides information on education.' By this he meant that the audit culture is overwhelming the public with information on the results of schooling, so that if, and when, failure occurs the blame will be either on schools and headteachers, or on parents who did not use the information wisely to choose the better school. This has already been noted by Whitty and his colleagues (1998), as the following quotes by headteachers caught between often-conflicting powers and bottom-up rhetoric followed by top-down policy illustrate:

> I should be accountable to students and parents … The governors are parents, they reflect parents' views. The LEA is the whipping boy. The government is passionate about education, but I'm kind of fed up of this rhetoric and the idea that we are not.
>
> (Superhead 2, 2000)

> Another [example] might be the national strategies you had for [the] growth of the use of a [pre-scripted] three-part lesson. The national strategy was aimed to control what teachers did in the classroom. How to get teacher behaviour to change. Another would be curriculum – the introduction of the NC in 1988. Again the legislation of that is about power. That's if you want to control it as a top-down approach if you want to shape an education system the way you want to shape it.
>
> (Superhead 3, 2001)

While the heads see advantages – for their school but also for their own professional status – in 2000–1 they are all social democrats, perhaps socialists, as was explained in Chapter 6. They show true yearning for state-controlled education:

> I am a true believer in the comprehensive all-inclusive school. Look at our area: we have an RC school down the road, and a posh grammar that's been around here since the seventeenth century in the centre of town. I believe a real Labour government should close these down: they are all a 'front' for segregation according to class. In the grammar school, first to be accepted are siblings, then children of graduates, then of the staff, then all the rest. You should see the expensive SUVs in the morning ...
>
> (Superhead 2, 2001)

In 2005–6 I still thought? Rethought?

Four years later the headteachers are celebrating eight years of New Labour governments. The policy trajectories of, first, the Thatcher–Major era and, second, two-and-a-half terms of the Blair governments, are sinking in:

> In a sense I think, for me, in terms of the school things are easier; I think the operation of schools had become smoother; some of the initiative is more structured and there is more consultation between the DfES and schools. The finances are better, they've stabilized the funding put into schools so I'm not struggling so hard in terms of what government policy means exactly. There is some evidence about monitoring performance and not how to do it. Schools have gained some control, things are easier to manage, such as KS3 but there are strange things, like when we tried to retain our 16–19 pupils we thought 'our 6th Form will be taken away' but just after we went on that track the government went to 14–19 so there is no consistency. The Tomlinson report said that but it didn't happen, it was good for us at the time politically. The evidence is that successful schools can set up their 6th Forms and academies are 11–18 so the notion that led to 16–19 change doesn't have the same force it had four years ago and that is strange.
>
> (Superhead 1, 2005)

Here the expectations from New Labour are huge, perhaps romantic and unrealistic. The superheads think that what they saw as important innovations to the old state system – mainly empowerment of schools and headteachers, and more autonomy – will remain, while the attributes of the comprehensive, state-controlled, but loosely coupled and supposedly egalitarian, system will be reintroduced. They are disappointed to realise that many of the new policies follow in the footsteps of the Conservatives, but that some of the novelties include impatient over-control by New Labour. Tenably, then, it all turned out to be a dream that was difficult to accomplish. Some, though, are eager for the government to further the separation between commission and delivery:

> My philosophy is working [well] in an academy. We assess them on our version of the national standards, the things that make a difference in a challenging school.
>
> (Superhead 5, 2005–6)

They experience a rude awakening, due to the understanding that the New Labour policies often contradict each other and that the system is now (that is, in 2005–6) over-legislated and burdened with detailed mandatory reform:

> ... another thing that has changed is that the government, before, the emphasis was on competition, and working to improve your own schools, competing with local schools on teachers doing better on exam results, there is a rationale. Now the emphasis is on collaboration, we are encouraged to share resources, ideas. In the 16–19 age group we came out of a consortium to a single school, but now we move children at 14 and this leads to a series of contradictions. What we now have is a federation of schools that contribute 30 per cent of the teaching to the 16–19 schools so now we retain some of [LEA X's] federation of five schools. The question is if you're in a soft or hard federation – hard is with one head, but we are a soft federation [with a more cooperative style].
>
> (Superhead 1, 2005–6)

> One of the things about education law within the policy process is ... ensuring that heads and schools carry out the policy, for example league tables and how one measures performance. That schools get to the actual measure of it is a moral hazard. A situation of vocational qualifications are offered to certain types of schools – and, for a battered qualifications system, legislating is a way of ensuring that what should happen, does.
>
> (Superhead 5, 2005)

The headteachers recognize that the problematic impact of local politics, that has perhaps weakened with the gradual stripping of LEA powers, is now replaced by close encounters with national politics that have increasing impact on life in schools:

> There are quite a lot of policies that this government brought in that could have been Conservative policies, but I can stick to my principles – a politician has to be much more pragmatic. Having been a Labour supporter all my life I ask how much do they have to sell their soul? There are 30 per cent that would vote Labour whatever happened, and 30 per cent who would vote Conservatives come hell or high water. So you need another 15 per cent. The present thing about admissions is a bridge too far, this can have a most adverse effect on equity. Some things are a lot of tosh, specialist schools just get more money, the notion that parents

> can choose is a con, but I can live with that if it drives the system forward. There are too many schools set up at the same time – that is a flaw, and to get around it is the wrong way, we recognize the flaws and then get around them. Banding is a non-runner, it's a ritual for the middle class. One of the first academies is close by, in … . It has a banding policy. They said that they will go on with it, but they have different banding policy. Local schools have three groups – a, b, and c [all calculated according] to local intake. The academy does this based on national data. That's going on along the whole country, and then the church schools, what is the DfES going to do with that? This is a notion of altruism, what school will change [and become a selective academy]? Academies cannot be named in Year 6 by SEN students.
>
> (Superhead 3, 2005–6)

Perhaps it is at this stage that the superheads understand that they not only need to apprehend national policy, but also harness it directly to their schools' needs, and perhaps be involved in its determination themselves:

> There are advantages in 6th Form funding; I will have good 6th Form numbers. It won't have any impact on admissions policy unless there will be the right to determine your numbers. In an open market, there is a lot of isolationism, which influenced the school a lot more than it has the wider community, and having a funding formula will have an effect for some inner-city schools that were well resourced compared to rural schools. The intensity of an inner city school is complex because the stamina for teachers is different. The demands on stamina are considerable when you have a lot of kids who suffer challenges such as poverty or no personal space, that have an influence on what you can learn and that bring to the family all kinds of issues. It's an adrenalin-filled situation, that's why we end up with more fighting and knife crime and gun crime, and teachers need different resources to deal with those things, it's a concentration effect. I think if you have a national funding formula you don't have that local context.
>
> (Superhead 4, 2006)

> [There are] many types of schools and many loyalties and ownerships. The system is diversified quickly and equality and equity policy do not catch up. Banding is a bridge too far, the horses are all gone. So a school like ours is left to do its own battle, when these are really situations that should be dealt with in legislation, by the government.
>
> (Superhead 2, 2006)

The headteachers have received something of a crash-course on the sociology of law. It is now seen as a tool and much less as a scripture.

> I've been a headteacher since 1986 in three different schools. The conclusion I've come to is that it's my job to advance the learning and wellbeing of my students and if I have to do, as a means of legal device, to ignore any type of legislation by government because it is destabilizing – I will. I'm a gatekeeper to allow in these initiatives and keep at bay these pieces of legislation that I think might work against the interest of the children. My parents are not as sophisticated as middle class parents. I have to work within the law, I will not break the law but I will bend it where I can.
>
> (Superhead 2, 2006)

Finally now I understand … that there's no going back to the past, but the future is unclear

So far as the superheads seemed to have grown habituated to the neoliberal education regime, in its several varieties; the legislation of 2010–11 left them lost for words. It was as if they could not believe what had happened in a very short period to the already significantly altered education system:

> Michael Gove has talked of the centrality of teaching but he's making big changes. Look at Pupil Premiums … we were expecting £3,000 [but] this is still a band aid. People underestimate the power of class and the ways your kids get affected by disenchanted aspirations. We stay here because the kids deserve a decent crack so we understand the expectations have to be a solid commitment and kids first, legislation second. So if I have to ignore the law to reach the kids I will do it. I'm not indifferent to what I'm doing but I'll do it anyway.
>
> (Superhead 3, 2010)

> One of the things that eluded practitioners was the level of intervention by the centre, it was overwhelming and it was necessary to avoid. Some of the schools were not run by our government, not even the LEA because they lost a lot of their power, but by a group of people in Sanctuary Buildings who set out to micro-manage everything, give you the full Monty, people got fed up and are not following any more.
>
> (Superhead 6, 2011)

Superhead 1 gives a detailed historic vignette on the involvement of politics in law-based reform:

> Politicians play a major part in how new legislation comes about. It's politically motivated. Look at the report on diversity and citizenship that came about because they were worried about 7/7 and using education

> to show they were doing something about a situation in the country. The academies movement had come from Adonis and Blair and their political will to change public services. Heads were angry about bog-standard comprehensives. Balls took back some of the powers and that was also political. Heads were not part of that debate. Gove has alliances that are outside the old education establishment, uses a lot of think tanks, ARK, Policy Exchange – this is where he's looking including other countries. But the charter schools are in an American context. I met someone from Sweden who said that schools in their inner city, children went to a free school but then the white kids escaped. There will be a big market of admissions.
>
> (Superhead 5, 2011)

These testimonies reflect, to me, a type of 'back to the future' encounter, somewhat similar to what headteachers said in 2000–1. Again the system is transformed very quickly in terms of governance, commission, and delivery, leaving large comprehensive secondary schools with fewer and fewer options in the comprehensive, LEA, public (in the US, Boydian sense) domain:

> If a school is struggling, they might die on their feet. There are politically-inspired things that are not inspired through discussion. Gove works with the most successful heads – mavericks – who work the system for their advantage, but the other heads, for them it's a struggle. A lot of where education goes has a strong political bias. The coalition, poor sods, they don't like New Labour things like citizenship and community cohesion, so these will not stay. Whatever happened in the New Labour years there was a lot of initiative, but if you take it from '97 to 2007, a lot of money went on, a lot of work went around assessment, behaviour for learning, training headteachers. It was higgledy-piggledy, but you couldn't free schools without this work. You need change but you need evolution, not revolution. When you got rid of the SEF, this made a real difference. Standards have improved.
>
> (Superhead 1, 2011)

> How school funding happens is going to be a key battleground. Having talked to various people in the current coalition government, it's my perception that there was a hope of a flood of schools opting out of local government. Michael Gove is moving into a national funding formula that will free all schools from LAs. So the way around that will be to fund directly. Legislation will have the same objective. Lots of heads are ambivalent, waiting to see what will happen.
>
> (Superhead 6, 2011)

But not all headteachers hold a similar apocalyptic view. There are those who see the new policy as a less-worse option, while others regard it as an aspiration to live up to:

> [Politicians from elite groups and schools have] a perception of society that is very limited to a particular framework they share, similar manners of etiquette to life, I suppose. If they want to make a real difference [theirs is] not a realistic look and [it is not] recognizing important aspects of society. Actually there is a lot of high-quality teaching and learning although attainment is not quite as high. [The current system] was forged in this melting pot, I went to a seminar with Gove, that after GM schools or faith schools, we now have academies and free schools, they [the heads at the seminar] weren't representative of London heads, it was a much more conservative [response] for a group of people arguing for independence and that's the group that were forming his think tank in a way, but it represents the group. It's a different experience; one has to account for that, that's why the academies bill hasn't yielded the particular response [in terms of setting up new ones, but also of critique and objection].
>
> (Superhead 6, 2010)

> Legislation does change the maps of power. What has been most revealing to me is exactly how much we depend on politicians. New Labour were much more careful on building their strategy, but Michael Gove is much more categorical in what he does, we don't have influence on that. They go to extremities and then have to back-track. It's interesting that the QUANGOs will be abolished, I wonder how they will come back.
>
> (Superhead 6, 2010)

> There is an agreement that we have to do not for the few – it's not altruism, it's an economic imperative. The education scene has changed a lot and schools are better now although there's a long way to go. There are figures to prove that social mobility has improved. Some say it hasn't changed for fifty years; I say the system has opened up and the consensus is that this can be done by giving headteachers more freedom and giving them more accountability through inspection and audit. This government believes that Blair's notion of academies and autonomous schools should be accelerated at the cost of diminishing the power of LAs and their bureaucracies, and produced a blizzard of initiatives that didn't come to much, and Ofsted will say that. The national strategies were sucked away by the department and will become a thing of the past but the question is who will hold them [the DfE] accountable? The challenge is autonomy, yes, who will hold them accountable? The mantra now is schools supporting schools, grouped

> together, hard and soft federations – they're all independent schools run through a common ethos, helping each other like a mini-LEA.
>
> (Superhead 5, 2011)

Superhead 5 discloses one of the drawbacks of New Labour's legislation: inconsistencies and contradicting initiatives and ideas. A real-life 'garbage can' (Cohen *et al.*, 1972; Kingdon, 2003) policy that expects discrepant policies to somehow mediate or balance each other. The Conservatives' legislation is simpler, more straightforward, and answers fundamentally to the free-market model of governance (Glatter, 2002):

> Some say despite the billions spent, it's now clear this wasn't spent well. Secretaries of state saying 'every child matters', of course every child matters, and all these crazy initiatives, we want them to achieve beyond national expectations not just beyond local norms. There was no continuity. My view is a fairly straightforward one: there is still a mobility gap but schools are much more accountable. Schools reflect the nature of society and local control transforms a mono-cultural education country into a multi-cultural country. It's a melting pot of a country. There's a real opportunity here because there isn't institutionalized segregation and racism in this country now people are more open and there's less tolerance towards talking about it. It was a defence mechanism, but victim mentality is going. This is social flux and education reflects that. We don't have this history of discrimination and this country should be proud of its legal heritage of racial equality.[7]
>
> (Superhead 5, 2011)

The headteachers are ever-more alert to their role in influencing policy. This role has several aspects. One aspect is the justified pride and honour they feel on being consulted. A second aspect is a growing feeling of responsibility – not being (just) at the receiving or implementation end any more – but involved in deliberation that impacts many schools, headteachers, teachers, and students. A third aspect that became evident during the New Labour administrations is the headteachers' mounting ethical concern regarding a 'Stockholm syndrome', in the form of an over-identification with the ministry. The reasons for this could either be because of a will to remain in the limelight, or simply a gradual adoption of a macro-policy synoptic view and loss of the authentic grass-roots view that comes from daily encounters with education at the school level:

> The balance of headteachers occasionally have the opportunity to talk to politicians and policymakers. We talk to department officials, and they are intermediary. I sit on the heads' reference groups and we meet regularly with department people, but occasionally a politician is there. They talk to the minister, then what we say is filtered and possibly presented these

> as their ideas. In the PM's delivery unit there is a new kind of breed. It's not a linear, direct relationship. Without being totally unprofessional, when someone like myself is asked to sit on a group like that you feel good about yourself, and the danger is what some of the people become, they might say what people want to hear, if they are not careful they become assimilated into the departmental culture rather than keeping their own position, because they follow suit into a culture, and you're afraid you won't be invited again. Some people maintain their individual opinion, but in some, the sycophantic quality is too strong but they move along the way. You realize that if you're responsible for 4,000 schools you have to view things differently; the people I see who talk to government and who government listens to sometimes become compliant. This government is quite good at looking at heads and talking to them, perhaps too much to them, and less listening to what they say. My biggest beef with Labour is that first they wanted to take control but then wanted to focus on what happens in all the schools across the country, so if we get good professional standards, and these were the national strategies, [then we would be] providing all schools with that central control over what a child is entitled to have as an educational experience.
>
> (Superhead 2, 2011)

Epilogue and concluding thoughts

In 2004 I wrote:

> The headteachers in this study, who were found to be highly committed to social justice and fair distribution of social goods, find the new deal of public education puzzling. What exactly should they be? Is it conservative masters of the schools committed to England's old class system? (Probably not). Is it neo-Marxist suspicious revolutionaries who see government conspiracies meant to appease the masses, while retaining power for old and new elite groups? (Perhaps, a bit). Is it managerial business bottom-line specialists who run an efficient and successful 'shop'? (Perhaps, quite a bit.) Is it communal leaders who assist a bewildered community in bringing up children for tomorrow's globalized, borderless, sophisticated and ever-changing world, while retaining human dignity, compassion, and fairness as much as possible and keeping an open eye for national educational policy? (Bingo!)
>
> (Gibton, 2004b: 146)

I now wonder if the crude applicability of these words in 2012 is a blessing or a threat. All but one of the six superheads whose case was presented in this chapter see the option of becoming an academy as viable and even favourable:

> It's hard to see where it's all going to. It's almost as if they say 'let's break down the system and then see where we are' – it looks like that, more than a clear, rational frame for our aspirations for our children. I've been trying to get a sense of where we're aiming towards, it's a fuzzy picture. I've taken a view to do what's best for the schools. We've done a staff review around Gove's consultation on how the school should respond to the new policy. One of the things was, should we become an academy? But I wanted them to consider what else the school could do so it remains a strong school in a context like this. I wanted the governors and staff to start thinking but very few do. Gove thought this will be blue-sky thinking, people talk about curriculum and not like the 2006 BSF. Our people are more conservative; also there are limits to the sorts of ways you can structure education for people. The responses were very direct and in contact to a particular individual who helps them understand a particular piece of knowledge … to further knowledge and learning you need individual people, so if that's the case there are limited ways, and people have to be in a real school there and decide on a certain path.
>
> (Superhead 6, 2010)

> Headteachers are valued more than ever before, we need to retain good teachers, not just recruit them. Leadership is essential for school reform. The teaching force is ageing and 40 per cent of heads will retire in a few years. All that is now fully understood. I would say that I'm a great supporter in what has happened in the last few years: the openness, the schools being accountable for money, I'm a great supporter of most initiatives and of the National College [NCSL]. In countries that value education and value teachers, schools are good places. In societies that value leadership and it's supported, schools are good places. There's general recognition that stand-alone schools don't succeed; our job is to bring schools together, any principal who said 'I don't believe in setting rather than mixed ability' is not accepted. An LEA has 150 schools and most of its money is taken away and they don't have the expertise; and being head of schools for an LEA is not seen as a prestigious job any more, being head of a school is seen as prestigious. Small groups of schools supporting each other are the future. LEAs will not be involved in school improvement, and perhaps imposing a fair admissions process [is] a residual responsibility.
>
> (Superhead 5, 2011)

So where are the six headteachers in 2012?

- Headteacher 1 works for a PFI that establishes academies and trains headteachers.
- Headteacher 2 still leads the same school as in 2000.
- Headteacher 3 still heads the same school, and is considering and negotiating academy status with school governors.
- Headteacher 4 is head of education at a large London LEA.
- Headteacher 5 worked for a PFI that sponsors academies and has lately accepted a senior government position influencing education policy.
- Headteacher 6 still heads the same school and is considering and negotiating academy status with school governors.

> I've seen these policies come through and they all seemed rational and could be implemented, and I found it interesting to see how they got to that point. When I studied my own school the teachers didn't know anything about whether it was the direction of the head and his practice and structures – they believed in him and it didn't matter if it came from government, or if you have a policy document with a wealth of things happening here, few had the time or patience to reflect on this.
>
> (Superhead 6, 2010)

Is this a clear victory for neoliberal ideology or a good example of, as Ball (2007) explains, not returning to the past but moving 'beyond the tyrannies of improvement, efficiency, and standards to recover a language of, and for, education articulated in terms of ethics, moral obligations, and values' (ibid. 191)?

Understanding this is awaiting further enquiry.

Notes

[1] www.standard.co.uk/lifestyle/secrets-of-the-superheads-the-teachers-that-are-saving-londons-schools-6561578.html (accessed 31 January 2011). See also www.actionmag.org/images/teaching.pdf

[2] www.guardian.co.uk/education/2010/sep/09/superhead-mark-elms-school-academy (accessed 25 October 2010)

[3] www.dailymail.co.uk/news/article-1195032/200-000-superheads-Best-leaders-chains-poor-schools–rich-rewards.html#ixzz28JsshWOq (accessed 24 June 2009).

[4] The powers for placing schools under special measures were introduced in the EA 1993 secs. 204–17 and especially 210–17. These powers were strengthened considerably in the 1998 SSFS (secs. 14–18), including explicit powers to close schools (s. 19). In the EA 2005, that is devoted almost exclusively to inspections, there is a large part on special measures (see especially secs. 13, 15, 17, 34–40, 44–6).

[5] In 2003–4 some 332 schools were under special measures; in 2007, 248 schools; in 2009, 255 schools; and in March 2010, 295. See
www.ofsted.gov.uk/resources/data-schools-causing-concern-spring-term-2010 (accessed 16 June 2010);
www.ofsted.gov.uk/resources/data-schools-causing-concern-autumn-term-2009 (accessed 10 March 2010);

www.ofsted.gov.uk/resources/data-schools-causing-concern-autumn-term-2007 (accessed 11 February 2008); and

www.ofsted.gov.uk/resources/data-schools-causing-concern-special-measures-and-serious-weakness-schools-end-of-200304 (accessed 16 March 2005).

[6] This sub-title follows: Elmore, R.F. (ed.) 2010, I *Used to Think … And Now I Think … Twenty leading educators reflect on the work of school reform.* Cambridge, MA.: Harvard Education Press.

[7] Race Relations Act 1976.

Part 3

Analysis and implications of England's law-based reform

Chapter 9

Legislation's role, short- and long-term impact, and governance

Introduction

This chapter analyses England's law-based reform from three angles. The first angle is that of symbolic action (Rosen, 2009); the second is that of governance (Balarin *et al.*, 2008; Ball, 2007; Glatter, 2002, 2003; Young, 2006); and the third is that of public policy (Kingdon, 2003). Based on the findings from the interviews, this chapter analyses the politics of education law and its roots in ideology, and tries to understand how legislation occurred.

The symbolic dimensions of law-based reform in England

Rosen (2009: 269) offers the conceptual base of the symbolic interaction of education policy. According to Rosen, every human interaction is mediated, human beings have a drive to create order, and reality has no inherent meaning other than that attributed to it by actors. Rosen presents several dimensions, many of which are relevant to England's law-based reform.

Table 9.1: Symbolic action and actors in legislation

Main symbolic dimensions	Sub-themes	Appearance in the findings and analysis of this study
Policy as a form of expressive activity	Instrumental failure and symbolic success	EAZs.
	Policy and status politics	Social cohesion policy; return to trust schools run by denominations.

Table 9.1 cont.

Main symbolic dimensions	**Sub-themes**	**Appearance in the findings and analysis of this study**
	Reinforcing articles of cultural faith	Circumventing the admissions/enrolment issue: 'the PM said "education, education, education", while he should have said "admissions, admissions, admissions"'; legislation that weakens LEAs.
	Policy as myth	Choice as a mechanism for improving education services and improving results; legislation and policy being 'colour-blind'.
	Policy as ritual	Volume and frequency of legislation; recurring legislation after each general election, and even for every administration and new secretary of state for education. The ritual of re-inventing schools over and over again in search for the perfect decentralized school that will redeem the system of its maladies.
	Policy as spectacle	This includes the detailed and dramatic white papers usually based upon one-sided and biased presentation of the education policy and results in a situation that is the base-line for the white paper – bias that usually includes strict criticism of the previous government's policy, and praise for the work of the current administration's past and present success. This rewriting of history is a perennial ritual with theatrical dimensions.
Policy as a form of constitutive activity	Intrinsically rhetorical view of language	The rhetoric of equality and equal opportunities in education that is consistently used to justify nearly any policy; the language of legislation is extremely complex and untidy in a manner that makes it nearly incomprehensible for laypersons who are not involved in the scholarly study of law but who need practical day-to-day interpretation and effectuation.

Table 9.1 cont.

Main symbolic dimensions	Sub-themes	Appearance in the findings and analysis of this study
	Politics of representation	Quite a few pieces of legislation attempt to represent various groups in England's socio-political scene. One example is BSF with regard to disabled pupils. Another is the idea of soft banding. A third is the emerging permission of trusts – including those that represent ethnic or religious groups – to establish schools.
	Framing	'Naming and shaming' ... of LEAs and a central inhibitor of change and reform, as are teachers' unions.
	The relationship between policy and science (including post-positivist conceptions)	All white papers rely heavily on data and research results. A lot of policy studies in the last 15 years or so are nearly equally critical towards the policy embedded in legislation, with slight favourable tendency towards New Labour policy, for a short while, which they then treat as scornfully as that of the Conservatives.
	The role of science in the politics of representation	A strong reliance on research by think tanks and international management companies.
	The tension between science and democracy	Legislation is quite separate and distinct – almost alienated from a growing body of research on the racist and discriminatory effect of policy.

Based on Rosen, 2009

The expressive aspect of policy is evident in many education laws. They 'constitute public expressions and exaltations of particular values and principles, rather than instrumental means to achieving particular ends' (Rosen, 2009: 270). English legislation is not titled formally as non-instrumental. But, as interviewees have remarked, it does have a robust declarative perspective. This fits most of the symbolic dimensions of policy. Rosen's model can be strengthened and validated in the findings presented in this book, with emphasis on legislation. The scope and rate of recurrence of England's education policy legislation entice the writer to challenge this legislation according to standards or results, feasibility, and accountability – and not only because the policy promoted by a greater part of this legislation is based on exactly these principles as principles worthy of modern education policy in a democracy. But irony aside, one can expect and demand from such an immense body of law, a truly far-reaching overall system of running education, to provide effects, outcomes, and perhaps solutions worthy of the effort put into the legislative process – certainly disproving the negative consequences of a system of policymaking as presented in Part 2 of this book. This is where Rosen's descriptors are useful, as Table 9.1 shows. The legislation is often declarative and symbolic, 'branding' change and renaming institutions and arrangements assuredly with the world-view of a new administration. Branding is likewise implemented in the dramatic and promising titles of change and of new types of schools. This, in itself, would not be undesirable, if these titles were not so short-lived. What pedagogical or organizational or managerial justification can there be for the renaming of projects and schools and even the department itself whose name has changed five times in less than two decades,[1] eventually returning to its original title from the 1980s?

Legislation has augmented a set of myths that are part of the culture and discourse in England's education system. By the word 'discourse' I mean in the way underscored by Ball (1994), namely what is *allowed* to be said, *by whom*, and *to whom*. Some of the preeminent myths are that the system is 'colour-blind' – a myth long-described as unfounded (Gillborn and Youdell, 2000; Gillborn, 2008). There is also the myth that choice (and more choice) will ameliorate or even serve as a panacea to most of the system's troubles (Ball, 2007; Harris, 2007; Whitty *et al.*, 1998). These myths are not unique to England alone (Boyd, 2003; Cohen *et al.*, 2007). Another dimension is the ritualistic quality of legislation, and the legislation cycle. This was quite attractive when I came to work in England as a fellow, each time new legislation or proposals (especially white papers) were declared or hinted-at. I quickly noticed the excitement of researchers and practitioners; the 'buzz' over the network in emails and in websites; the 'race' to get a glimpse at the green/white paper or the bill; the inevitable critique or praise in the *Guardian* and the *Independent* from one side of the socio-political debate, and from the *Times* and the *Daily Telegraph* from the other (usually disapproval from the first pair and praise from the latter); and the symposiums and debates organized ad hoc. And no sooner did the 'hype' cycle expire, when a new white paper or law emerged on the horizon. For instance, in July 2010, the debate on, and analysis of, the Academies Act was tangled with talk on the upcoming white paper – 'The Importance of Teaching' – and the EA 2011 that followed soon after. This is a policy cycle (Ball, 1994) that determines, and in fact rules, the lives of policymakers, academics, policy-implementers, and educators over and over again. The participants in this study, even those directly involved with, or in control of, this cycle, treat it as a force of nature, something altogether external and out of their (or anyone else's) ascendance. This is a spectacular ritual, and another of Rosen's dimensions.

Legislation harnesses myths to frame problems recurrently. Framing is the process of pinpointing problems by creating a 'favourable impression of positions' (Rosen, 2009: 277). LEAs are one such frame that foreruns every white paper as the pallbearer of failure. Most of the interviewees in this study were also of this opinion. The teacher workforce is another long-framed factor that is blamed for poor results (Gunter and Rayner, 2006). And finally, perhaps the most pertinent topic that is framed by the participants in this study is that of admissions policy. Admissions have a ceaseless presence in the participants' narrative, as in the policy arena. The procedure of framing is an immanent component of legislation and has been discernible in most education laws since 1988. However, the solutions offered in legislation are relatively conservative and astoundingly unchanging vis-à-vis the poor results on all the framed fronts. This bespeaks the relation between myths and frames, because the solutions designed by legislation seem to persistently ignore the findings of the literature in the UK (Ball, 2007; Fitz *et al.*, 2006; Gillborn and Youdell, 2000; Gillborn, 2008; Harris, 2007; MacBeath *et al.*, 2007; Olsen, *et al.*, 2004; Whitty *et al.*, 1998) and the US (Cohen *et al.*, 2007; Fuhrman *et al.*, 2007; LaFever, 2006; Mickelson and Southworth, 2008). The solution to poor results is often even further and deeper decentralization and weakening of LEAs, while admissions policies are loosened. Due to the EA 2011 being the definitive and latest yardstick for these standards, it remains to be seen if, and how, the myths and frames will prove themselves as valid or not. Nonetheless, researchers are less confident than legislators and policymakers.

Identity politics and 'politics of representation' are another ingredient of legislation, although the white papers dwell on related issues much more than legislation. A lot is said on race and faith. Some policies address these, the most apparent being the community cohesion initiative (mentioned in abundance in the EIA 2006 and remarkably non-existent – as such – in the Academies Act 2010 and the EA 2011),[2] that endeavours to prevent discrimination against ethnic, religious, or immigrant minorities, and to promote mutual understanding and positive relations or attitudes among the members of such groups that comprise the student body. Notwithstanding, and parallel to this, is the recent further authorization of faith-based trusts and charities to set up new schools, the recognition of which is done negatively – that is, by permitting religious affiliation of academies. These two forces clash, of course, and represent an avoidance of the issue of integration within the maintained system. The colour-blindness of England's legislation can be interpreted from two very different viewpoints. On the one hand, it is a virtue, that legislation tries to assure that schools will have as few opportunities as possible to administer race-based, or faith-based selection, including the implementation of a Euro-centric curriculum. On the other hand, the (in)famous words of the US Supreme Court's Justice Harlan, in his dissent in *Plessy v. Ferguson*,[3] and Prime Minister Thatcher's equally infamous words, that 'there is no such thing as society',[4] emphasize the essence of the argument on social policy, including, and especially, in education, with regard to racial issues.

At one end of the spectrum is the opinion that complete disregard, coupled with strong legislation – for example strict admissions codes in an open enrolment system and policy that forbids any racial discrimination or preference – are both just and effective in creating equal opportunities and preventing racial segregation. At the other end of the spectrum lies the understanding that without affirmative action, and without legislation that addresses race issue proactively (that is, purposeful and deliberate monitoring of racial outcomes of policy, and proactively attempting to overturn them), equality cannot be addressed. The debate is around whether such proactive legislation and the policy that follows might necessitate certain practices of singling out the members of an underprivileged or disadvantaged racial, religious, or ethnic, group or minority, or limit parents' school choice processes. This tension, which is part of a fierce debate in the American legal and educational sphere (Orfield, 1999; Smrekar and Goldring, 2009; Thompson-Ford, 2004), comes across as much more insidious when interviewing policy figures in England, and, in view of that, much more restrained, or subtle, in legislation and in education policy and reform. This subtlety has not gone unnoticed, nor is it free from critique by English scholars, particularly critical sociologists (Fitz *et al.*, 2006; MacBeath *et al.*, 2007; Olsen *et al.*, 2004) and especially in the comprehensive research on this issue. Particularly noteworthy in this regard is the work of David Gillborn (2008) who has been critical of England's racial education policy for over a decade and has established sound and powerful empirical foundations for his analysis:

> There is no inherent reason why members of one socially defined group should not achieve average results on a par with any other such group. This is not to say of course that every member of the group will achieve at the same level. It simply means that, on average, and all other things being equal, it is reasonable to assume that members of each group are equally capable of success. Consequently, if the average achievements of one group (based on class, gender, ethnicity etc.) are significantly below those of another then there is prima facie evidence of discrimination – a clear cause for concern that should be examined. Such an approach is totally incompatible with hereditarian notions of 'intelligence' (as a genetically based and fixed capacity) and with social Darwinist philosophy.
>
> (Gillborn and Youdell, 2000: 3)

Put simply, there can be only two explanations for consistent under-achievement of certain ethnic minorities. Either there is an inherent lack of capability among the members of that group, which itself is a racist idea, or there is racially-inclined discrimination embedded in structures, practices, and policies, such as streaming to worse schools, less provision of public funds, and, finally, covert practices in teaching–learning relations within schools (such as lower expectations, fewer opportunities for tutoring and encouragement, and so on – Gewirtz, 1998) that widen gaps. Altogether these policies and processes, whether purported or unintentional, eventually produce gaps between groups. The gaps, in turn, manufacture what Gillborn (2008) labels 'gap-talk' (ibid. 2008: 65):

> Such a view ignores the real diversity of experience and achievement nationwide and, perhaps most importantly serves to remove racism from the agenda allowing racial inequalities to go unnoticed and unchecked. Within such an approach it is still possible for policymakers to acknowledge that racism exists … however, when racism is spoken of in policy debates it is usually positioned in terms of individual prejudice and ignorance – as a kind of personal aberration. Such a perspective serves to marginalize racism … denies the social and economic processes which remake and reinforce racism on a daily basis.
>
> (Gillborn and Youdell, 2000: 50)

The findings in the study presented in this book coincide with, and reinforce, Gillborn's (2008: 65) notion of 'gap-talk', in the case of many interviewees. But not all of them. Headteachers, in particular, and LEA senior personnel (as well as academics) address the racial gap uncompromisingly. Government officials I interviewed, in all periods, are much more hesitant, cautious, and elusive on this matter, as are think tank personnel. I believe the reasons for this may be that, on the one hand, they feel much more responsibility for nationwide gaps than headteachers, and, on the other hand, much more bewildered as to what can, or should, be done to minimize or avoid them.

Crises or long-term planning and the pitfalls of adhocracy

Following the symbolic dimensions and due to the frequent reformulation of the law, legislation is used in England for an array of purposes. Figure 9.1 highlights some of the conflicts surrounding, and motivations for, law-based reform.

Figure 9.1 shows the tensions between the political and ideological dimensions of legislation, and the degree of adhocracy involved. 'Adhocracy' is a term connected to organizational theory by Mintzberg (1979). It usually refers to innovative organizations that react swiftly to change, usually as an opposite term to bureaucracy. Notwithstanding, in this chapter I refer to adhocracy as a form of policy and governance that is characterized by ad hoc, hasty, perhaps superficial, responses to a social or political situation or crisis that the political level of an education regime believes it needs to react to (Bowen, 2011; Dolan, 2010). Lundqvist (2001) analyses governance as set between the idea of governing without governance and the (still) important role of hierarchal control. He points at the contradiction between decentralization processes, such as are becoming pivotal to public policy in many areas, and the need for governments to react in the face of specific crises and circumstances. The findings

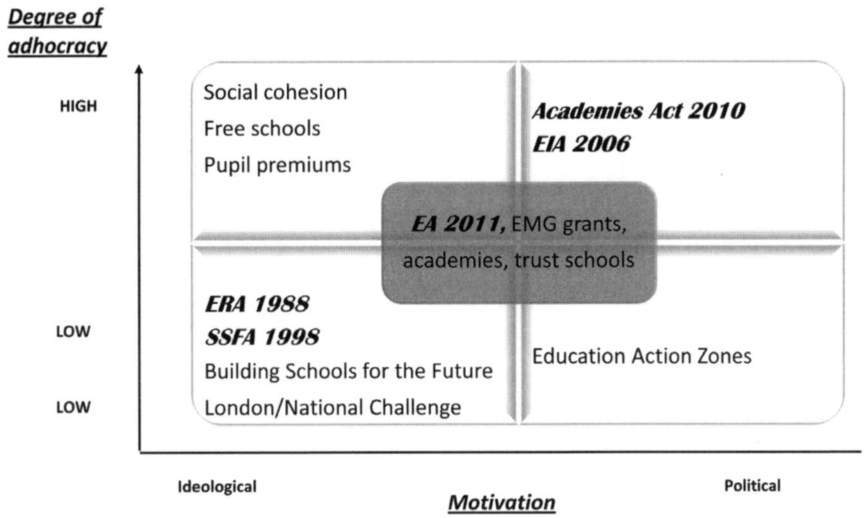

Note: Legislation in bold italics; policy and reform in regular font.

Figure 9.1: The field of adhocracy and long-term planning, politics, and ideology in law-based reform

in the present study show that in such contexts governments resort to old tricks and methods of control – sometimes forgetting that they are reacting to a different, new world:

> The creation of new structures for governance – 'adhocracies' such as special delegations, commissions, or units like … – are often specifically designed to secure central political control over processes of program implementation … However, what government gains in direct control over the process by changing the structures of governance, it may well lose in terms of the end results.
>
> (Lundqvist, 2001: 334)

Crisis-management through law-based education reform is a trait of all governments, including that of New Labour (including their two main Blair and then Brown administrations) and the current Conservative–Liberal-Democrat one. Democratically and politically this is probably reasonable, for no government can rely on long-term planning alone, and has to react to unexpected crises, mounting problems, and deteriorating situations. The education system is often held responsible, blamed, or expected to compensate – not only in England – for a range of malaises. Typical issues, that are not *directly* the assumed result of education policy such as retention and attainment, are: social unrest; racist or religious tensions; violence and yobbery of all sorts; economic decline of industries and technology; and changes in democratic understanding and participation (Strike, 2003). While the ambition to address such problems when they erupt or worsen is sensible, such attempts are seldom aligned with the immense tasks that lie ahead of the problem and the complex change – not just in organizational or financial terms but more often in the deep social and political change – that is necessary to make a difference in the issues on the current agenda. This is a problem for every democratic government, certainly in a postmodern age where governments weaken just as demands of them are rising, and impatience becomes a constant factor in the public response (Brighouse *et al.*, 2002). Some of these reactions are extremely ambitious and overly linear; perhaps the most striking is that of community cohesion policy. Admirable and noteworthy in terms of fairness and equity (albeit with unknown equitable effects), this New Labour enterprise only just fell short of an experiment in social engineering. A reaction to social and ethnic unrest, this initiative, announced and legislated by the government (complete with directives to Ofsted – which issued a standard inspection form for schools – to include community cohesion in its inspections),[5,6,7] was quickly scrubbed by the Conservative–Liberal-Democrat government that followed. Another example is that of EAZs. As early as 1998, Education Action Zones were arguably less challenging and comprehensive than community cohesion, but just as problematic.[8] Going back to Figure 4.1, entitled 'The evolving freedom of government-initiated schools', adding some of the 'adhocratic' reforms, does conceivably mediate and moderate the angle of the graph in Figure 9.2, but the interviewees in this study thought that they achieve exactly that: a temporary moderating effect. Possibly this is a worthwhile effort, but the interviewees perceived there to be a chasm between the dramatic, long-term effect declarations, and the short-term effect, often followed by a hasty retreat from the policy. This is also the reason, according to the participants, why these reforms are persistently replaced by new ones. One senior adviser to political figures said:

> To this day I do not understand the difference between grant maintained schools and foundation schools or between CTCs and specialist schools. For that matter I also never figured out the great change from EAZs to EICs. Academies are a big change – but how are they different from trust schools and how are these two different from free schools? This is a process of rebranding and repossession.
>
> (Senior adviser to the government, 2)

The eventual amalgamation of one reform or structure into another validates these observations and suspicions as to the 'branding' effects of adhocratic reforms. In the early stage of this study (2001) I documented a participant observation, in case-study format, of a leading EAZ in a well-known area of London that is often mentioned in the media as an ongoing example of failure in education and a habitual target for various education reforms:

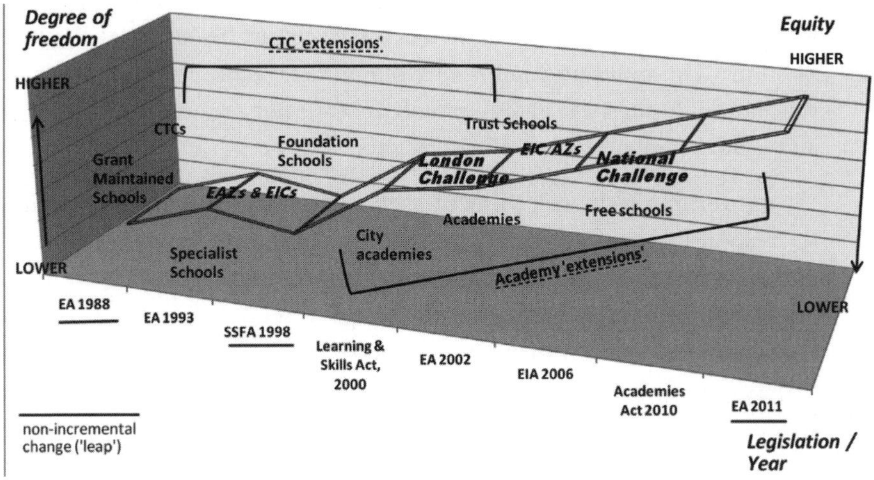

Figure 9.2: Targeted projects and long-term schools

The EAZ headquarters' smart, modern building stands out against the run-down area in which it is located. An enclosed car park for the EAZ's workers welcomes the visitor into a reception area on the ground floor. This floor is divided into two parts. The first includes a bank-type counter, in front of which a weaving line of citizens – prospective students' parents – are waiting for service. Interpreters stand beside the secretaries, and it quickly becomes clear that only a few of the conversations are in English. Around the edges of this reception area, a few empty offices await EAZ officials, who use them to meet their clients. In the middle of this large hall, an electronic barrier manned by a security guard prevents the citizens of the zone from entering the building itself. Once this barrier is crossed, you will find numerous offices, brand new, with state-of-the-art IT equipment and smart furniture. The visitor enters an enclave of professionalism, efficiency, and tranquillity – quite a contrast to the commotion in the entrance area. So the citizens – the direct clients of the zone – cannot enter the offices beyond the barrier, and the EAZ officials come down to meet with them in these empty offices in the reception area. This system is not unique to the zone, and can be found in other government or local human-services headquarters. Nevertheless, it is still a statement, even if not intentional, that is bothersome, especially in this neighbourhood. The lobby area, crowded with parents, is in stark contrast to the quiet and spacious upper floors.

Christine, the headteacher of a primary school in the same EAZ, sees it as a mixed blessing. Her school is on one side of a street with small, two-storey Victorian black-brick buildings. A high-wire fence surrounds the school. The gate that opens into the playground is a heavy-set metal door with CCTV, and the same surveillance system can be found at the main building. The building itself is very old and the halls are in bad need of renovation. Some new IT equipment is scattered around the classrooms and is not in apparent use. Christine says:

'The government doesn't think of itself as the sole provider of education. It's responsible for standards and monitoring those who do it. We heads are the socialist few. Look at this EAZ: I get a lot of money from them, but we were forced to get together groups of schools that have common characteristics and produce such detailed programmes and employ an expert out of our own budget. The EAZ has this new building – the only decent one in the borough. We're about to go to a private finance initiative [known as a PFI]. I get furious letters from unions. But it's the only way to get money to the school. They'll run it, clean it, develop it, and secure it. In the first five years, they invest money in the building and it's a 25-year contract. The profit will come in the eighteenth year. Will the EAZ still be around? Pragmatically, I can't get the gutters fixed, but I have a fast Internet line. First, it's already far from enough. Second, will I be able to pay for it once the EAZ is gone? I doubt it!'

Christine mixes her fears and hopes, with regard to EAZs. One of the problems is that headteachers in areas like Christine's are weary of initiatives and promises. Each time a new idea comes up, they muster the resources, boost the staff's moral and hope for the best, only to be disappointed. This observation is not intended as a criticism towards law-based reform under Labour. It is a world-wide finding from numerous studies on educational reform (Macdonald, 1991). Christine continues:

'Local management of schools and the National Curriculum were the big change. We just got a big grant from Excellence in Cities to begin a learning support centre. How does this coincide or collide with the EAZ? No idea. I like the autonomy. The school is better run since LMS. I like doing the budget – though it's a lot of work. But I think there is place for the LEA, I wouldn't go the Tory way of abolishing LEAs altogether. From my view, collaboration and cooperation are important, we shouldn't be fighting each other. The LEA isn't always efficient, but it represents the people. How does the EAZ fit into this? For example, we went on to hire an independent staff provider. They cost half and are just as inefficient. LEAs have a role in supporting schools. They tried to set up a school development advisory model but it didn't work. Advisers are making good money. I lead the school in a different way. My job has changed. It's obviously different being in charge of the budget, having control of the building – but now the EAZ brings in money. Will it ask for control?'

The fragile, volatile, situation of the inner city school headteacher in a poor area is presented here at its worst. Need for change – fear of change. Self-efficacy – powerlessness. A sense of hope – a sense of despair. EAZs carry this entire burden on their back when entering the area. This background may serve as a mitigating factor when judging EAZs as part of law-based reform, but it also means that they have to be extremely sensitive. Condescending 'we know it all and are going to set things straight' attitudes are not helpful.

When interviewing EAZ officials the picture became even more complicated:

'The idea of EAZs is to raise achievement and reduce deprivation in bad areas. Some money is set aside for EAZs; however, hardly any EAZ has acted outside the statutory areas because these are the most problematic around employment of teachers and governing bodies. An EAZ can change national employment requirements and the government thought this is more exciting. I think they are actually trying to break the unions, have them work more hours for more money. But hardly any EAZ did that because their teachers were working flat-out already ... Our schools joined the EAZ knowing that working standards wouldn't change. They thought teachers would work longer days and have fewer holidays. They are stressed out to the eyeballs. Most staff are prepared to run an activity after-hours once a week, but they won't do that every day because they would burn out. As for governing bodies, they were supposed to surrender their powers to the EAZ but no one in the country did this. No governing bodies would do this if they had any sense of pride. ... The main way we promote higher achievement and less social exclusion is through programmes and we do have additional funding. I was a head for 11 years, and what I thought the idea was, was to create an emerging dynamic within schools. I saw the school as a mini-EAZ. I wanted to work with my neighbouring schools in the primary sector in particular, and with businesses and my community, and generate income. Every head should do that. This was good-practice promotion. So EAZs help you to do something you should have, or could have, done in any case. Combined with other initiatives there might be an outcome when there is an initiative to maintain the exclusivity of the middle class. People like Chris Woodhead were talking like this. When the level went up, they made it harder. People talk of a gold standard, which is protecting elitist groups.'

This means EAZs are about power and politics, and not only about promoting education. But they are also an impressive tool to create new sources of money, and perhaps, as the following statement by an EAZ director shows, to introduce some new managerial practices into schools in decaying areas:

'Education is a complex and complicated issue, and is the only chance for young people in poverty to better themselves, so having democratic involvement is important. But business gives new ideas like private leadership partnerships, where heads link with corporate managers and learn about finance and business and business people, and have learned a multi-skilled approach. [They have learned about] the complexity and intricacy of their [corporate managers'] jobs. One of the things a headteacher said here is that having a business partner was a good thing because it gave her the courage to bend the rules. I think the government has carefully ensured that business is just complementary. Anyone who accuses Michael Barber about not caring for the provision of education is wrong. The initiatives are coming from the government! They have the aim of raising achievement and increasing social inclusion. This is a global dichotomy – some people have more money and others are in poverty. We might have a two-tier education, private education for the rich. EAZs balance this a bit by equal funding in inner cities, where there is a massive set of impossible economic and social conditions. We cannot afford having schools with 5 per cent GCSEs and it's not because teachers are not working hard, it's because there is some ideological teacher who should have been updated and are unaware of recent developments that can change achievement levels. It's an issue of recruitment and here they had the lowest performance management. We should give teachers more support: housing and travel cards. We should engage parents who are apathetic and antagonistic towards education. It was Bernstein who said, "you cannot compensate for society". We should be careful how much of a social engineer we should be.'

This passionate monologue is typical of the ambivalence EAZs cause. They offer a mixture of high hopes and fears; a fresh approach to education with the most common political power struggles, not to mention the bad experience with faddism that wears off and leaves the underprivileged in the same shape, or worse.

Several questions arise on EAZs:

1. How do EAZs coincide with LEAs? How are cooperation and control issues over schools organized between the two authorities?

2. How are EAZs empowering schools? How are they incorporated into the big law-based reform of LMS? What happens with contradictions between the two?
3. What is the lifespan of EAZs, and how will schools in low-income areas be able to cope with the upgrade of their conditions after the EAZ expires?
4. How are the private economic aspects of EAZs planned and controlled, concerning school financial autonomy?

This case study presents the dilemma of adhocratic law-based reform. Reading this text from over a decade ago raises deplorable thoughts. The headteacher who wondered whether EAZs would be around in 18 years was grossly optimistic, as EAZs became obsolete much sooner. A lot of what has been said by critics (Whitty *et al.*, 1998), not just in this account of mine, has proven to be true:

> Who remembers EAZs today? Some have withered down completely. Some are part of some other project and some are still a funnel for acquiring funds – though a trickle now. What is left behind is mainly despair and more suspicion towards reform among LEAs' departments of education and heads and teachers in schools. Each of these things makes the next reform more difficult to adopt and believe-in. When hope is replaced by cynicism the result isn't good.
>
> (LEA head 1, 2011)

Looking back at the EAZ experience reveals a grim picture. This was a hasty reform, expected to become the cutting edge of the system forthwith, through exemplary, localized, tailored solutions that involved the educators in the field and channelled money to the end-unit, cutting 'red tape' and circumventing 'annoying' and 'old fashioned' civil servants in LEAs. At least, that was the idea that was quickly implemented and put into primary legislation. However, this upbeat picture differed considerably from the reality. The reality was, as was presented here, sobering. First, the initiative was not aligned with 'big' legislation and sweeping reforms such as LMS and the National Curriculum. Second, the managerial rationale of EAZs ignored – and not for the last time – the powers of tradition, local politics, and teachers' unions, and tried to brush these aside through administrative and legislative mandates. Third, as often happens with new, stylish reforms, the implementers in the field quickly realized that the extra funds that were supposedly attached to the new toy were partly 'skimmed' off other reforms. These previous introductions into the system were often quite recent themselves, thus causing chaos, savagely cutting back on change that had begun to be implemented or attempted to be implemented in schools, involving extensive efforts in terms of staff preparation and training. Fourth, another part of the newly-acquired funds, publicized as 'cutting red tape' and placing the power in the hands of staff in the field, were quickly channelled to the reform's headquarters, advisers, consultants, and so on. Fifth, when the EAZ head was interviewed, the age-old 'name and shame' culture was clearly present: unions, local government, and traditional superannuated teachers were the source of failure – never a short-sighted reform, or the managerial agenda that was imported from an alien culture and then superimposed on an education setting. Finally, the adhocratic nature of change probably prescribed short-sightedness and impatience regarding results, thus emphasizing the different pace of the political and pedagogical clocks.

Ad hoc policies create ad hoc change, and education – being a long-range process that needs deep cultural and political change – does not accommodate instant solutions without consequences. Some problems of adhocracy are the result of problems of scale (Elmore, 2004). An innovation is experimented with; the results are impressive; but then when the idea is implemented on a larger scale, success withers down in reverse proportion to the scale of implementation. One participant, a professor of education policy who is involved in pedagogical changes in schools, commented:

> It's one thing when I work directly in one school with a team of doctoral students, and another thing when a company of consultants wins a tender to intervene in schools and trains x number of people in the principles of reform, and the investments in implementing the change in each school, in terms of hours and other resources that are allocated, are half of what they were in the original first school. Moving from three schools to fifty, not to mention five hundred, happens too hastily. Some of this downsizing is justified because there is some accumulated experience, but this does not compensate for the overall thinning out of resources. Later when the results are poor, no one really knows if this is because the initial idea was wrong, or the system didn't wait long enough to have valid assessment results, or because the implementation process has gone sour. The damage, to the teachers and to any future change attempts, is done.
>
> (Academic consultant 3, 2010)

Adhocracy, according to the findings in this study, is often followed by ad hoc implementation. This is a contradiction to its establishment in legislation. Studying Figure 9.2 shows that despite the relatively frequent changes in structures, titles, and other ingredients of the respective policies, quite a few become part of legislation. This gives the law, which is supposed to broadcast a feeling of security and stability, a quicksand quality. The volume and frequency of legislation create impudence towards it. There is a price being paid for the 'upgrading' of detailed policy from secondary legislation (regulations, directives, and circulars) to primary legislation. On the one hand, the political echelons have tighter control over policy and regulation, but on the other hand the status of legislation becomes weaker, and it is treated with less respect by precisely those trusted to see it through and safeguard it after the first few weeks of publicity and public debate.

Public policy theory and law-based reform

One important theory that can shed light on the political, adhocratic, and ideological attributes of law-based reform in England is that of John Kingdon's work on public policy. He rocked the field of public policy research with his development of the 'garbage can model' (Cohen *et al.*, 1972), which originated from organizational theory but was adopted by Kingdon for his study on public policy. The model pertains to a loosely coupled system of government, much less hierarchical than it may seem, for instance when one visits the busy headquarters of the department in Sanctuary Buildings, as portrayed in my introduction. According to Kingdon, the system has people moving in and out of the formal boundaries of decision-making. Policy created under this movement consists of a 'loose collection of ideas' (Kingdon, 2003: 1) that characterize an 'organized anarchy' (ibid. 2–4), somewhat similar to the organizational theory of 'loosely coupled systems' (Orton and Weick, 1990). Kingdon describes policy as a coincidental result of clashes and coalitions between ever-changing and ever-shifting groups (politicians, interest groups, academics, consultants, and so on) that fragment policy and policymaking. Kingdon explains how adhocratic reform emerges, how problems become the nub of change, and how ideas are brought to the front or discarded. Much of the selection process with regard to those issues worthy of policy change is due to indicators that cause government to react.

Committee reports that gather media coverage and public debate are important catalysts of change. During the time span covered by this study (approximately from 2000 to 2011, with some attention to policy since 1988), many committee reports influenced legislation.[9] The reports highlight problems and may also act as an accompaniment to crises and other indicators. Indicators include: the results of international tests such as TIMSS or PISA; OECD indicators from its high-profile yearly report;[10] indicators on levels of violence in schools; approaches to higher and further education; Key Stage results; GCSE grades; retention and drop-out rates; teacher and other staff turnover; public expenditure on education both nationally and locally; and many others.

Legislation is, therefore, according to Kingdon, often the result of the convergence of three forces, namely: (1) problems (that is, the rise of a certain concern from the general public brought to the attention of policymakers); (2) policy – a set of alternative solutions to the problem, often constructed by a 'community of specialists' that include civil servants, researchers, and think tanks, all of whom, with their 'pet ideas and axes to grind; ... float their ideas up and the ideas bubble around in these policy communities. In a selection process some ideas or proposals are taken seriously and others are discarded' (Kingdon, 2003: 87); and (3) politics, 'composed of things like swings of national mood, vagaries of public opinion, election results, changes of administration' (ibid. 86). New or changing ideologies in parliament and 'interest group pressure campaigns alert politicians to discern a new mood among their constituents'. Kingdon explains that 'each of the actors [on all three levels] can operate either as an impetus or as a constraint' (ibid. 87). A look, both synoptic and detailed, at the legislation studied in this book and the interviews with participants shows that Kingdon's theory is valid in England's law-based education reform scene.

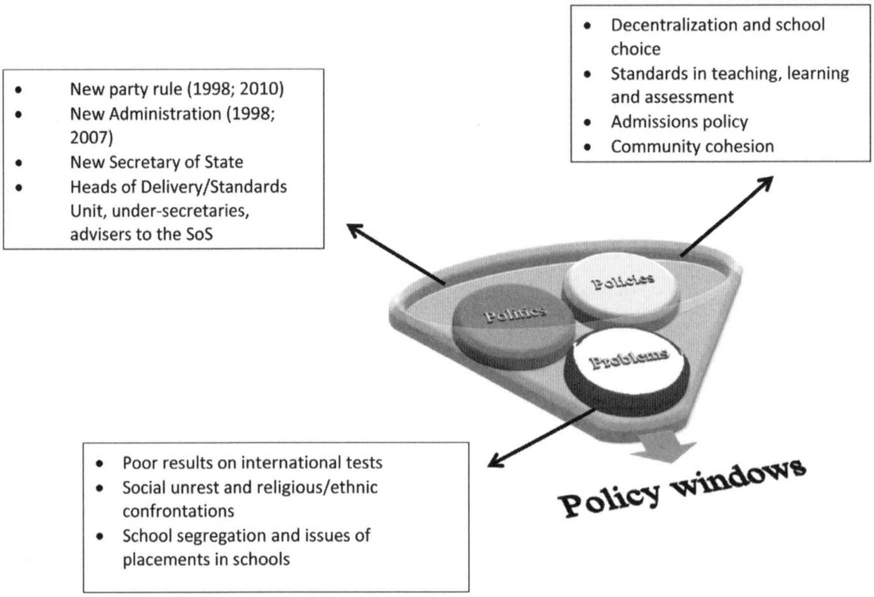

Based on Kingdon, 2003

Figure 9.3: Kingdon's model and England's law-based reform

As shown in Figure 9.3, the policy problems and debates that dominated education policy were quite constant, not only between 2000 and 2011 but also, as can be traced for the sake of this study, as far back as Callaghan's Ruskin speech in 1976, and are not unique to England at all. Since the Second World War and the realization regarding the role of education as – in Horace Mann's words – the 'great equalizer',[11] the basic questions still remain:

1. What is, or where is, the moral authority on education? Who controls education? What are the roles of the centre and the periphery? The authorities or the schools? The professionals or the parents?

2. Who should own and operate schools? What model of regulation is right, fair, and efficient? What is the division of accountability between the government,

local authorities, alternative providers such as trusts, chains and federations, and communities, whether local groups of parents, religious or ethnic groups?

3. What are the viable answers the education system offers to issues of equity tools, attempting to achieve proximity of equality?

What, therefore, allowed these problems to become part of policy or be discarded? This is where the two other sides of the Kingdon triangle shown in Figure 9.3 kick in. In 1997, Secretary of State Blunkett pledged to implement policies that would 'be designed to benefit the many, not just the few'.[12] Although the politics at that time avoided policies that included any factor of desegregation, the political situation in 1997 allowed for the 1998 SSFA to introduce several novelties in harmony with the principles of the Excellence in Schools 1997 white paper. The drastic 'freeing up' of the system under Prime Ministers Thatcher and Major opened a definite 'policy window' (Kingdon, 2003) for the first Blair administration in 1997. Two of its more prominent figures were Secretary of State Blunkett and Michael Barber, whose book *The Learning Game* became, according to many of the interviewees I talked to, a portfolio for the education chapter of New Labour's manifesto in the successful upcoming 1997 campaign. The policy window opened thanks to the education system being under severe shock due to the Conservatives' opting-out, open enrolment, and National Curriculum changes, and the introduction of Ofsted in 1992–3, which allowed the Blair administration to legislate a regulatory 'steering, limited rowing' (Bottery and Wright, 2000) or 'quality control' (Glatter, 2002) model. The professionals within schools, even the few headteachers (Gibton, 2004a) who welcomed the decentralizing shock of the Conservatives, and certainly those who opposed it vehemently, were willing, if not eager, to gain some control by the regulating hand of government, and legislation that would balance the one-sided neoliberal policies with a 'softer' approach that reminded them of more social-democratic times. This period was also open for the idea of EAZs. Although there was some criticism of the heavy involvement of the business world in education, targeting the weakest neighbourhoods and allowing the schools themselves to come up with important parts of the local change plan made this idea favourable despite its both neoliberal and adhocratic nature. The warnings of experts on the short-term influence that would lead only to short-term results, if any results at all, went relatively unnoticed, and were realized in the field, according to the participants in this study, only several years later, in around 2005. It was then that a second policy window, though not as wide and inviting, opened in 2006, when it seems the interviewees agree that the government's impatience, that had risen since about 2002, did have foundations in (poor) results. This allowed the introduction of academies and trust schools in significant numbers as the new panacea for boosting results and improving education in SES-weak areas. Again, there was an outcry both from researchers and also from the field. Headteachers, most of whom saw academies as an outright attack on comprehensive education and as a further infringement on public education by the business or private-sector world, were strongly against them. Researchers (Woods *et al.*, 2005; 2007) warned of the dangers of 'cream-skimming', a controversial but well-known side-effect of charter-type schools (Stein *et al.*, 2011). But despite the resistance, academies became an important part of reform, and grew in number. This allowed a third policy window to open in 2010–11 when the Conservative–Liberal-Democrat coalition made academies the standard model for new schools throughout England. I believe the opportunity to open this window, that is expressed in the 2010 Academies Act followed by the much more comprehensive EA 2011, was based on two forces that allow such windows to open according to Kingdon. The first force was the bed that was made by the EIA 2006 and its reforms. Just like the 1998 reforms that were made possible by the platform and culture set by the Conservatives in the 1980s and early 1990s, the EIA 2006 formed the platform for the Academies Act and the EA 2011. Interviewees in 2010 – though stressing, on the one hand, that the new legislation and policy were the dawn of revolutionary, not evolutionary, reform – also reminded me, on the other hand, that academies were introduced under New Labour and that the new legislation was, in significant ways, a mere follow-up on New Labour law.

Just as some large policy windows opened in 1997–8 and 2005–6, other reforms withered away, due to their not being engrafted in all three sides of the Kingdon triangle. For instance performance-related pay, formally known as performance management, which was introduced in 2001,[13] struck a weak chord although it was followed by considerable government hype and a lot of concern among headteachers and teachers, their respective unions generally being exceedingly opposed to this change. First, they viewed it as a violation of collegial solidarity. Second, it placed an impossible bureaucratic burden on headteachers and senior staff members already bogged down with bureaucracy due to other decentralization policies, posing a danger in terms of potential staff discontent and uprising. Concern was amplified in primary schools, due to the intimacy of small teams and the short hierarchical distance between the headteacher and the staff. Another lost cause in policy window terms was the attempt to introduce soft banding through legislation.[14] This reform was an answer to some of the criticism against the growing SES- and ethnic-based segregation of England's school system, and especially to New Labour's 1997–8 policy that kept most of the decentralization policies of its predecessors, while avoiding the controversial issue of grammar schools and their selective admissions policy (Levačić *et al.*, 2002). The answer consisted of allowing 'soft' (non-compulsory) SES-based banding – that is, accepting pupils according to 'bands' of SES. This was encouraged with public funds but had minimal influence on schools. According to the interviewees, soft banding allowed schools that were practising this policy already to receive some compensation, but had very little impact on the system as a whole and certainly did not create a policy window for real integration – a subject that will be discussed further in the concluding chapter of this book.

Finally, Kingdon explains, problems can weaken or disappear just as they float on the surface of policymaking:

> Failure to solve or even address a problem, as well as success, may result in its demise as a prominent agenda item. It takes time, effort, mobilization of many actors, and the expenditure of political resources to keep an item prominent on the agenda. If it appears, even after a short time, that the subject will not result in legislation or another form of authoritative decision participants quickly cease to invest in it ... addressing or not addressing the problem the subject fades: people figure either they solved it, or they did the best they could and the issue must lie fallow for a time until they make another try.
>
> (Kingdon, 2003: 104)

In the current study it seems that a lot of the debate that went on during the first two stages of this study, that is, in 2000–1 and 2005–6, had withered down by 2011. Presently, issues of desegregation, integration, and possible banding are all gone. A lot of faith in the public school system (in the US, Boyd, 2003 definition, as explained in the second chapter) is gone too, and the expectations from academies and free schools are generally running along the range from careful, hesitant support and curiosity, to open support. There are some social-democratic strongholds but they too are so critical of the last years of New Labour administrations that they set the field for acceptance of the new types of change, perhaps unseeingly.

Comparing Kingdon's range of participants in policymaking shows that in England, compared to the US, the range is wider, or perhaps the fact that Kingdon wrote the second edition of his book before 2003 can explain this. The role of politicians and civil servants is emphasized in his model a lot more than in the picture that emerged in this study.

Regulation and governance in law-based reform

How, then, does legislation regulate the education 'market'? First, the participants in this study are aware that *it is a market*, more so than ever before, but yet it is also an emphatic result of two decades and five administrations of law-based reform:

> If society derives a benefit from education and training over and above that acquired by the immediate recipient, then it also has an interest in the quality of the product, and that may justify subjecting the contract between supplier and purchaser to the imposition of public quality standards.
>
> (Ogus, 2004: 35)

The last two decades of legislation, and certainly the period traversed in this study, show that there is a serious effort by government to do just that. But the attempts to regulate some of the factors of education have become, according to the participants, cumbersome and not altogether fruitful. The example of asking Ofsted to assess and monitor community cohesion is one debatable example. Reducing such a complex, long-range, social and political process to a form signed by a HMI exemplifies the gap between the will and the way. The attempt to control admissions while at the same time weakening the adjudicator's powers to look at the overall policies of a school or cluster of schools, instead of solely at a specific case, and the never-ending battle against the control of LEAs over schools, are another example. The educators and policymakers who took part in this study (Ofsted officials, some civil servants, and some political appointments) were, at best, cautiously optimistic but often sceptical, and sometimes despairing (headteachers and LEA officials), about the chances of the endeavour to control admissions being successful, once regulation is confronted by the forces of cultural and social capital. Ogus cautions of this very hazard:

> A sceptical attitude to the assumed 'public-interestedness' of legislation and a recognition that regulation typically benefits particular groups in society – not always those groups that it was apparently designed to benefit – has led to an alternative private interest theory of regulation.
>
> (Ibid. 4)

This is where it is essential, I believe, to offer some real measures of equity in England's system, to retain strong residual powers that 'review agency rule making' (Ogus, 2004: 106). The regulating powers of Ofsted inspections and admission codes are, to the best understanding of the participants in this study, from all levels and groups of England's policymaking, far from adequate. Thus, large loopholes that can be easily manipulated to provide public funds to better-off schools are preserved (and sometimes extended). Such a form of 'substantive' accountability' (differing from financial and procedural forms of accountability – the terms by Ogus, 2004: 111) is therefore a necessity. This can be a fundamental role of legislation.

In the second chapter of this book, I mentioned Paul Hill's work on educational governance. Writing on governance in education is much more complex and multi-faceted in the UK than in the US, where the focus is often on the legal structure of the system. Perhaps one reason for this is the domination of the field in England by critical sociologists and political theorists of education (Balarin *et al.*, 2008; Ball, 2007; Glatter, 2002, 2003). A second reason could derive, as emerges from the findings in this study, from the messy arena of governing education in England. Structurally speaking, the US has a much more complex system, both organizationally and legally. England has one basic system of public schools, and one ministry of education that, since the late 1980s, has devolved power to LEAs, partly to the schools themselves, and lately, little by little, to various clusters of schools. The US has a federal, a state, and a district system, mixed with a 'mayorization' process in many big cities (Cibulka, 2003; Kirst, 2003; Wong, 2011). Both countries have seen the appearance and growing numbers of charter-type schools of sorts, and the emergence of forms of control and organization. Legally, again, England has one education law for all, crafted by the ministry and affirmed by parliament. The US (Cohen *et al.*, 2007; Fuhrman *et al.*, 2007; Hill, 2003) has a maze of federal and state legislation, district directives, and secondary legislation, all influenced heavily by a large body of case-law from both federal and state courts. Still, governance in England has become undeniably complex in the last two decades (Balarin *et al.*, 2008; Ball, 2007; Glatter, 2002; Ranson, 2011).

While in the US the experience of having non-municipal governance (through school districts) is becoming more and more negative, in England there is growing interest in federations and chains that are not inescapably connected to a certain community. Recent research, both in England (Ranson, 2011) and in the US (Wong, 2011), cautions against the second part of this wave. Ranson (2011: 410) suggests a level of governance 'above the cluster and below the authority', especially suited for local authorities comprising distinct towns and villages. Wong (2011) and earlier Hill (2003), Kirst (2003) and Cibulka (2003) call for the strengthening of mayoral authority over education while allowing for a diverse assortment of providers. From the interviewees in this study, it is impossible to avoid the suspicion that the changes in school governance are no less about a power game of weakening local political control than about improving education; hence the warning by some of the participants that England's system is gradually slipping down a slope that ends in governance chaos for parents (especially those from underprivileged parts of society) attempting to find a place for their child in a decent school.

However, a lot of the writing on governance falls prey to the second principle of education reform that was presented in the second chapter of this book – the principle that legal, economic, and organizational macro-change can influence micro-change in teaching and learning. This principle – perhaps inevitable when planning policy on a large scale, especially with political goals in mind – has so far not proven itself to be scientifically valid. The interviewees in this study are the victims and survivors of the 'squeaky wheel' effect of governance (Hill, 2003: 62). This effect is magnified by the volume and frequency of legislation, regardless of its content.

Despite the volume of legislation, little attention is given to the aspects presented here. It is not clear, when reading through the law, what map, or schema of education lies in the background for English lawmakers. Instead, the legislation is a compromise between strong forces – a compromise that produces, especially for schools and at the local (LEA) level, problematic situations and uncertainty. When all this is under the influence of fast-paced and high-frequency legislation, the result is difficult. In Israel, where governance is perhaps even more chaotic, again in contrast to the centralized and supposedly straightforward legal situation and structure, there is a saying that a camel is a horse planned and constructed by a committee. Sometimes it seems that English law-based reform produces a creature much more imaginary than a camel. A similar scenario arises in the US:

> Unfortunately much of this experimentation is ideologically driven and builds on acts of faith; policymakers are designing policies without solid evidence that any of these approaches to reversing failing schools (and school systems) will be successful. ... accountability policies have become more complex, incorporating standards for students, complex student assessments, standards for teachers and administrators, and myriad other requirements. All these pieces must be coordinated in a meaningful manner.
>
> (Cibulka, 2003: 267)

From talking to the participants and reading and analysing the legislation referred to in this book, the feeling is that reaching such coordination in the huge body of frequent law existing in England is impossible.

Notes

[1] Department for Education (DfE); from 1995: Department for Education and Employment (DfEE); from 2001: Department for Education and Skills (DfES); from 2007: Department for Children, Schools, and Families (DCSF); and more recently, from 2010 Department for Education (DfE) once again.

[2] EIA 2006 Section **33: Foundation and foundation special schools: requirements as to foundations**

... (6) The foundation of a school to which this section applies shall, in carrying out its functions in relation to the school, promote community cohesion.

Section **38 General duties of governing body of maintained school**

(1) In section 21 of EA 2002 (general responsibility for conduct of school) after subsection (4) insert –

(5) The governing body of a maintained school shall, in discharging their functions relating to the conduct of the school –

... (b) in the case of a school in England, promote community cohesion.

Section 154 Duty to report on contribution of certain schools to community cohesion

In section 5 of EA 2005 (duty to inspect certain schools in England at particular intervals), in subsection (5) (which lists matters on which the Chief Inspector is under a general duty to report) –

... (b) at the end insert –

(g) the contribution made by the school to community cohesion.

[3] In the landmark case of *Plessy v. Ferguson* the racist doctrine of *separate but equal* was challenged by a one-eighth black plaintiff who was ordered to sit in a black-only carriage of a train. The US Supreme Court affirmed this doctrine that allowed de jure and de facto apartheid between whites and blacks especially in the former secessionist states of the southern US. The *Plessy* ruling was practically overturned by the Brown decision in 1954. Justice John Marshal Harlan, from Kentucky, who dissented from the majority opinion of the court and thought the separate but equal policy to be unconstitutional, wrote in his opinion: 'The white race deems itself to be the dominant race in this country. And so it is, in prestige, in achievements, in education, in wealth, and in power. So, I doubt not, it will continue to be for all time, if it remains true to its great heritage, and holds fast to the principles of constitutional liberty. But in view of

the constitution, in the eye of the law, there is in this country no superior, dominant, ruling class of citizens. There is no caste here. Our constitution is color-blind, and neither knows nor tolerates classes among citizens. In respect of civil rights, all citizens are equal before the law. The humblest is the peer of the most powerful. The law regards man as man, and takes no account of his surroundings or of his color when his civil rights as guaranteed by the supreme law of the land are involved. It is therefore to be regretted that this high tribunal, the final expositor of the fundamental law of the land, has reached the conclusion that it is competent for a state to regulate the enjoyment by citizens of their civil rights solely upon the basis of race'. (*Plessy v. Ferguson*, 163 U.S. 537 (1896), 559.)

[4] 'I think we've been through a period where too many people have been given to understand that if they have a problem, it's the government's job to cope with it. 'I have a problem, I'll get a grant.' 'I'm homeless, the government must house me.' They're casting their problem on society. And, you know, there is no such thing as society. There are individual men and women, and there are families. And no government can do anything except through people, and people must look to themselves first. It's our duty to look after ourselves and then, also to look after our neighbour. People have got the entitlements too much in mind, without the obligations. There's no such thing as entitlement, unless someone has first met an obligation.' Prime Minister Margaret Thatcher, talking to *Women's Own* magazine, 31 October 1987.

[5] A joint plan by the Department for Children, Schools, and Families (DCSF) now the DfE and the Department for Communities and Local Government.

[6] Ch. 3 (beginning with section 10 'Establishing Education Action Zones') of the SSFA 1998.

[7] Equality Impact Assessment Action Plan, 22 July 2008

[8] Sections 33 (1) (amending section 23A of the SSFA, 1998), 38, and 154 of the EIA 2006.

[9] *14–19 Curriculum and Qualifications Reform: Final report of the working group on 14–19 reform* (2004). Presented to the Secretary of State by Sir Mike Tomlinson.

Diversity and Citizenship Curriculum Review (2007). Presented to the Reading Committee by Sir Keith Ajegbo.

Independent Review of the Primary Curriculum: Final report (2009). Presented by Sir Jim Rose CBE to the Secretary of State for Education.

Independent Review of Key Stage 2 testing, assessment and accountability: Final report (2011). Presented by Lord Bew to the Secretary of State.

Learning Behaviour: Lessons Learned. A review of behaviour standards and practices in our schools: Final report (2009). Presented to the Secretary of State by Sir Alan Steer.

[10] Education at a Glance (2011). OECD indicators.

[11] 'Education, then, beyond all other devices of human origin, is the great equalizer of the conditions of men – the balance-wheel of the social machinery.' Horace Mann on education and national welfare, 1848 (Twelfth Annual Report of Horace Mann as Secretary of Massachusetts State Board of Education). See also www.guardian.co.uk/education/2000/mar/06/educationincrisis.uk (accessed 6 March 2000).

[12] Excellence in Schools, July 1997 white paper, p.11.

[13] Education (School Teacher Appraisal) (England) Regulations, 2000.

[14] See sections 99 and 101 of the SSFA, 1998.

Chapter 10

Think tanks, local government, and the career cycle of players

The policy network and law-based reform

England's extreme legislation could not have come to life without a power grid of mutual interests. Although these interests may have developed from initially contradicting conditions, they have some basic pursuits in common. This chapter explores the power grid more deeply and attempts to outline how it is linked to issues of governance and regulation. In 2007 Ball presented a map of a 'new governance' network in which quite a few of the bodies and organizations I have mentioned in this book are laid out (ibid. 128–9, although without any overlap in the list of interviewees and a different time-span). My argument, which forms the main contribution of this book, is that legislation has had, and continues to have, a pivotal role in this process. This is because of two policy–process trajectories, common to both New Labour and also the Conservatives, that could be pursued only with, and through, the law. The first trajectory is the idea of decentralization which required a redefinition and restructuring of the commission, delivery, and regulation of education. The second trajectory, not separate from, or alien to, the first, is the deconstructive agenda of both parties regarding the three forces within the education system. This deconstruction involved the weakening, if not complete removal, of LEA involvement in education commission and delivery; the harnessing of the ministry and especially its senior staff to party politics – whatever they were; and the disenfranchising process of teachers' unions. All three required vast legislation. The interviewees in this study stressed the dramatic change in the stance of ministry senior staff, from being guardians of professional policymaking, to those responsible for 'making it happen' – 'it' being the agenda and will of politicians.[1] This is not a criticism. One could argue that the current situation is the true materialization of democratic processes. The use of legislation was a central component in the constant re-shuffling of power: first, strengthening the ministry to weaken LEAs and unions, for instance by reinstating and reinforcing regional offices – a process that reached its peak around 2006; second, by encouraging alternative structures of commission such as chains and federations; third, further on, by weakening the ministry itself by setting up the standards unit and the delivery unit that allowed the Prime Minister direct involvement in education planning and implementation; and finally, by weakening the power of rigorous, peer-reviewed academic research by relying more and more on research findings produced by think tanks. A senior policymaker explained:

> For LAs the intention was by and large to reduce their power. But there were some exceptions such as the child services, but there was a tendency to give more power to schools. Now they will not be able to establish their own schools without the secretary of state's permission. We pushed LMS further and we published how much money is used, and the schools grant that allowed a national funding formula can be introduced if the coalition can and will do it and can afford the compensation necessary to do that. So on this structure level you get a lot of legislation. In school governance the civil service came up with all these clauses and we put in all this about the responsibility of governing bodies that had to be repealed thereafter. Most things in teaching happen through accountability and cultural mechanisms.
>
> (Senior political adviser)

The legislation has succeeded in re-mapping power in England's education policy. Foster (2005), in his comprehensive analysis of British government, presents the specifics of the process by which it went through a transition towards managerialism. Although the Thatcher–Major administrations provided an ideological drive to this process, its actual implementation in the tiers of government was crafted by Prime Ministers Blair and Brown. Foster cautions that there is a:

> ... fundamental difference between private and public sector ... Making a greater profit is the private sector's only objective. Every intermediate target can be seen and evaluated in terms of the contribution it is expected to make to a firm's profit. Little attempt has been made to develop similar valued non-profit objective for public bodies.
>
> (Ibid. 200–1)

Like the executive who was outraged that a member of a public reform committee could discuss its shortcomings in public, the managerialist and corporatist qualities of government took over the human service quality of education policy. This observation by Foster is exceedingly important, for one of the main problems associated with planning education policy is the basic disagreement on the values and targets of education policy. The dilemmas between excellence and equality, between a mainstream canon of knowledge and multiculturalism, and between public and quasi-private or private education, are never settled in any society and are simply endured, with episodic tips of the scales to one side or another according to who is in political power, or what crisis has occurred at any given time. Superimposing the managerialist ideology that is based on a system where, as Foster and others explain (Harris, 2007; Whitty, 2008), there is no constant debate on what constitutes success or failure and what its basic values are, creates chaos. Add to that the gap between the political 'clock' that ticks at a quick pace of four–five years between general elections, and the structural, cultural, and pedagogical 'clock' that ticks at a much slower pace, and the impact of large-scale and frequent law-based change is clear. The overwhelming managerialist discourse of policy is well embedded in education law. The regulatory lineament of legislation is a type of 'newspeak' that carries with it a make-believe or real image and agenda of a market-based corporatist system in which vigorous, excellence-oriented, successful professionals strive for results that are undisputed in their contribution to achieving the overall objectives of the system. This is similar to the Marxist critique of democracy, namely that the image carried by legislation is of a system that supposedly has always been here and will remain here in the foreseeable future, and is therefore just and prosperous for all. The truth is, as research shows, quite distinct and, at best, controversial (Ball, 2007; Berends *et al.*, 2011; Boyd, 2003; Fitz *et al.*, 2006; MacBeath *et al.*, 2007; Smrekar and Goldring, 2009).

The think tank and the flattening of governance

Welner and his colleagues (2010) led a unique project of analysis and evaluation of think tank research quality in the United States. The findings of the project are troubling. First, the researchers raise serious concerns about the methodologies employed and the soundness of findings and conclusions, and especially about the lack of rigour, both in the research process itself and in the availability of the studies to objective impartial scrutiny. Second, think tanks' studies are, perhaps strikingly, financed and promoted because of their agendas, not because of their validity. 'Values are instead tightly linked to the ability of the research to gain attention and influence policy' (Welner and Molnar, 2010: 312), the main problem being the seeming objectivity versus the agenda-based intentions and practices. Welner and Molnar explain that nearly all think tank studies are enthusiastic supporters of decentralization, managerialist patterns such as quasi-privatization, competition between schools, and aggressive criticism of public education, desegregation, affirmative action, and other centrally-controlled mechanisms designed to offer equitable solutions to social justice issues in education:

> These reports are generally not aimed at experts in the field, who know the other research in the area or can easily recognize methodological flaws. Instead they are aimed at policy-makers, reporters, bloggers and others who are predisposed towards their ideological conclusions and recommendations or are simply receptive to use 'research' that is slickly produced and well packaged.
>
> (Welner and Molnar, 2010: 315)

One interesting influence of think tanks is, as Welner and Molnar explain, a market and branding quality of policy, part of the 'newspeak' often introduced by a public relations media culture into, and onto, education. The findings of this study and the analysis of legislation affirm this. Nearly every law has lengthy sections on renaming and rebranding bits of policy, programmes, and bodies, often without changing their real content, targets, or areas of operation. The most obvious are the changing titles of the ministry itself, and the renaming of the types of 'charter' schools as explained in Chapters 4 and 9. But there are many other examples, such as the renaming of QUANGOs, departmental bodies, and policies. Another important aspect is what was labelled by interviewees as 'budget-neutral' policies. These are changes in curriculum, in practice, and in organization introduced by legal mandates, whether primary or secondary legislation, circulars, or directives, that require schools and headteachers to implement change without accompanying it with specific funds, sufficient funds, or any funds at all; or even when there is money, there is insufficient training, facilities, 'scaffolding', and expert consultancy and supervision regarding the new policy. This creates a bipolarized situation, of having a legal mandate, on the one hand, and no financial or professional support, on the other, that therefore strains the already stretched-out budget of schools that is the result of two and a half decades of LMS, autonomy, 'opting out', and related changes. The amount and scope of legislation render it doubtful whether anyone ever took an overall look at the total list of financial obligations that legislation places on the shoulders of each school. These just pile up, one on top of another, often without being replaced. 'Lingering policy' (Hill, 2003: 60) is the most accurate term for this phenomenon, in other words small 'bits' of policy that are left over from previous reform and for some reason remain in the system although the rationale or the framework or the overall programme have since been replaced. Some of the more notable examples of lingering policy are: EAZs and Excellence in Cities; SIPs and SEFs; key stages strategies; QCDA; OfQUAL; the STA, GTCE and TDA; and SEAL and behaviour management. The following account gives a flavour of this cultural change:

> How independent is Ofsted? [David] Bell has created some base. They are having to fall behind on core aspects of education. The white paper does give a role to LEAs, a role of commissioning and regulation, but it should not have a role in provision, it's unrealistic that all these private and faith providers will spring up. People thought the government couldn't control 25,000 schools, but law says they can and to some extent they have succeeded. The role of think tanks, and the fact that the LAs did get a role means they couldn't get rid of them completely. If you look at the history of English education they say 'we want to make them autonomous', well of course they always were, and this has increased – the question is at what point this becomes too much in terms of enrolment. But the more you do

> that [increase autonomy] however you hedge it around with a national regulatory idea, it would forever fix the intakes, especially in a context of league tables. However uncomfortable you are, and however [much] less than others you may do it [regulation], this is still being accountable to the governors. Unions are less influential in bargaining, but more so on other things. Consultancy firms are extremely interesting, there are key projects they have taken upon themselves, or handed by government as they have a human resources background, and evaluation was given to an account management firm. The first report was not published and the *TES* and the *Guardian* made an application under the Freedom of Information Act ... and the consultancy firms are now doing work that was reserved for academics, there's no reason we should have a monopoly. If you're a government commissioner or procurer [you can't afford to wait], because academics take too long with their report and often don't come up with clear conclusions for practice.

Many interviewees in this study stressed that they feel legislation is declarative and trendy, often enacted to give the public a feeling something is being done, but too often not accompanied by the deep economic, structural, pedagogical, and cultural changes that are necessary to implement it. This is the influence of the managerialist culture encouraged and implied by the proposals of think tanks.

Blinking in the headlights: the dilemma of local control over education

As early as 2005, a head of DCSF regional office provided the following vignette. The parts in bold will be analysed further on:

> During the Cons [the Conservative administration] they said 'here comes the policy, we know what's good for you' but this has changed dramatically. I read this story of health and wellbeing thought to improve the quality of life [in a third-world village] by improving the water. They put the well in front of the headman's hut, and six months later the pollution and disease was the same. The women went down to the river and brought the water on their heads and the villagers said, 'the pots are our framework, our way'. You know the Sure Start programme, before the regional themes and such, we targeted [several cities]. There was an estate outside ... there was poor attendance, poor standards, distracted, grumpy students and teachers, the classic combination would be to get rid of the head but we sat down with the shopkeepers and parents and it turned out that if [local people] had toothache they couldn't travel to another dentist because it was a £5 return, and the local dentist had closed and the parents kept

the children at home, [yet despite these kinds of difficulties] one year later KS 1 and 2 were the best-ever. Our framework and 'do it your way' legislation that is not across the board (... EAZs and Excellence in Cities, New Deal for Communities, Sure Start, all [of which] are [a] challenge for traditional civil servants) [are] great in [our LA]. We were doing ... a £60 million project. These people were used to low-skill economy and garrison-type living. Getting the community to spend money was very difficult, there were factions, rivalries, you wouldn't go with your suit and you went to evening meetings, people had a culture shock, we had a chronic level of under-spending **because people couldn't agree about how to spend the money so legislation has brought LAs out from the cold, you had a whacky tiny charity running a £60 million programme. We're getting on fine with it now: the government is encouraging the voluntary sector to take on the thing. You had two or three cultural eclipses, these communities didn't know how to manage themselves and the government gave these ambitious urban renewal programmes that were community-based totally and you had to make sure that pushing out to communities all at once was working though it was a big risk.** This is the worst performance in the country: 16–19 do as well as anywhere else so how is it in the secondary level? The schools are poorly led, the LA gives 23 per cent for education which is a very poor level of challenge and drive, doesn't have the people, doesn't have the clout. One of the things that is interesting in educational legislation is the first Labour administration was a bit ambivalent on LEAs setting up EAZs. They never set the real clout and drive and, as time went by, they saw better what LEAs are doing and the education system is still blinking in the headlights about local education. **Now they are talking on diversity of provision, promoting parent-owned schools, other schools the communities are now sufficiently competent to stand up and deliver, and who is going to get the schools built? The people who built this policy are those who built the GM experience, it's the emperor dressed in new clothes. Can you imagine the government talking about banding, they have become so populist, very much like the Conservatives.** In the third term it's very 'schoolish', we have more in the FE than we have in the 16–19 sector but it's underfunded and not enough voting material, not enough *Daily Mail* people. I had doubts on FE: it was badly explained, we struggled to figure out what top-up fees are and we went up to 37 per cent in our HE sector. 16–19 EMAs have worked, if you are on a £13,000 [family] income you get £30 a week; in parts of XXX 80 per cent live on less than £13,000 a year per household but there are better colleges that lift people's hearts a bit, especially in a deprived community. The LA won't have the role, they will knock on the door of an academy, the powers of the LA will be

> sharpened up, got to be, I cannot take care of a child in XXX ... you need a local democratic process that will determine how things happen. According to government agenda there is a government expectation that the LEA will operate in a more dynamic way than before, children's trusts etc., but not fulfil some of their more traditional roles that they had in the past.

This vignette captures the hopes and disappointments, the aspirations for social engineering, the attempts to penetrate the most difficult urban and rural areas in England and change the basic conditions, and the concern regarding paternalism and megalomania. And all in the context of New Labour law-based reform.

One of the attempts in the evolutionary quest to weaken LEAs is the short-term empowering of regional offices. As can be seen in this vignette the text is ridden with controversy, contradictions, and irregularities. The interviewee is torn between several forces and ideas. From one point of view he is the enlightened educator who brings the well to the headman's hut – not a picture of equality and collaboration but perhaps one of compassion or condescending attitudes. Another point of view is that the failure of local government forces central government to step in. A regional office may be seen as a compromise between the role of a distant central government, which finds it difficult to adapt to local needs, and a dysfunctional local one. However, when the official realizes that his own role is, itself, soon to be legally replaced by a further empowerment of schools, a democratic communal viewpoint sets in. All this happens when a few years prior to this account, and a few years later, regional offices go from non-significant to extinct.

Here is a second vignette on what happened to the role of LEAs. Again, the core categories are highlighted:

> When the 1988 legislation came about there were two reports, the national primary and the national secondary surveys, which were a stratified sample of schools, and that painted a picture of what was happening as far as the data at that time could give. **What came out was that you couldn't leave curriculum decisions to local authorities, and where a student was in various points in their life.** Keith Joseph said it was not about de-professionalizing the profession. He wanted to improve schools. When it came to Thatcher's time she wanted to get at all the professions but there was no serious objection for a national curriculum – we were one of the few countries in Europe that didn't have one. The risk is that, by accident, that by design, you create an orthodoxy that leaves those standing at the front [isolated]. Teachers would say that Ofsted and the NC curb their teaching methodology, but **when you look at legislation it doesn't say that, but it is being blamed inaccurately because a culture is created. We rather had a whole bunch of laws, taking further education,**

> **Ofsted, key stages ... Academies have been put forward – an experiment on something that has not been solved anywhere in the world: how do you provide good education for young people in inner cities?** The concept will take over the whole of the system. The unanswered question is a serious concern with the function of LEAs. It wasn't anticipated that the Labour governments would come down so hard on LEAs, they did not expect the learning trust to take over education from the LEA. The first initiative of the government was to bring in two private companies that take care of two issues: one was education, the other was ethnic minorities. They offered the government a series of possibilities, with an education twist, as to what the community preferred, and out of that came the idea for a not-for-profit trust that will deliver the service to the public, and this was accepted under a government directive because they [our LA] were bankrupt. ... The trust came around [in] 2002, [and] since then ... in effect [has had] no political input. Our plan should be approved by the council but cannot be rejected or amended. The performance of GCSEs has improved by 50 per cent, attendance has improved. The EAZ just finished. We took those parts [left over by the EAZs] into [our jurisdiction] – the headteachers were pulling up the drawbridge and operated as a separate entity. A lot of people have been interested, I don't think other LEAs will want that [a trust to take over the LA] and the government has lost its appetite for this.

This account depicts one of the deepest controversies in education policy, not only in England but elsewhere as well. It is the dilemma of the middle tier of education policy. There is widespread understanding and acceptance that, being a key human service that is financed, if not delivered, at a national level and that provides a 'good' that bears foremost ramifications for the well-being and flourishing of every citizen, every country needs some central body that controls it, for example a ministry. Putting aside for the moment the issue of the powers of this ministry, there is also common agreement that the system needs a school – that is, a locally-based institution at a reasonable distance from students' homes and of reasonable size, that can be autonomous and at the same time controlled and governed without losing control of the education system or causing excessive alienation or violence. These two pillars of the system may disappear or change in the future, perhaps with the assistance of technology. Notwithstanding, without being too futuristic (an area outside my expertise) it is clear that these two tiers – the national level and the school – are here to stay and have established the justification for their existence. But the role, structure, and basic rationale for a middle tier is, to this day, unclear. Certainly in England and in the US this tier is constantly changing, and is criticized for many of the system's ailments:

> The secretary said: 'you people don't understand that the LAs are there purely by grace and favour of parliament', but he meant the executive, and we all looked at him. The idea that someone could take away their powers ... and this was a prophetic statement. The constitution [England's material, in contrast to the US, formal, written] doesn't have distribution of power through the levels and doesn't have a system of checks and balances, but 'til the late 70s there were gentlemen's agreements. I read someone who wrote about Derek Birley, deputy education officer in Liverpool, he's analysing the different powers, he said 'there is no source of power from which change can spring'. This indicates the huge transformation to where the centre is in tremendous control.

All along the three periods during which I collected data in this study, one of the consistent themes was that LEAs were, and often still are, blamed for many types of failure – from slow and incompetent bureaucracy, through helplessness and impotence, further to corruption and over-politicizing education, to providing outdated reactions to new problems. Specifically, the fact that it was New Labour governments that led the drive to weaken LAs surprised many, as the previous vignette shows. The extreme example of taking over the entire range of education responsibilities from an LA, and handing them over to the trust in return for avoiding bankruptcy, is the administrative equivalent of appointing an official receiver to a failing company, and another example of the legal culture seeping into education policy. As the interviewees reflect:

> LEAs were able to control the delivery. In 1986 there were two types of VCRs, Betamax and VHS and you could only buy Betamax, they got the wrong one of course.
>
> If you think on LEAs, they focused on commissioning. This is powerful within [our LA], most schools would not choose to go down the trust route. There are partnerships, there is a balance; why would we as schools want to get out of that?

But, as one participant explains, an LEA community comprehensive school is, as early as 2005, just one option – part of a struggle with a remarkable continuum of schools that offer degrees of selection, rendering LEA commission theoretical:

> Because within ... [our LA] there are several schools that can select 10 per cent – foundation schools that select according to music. Single-sex schools may work; [there is] some competition from a specialist sports college that improved hugely, going from 20 per cent to 40 per cent [5 A–Cs on GCSE results] throughout a change of head and change of style; and [there are] the independent schools, [and] our 6th Form. The 14–19s: it's

> interesting that the Tomlinson report has been rejected but Blair mentions the word diploma – it has in fact been mentioned. We have a strong science department, still do, it attracts applicants.

Taking into consideration all the criticism flung towards LEAs, the various alternative middle-tier solutions have, so far, neglected to deliver on two essential levels. The first level is that of local community control or influence over education. This idea is age-old and is perhaps most evident in the American idea of a frontier community, in which the parents, often led by a religious figure, hire the teacher of their choice to educate their children in the most technologically advanced building in the village or settlement: the school. It is considered advanced because it has a dry roof, some heating, perhaps, books, and the most educated person in the community. The teacher and the school base their legitimacy on the parents and the community who provide the moral foundations of schooling. This idea has, of course, come a long way but is still at the centre of debate, not only in England. The changes in the role of school districts in the US (Smrekar and Goldring, 2009; Berends *et al.*, 2011), and their replacement with mayoral control, are perhaps the robust manifestation of this dispute. Nevertheless, one of the more forceful comments against LEA control is precisely that LEAs no longer represent a viable community with specific common demands and needs. The second, perhaps more sustainable response, to the alternative commissioning solutions, is that the LEA has the ability to provide fairness in the distribution of education in a given area. According to most participants in this study, the alternative solutions have, so far, failed to deliver on this point. As they represent a large group of senior policymakers from all echelons, tiers, and groups in England's education system, I think this is a warning worth listening to. Even those who condemn forms of public control and enthusiastically support marketization and complete autonomy of schools, and belong to the third way or neoliberal side as presented in Figure 6.2 in Chapter 6, are genuinely worried. The concern is that the current legal structure, especially under the recent 2010 Academies Act and 2011 EA, does not offer solutions to the danger that in a few years there may be no public authority in charge of promising every child a place in a decent school, and certainly any type of SES or ethnic integration will be diminished:

> Directors know that under this current regime LAs don't have any power to influence the best schools. I know one outstanding school with a deliberate non-deprived catchment area and an LA that would love to tell the school to change the catchment area and take in children from deprived families but then the board of governors would push the button and become an academy.

True, some educational ideologies completely refrain from the need to create – or even the possibility of creating – such a fair system, and turn exclusively to market-regulated ideas. Such ideas really could do without LEAs. Legislation has, and will continue to have, an important role in this new type of education regulation – a topic that will be explored in the concluding chapter of this book. One strong point presented by the critics of LEA control over education are the discrepancies between LEAs in terms of educational and pedagogical experience and support, the level of politicization and efficiency, and their track record in policymaking. But how the alternative solutions will be able to provide support for schools in these areas in a better way remains unclear. The fact that so far some education organizations show signs of succeeding – signs that are hitherto unsubstantiated by unbiased and rigorous studies – does not, according to the recent research, promise that this quality can be retained on a larger scale (Elmore, 2004).

> In the tipping point there's an optimum size for a community. It may well be that the scale is about that. There is scale people have got to feel. When I was on the local end I thought about it that there are teachers listening, then parents listening, and then I thought how wonderful it is about working for the council. Estelle Morris said 'it's about looking good in the interface between media and government'. I think there should be networks of schools. A kid can be a member of more than one community.

The constant reinstatement of government and governance: Democratization or fragmentation?

One interesting outcome and application of legislation is the attempt to use it in the constant battle to repossess and redistribute power. Foster (2005) explains that this has happened in many areas of British government, not education alone. But legislation in education is a distinct example:

> There was a clear acceptance that it is not bad to legislate in education. This was established in the 1980s; some ministers were suspicious towards the people in the DfES, whether they will work with Labour or be 'Sir Humphreys', and some of these became DfES people. David Blunkett set up the standards unit which was seen as a Trojan horse, and they brought in people who had not been civil servants. There were some positive things that came out: Labour brought in a corporate culture; the considerable strength of the No. 10 policy units; because the treasury has shadow units for all government departments the chancellor wants to have his own influence. This is new and did not happen in any government prior to Blair. **If the corporate government will have better cooperation between services it will be a blessing. We haven't got to the end point of delivering child services.** This has never been seen in the structure of the DfES, there is no single department for 14–19 or the curriculum. There is much

greater use for outside consultancy. I'm not sure if this is a product of change or a direct initial decision or just happened along the way. **There is a mix of people, which is a good thing**.

The government may, or may not, have become corporate, but, as explained earlier in this chapter, education has not. There are some education policy and leadership figures (often individuals, not even groups of policymakers) that speak the corporate language and understand it. But many educators, though aware of the cultural change, both distrust it and see it as alienated from pedagogy, and do not understand some of its possible attributes for schooling (Ball, 2007). The frequency of legislation does not help: the swift, law-based change, attempting to consolidate all child services under LEA education departments and under schools, initiated in 2004–6, is a striking example. This change, which barely lasted five years as discussed earlier, was carried out while pursuing, simultaneously, the two-and-a-half-decade-long process of weakening LEAs and stripping them of their responsibilities in education. It provides a solemn illustration. One thought-provoking and perhaps fruitful result of the reinstating process and corporate culture in governance is the recent movement of policymakers and educators into new professional terrain, as Figure 10.1 shows.

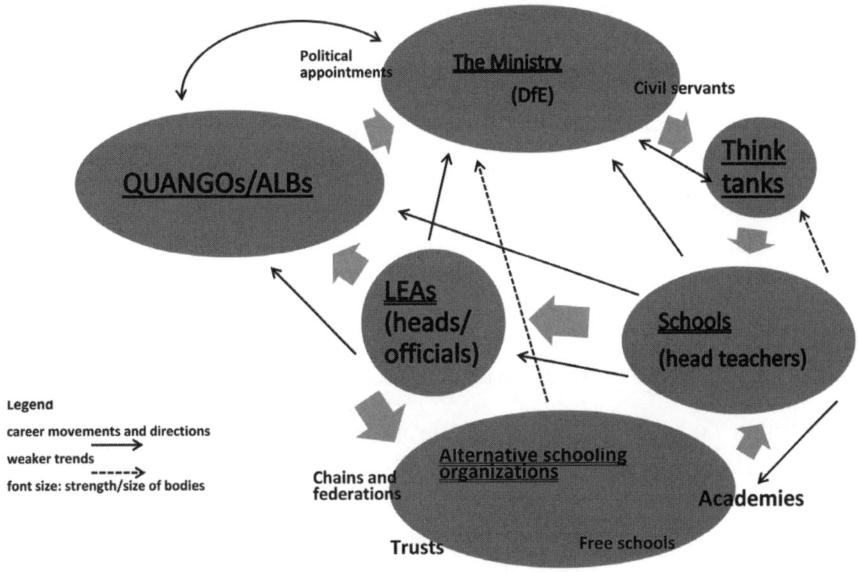

Figure 10.1: The career and influence cycle in law-based reform

According to Figure 10.1, the character of a headteacher or civil servant who remains in their post for many years and then retires is all but gone. While most of the superheads and policymakers I interviewed in 2000–1 were still around in the same position in 2005–6, they had all moved on by 2010–11. Many educators now work for PFIs, whether in the provision of education, or teacher and leadership training.

Moreover, many of the civil servants who were previously involved in policymaking for government have moved on to work for PFIs too, or become consultants and advisers to schools and LEAs. This is not a one-way street, as many of the consultants, headteachers of academies, and think tank personnel have decided to work for the government or for LEAs. This interesting process requires further research but, initially, can be either criticized as a spreading of the corporate culture, or a constructive phenomenon that allows knowledge, experience, and viewpoints to move around to the various components of the 'new governance' network:

> Consultancy groups have more significant impact on policy and legislation than they had. Teachers' and heads' unions didn't have much influence to begin with but had a growing influence – more than the headteachers and deputy heads. The really interesting development is the influence of a small number of headteachers, who ... have exercised more influence on policymaking but not through their associations but as individuals [superheads]. You can see that government committees do not have formal representatives of unions and still have policy closely related to work on the ground. The recent committee on behaviour had only people from the floor instead of professional or DfES officials. The LEA power has declined substantially, individually, and as a group. A regional structure is much more likely. The North-east decided not to go for it. It was a serious blow, but I think it will happen. How it works on the local level I don't know. In London, when you look at it logically and legally, the idea for having twenty local authorities is that we want people to cross boundaries all day long. I wouldn't underestimate the problems of getting there. The population is suspicious towards bureaucracy and the democratic issues.

This quote on regional governments – from 2006 – seems archaic, almost obsolete, in 2011. The current 'governance network' has done, it seems, a better job of reshuffling power than of creating a sound base for the regulation of education:

> SIPP is taken per capita, and the improvement [bonus] is taken away, and the LEA might be responsible for failing schools only. And we have a schools forum, of which I'm head, and we discuss the LMS formula, how money is delegated, and now this forum has been given more power, there's no LEA member on the board and if there is controversy with the LEA, by law we have to go to the secretary of state, so the LEA's power is diminished. The power of the DfES is invested through Ofsted so if schools want to be good, they need a good Ofsted – so heads have a great deal of power, if they are successful they have a wide parameter to change the school. In an ideal world the school would be able to set its own pay and this makes the successful schools more successful, but the question about

> gaps between different schools remains, how to improve the unsuccessful ones. Unions did weaken as well, they are not looking on curriculum any more, I don't think any head would go to the NUT for anything except teacher pay conditions. Now the NUT and the NAHT are not on the remodelling of the workforce, and you have people that are not qualified working in the classroom, doing work instead of teachers, and sometimes it's better and cheaper work. When I was a head I had my own payroll. I had a good physics teacher; I gave him four management points and a PA or else he would have gone.

The appeal of the corporate culture is clear, indeed many interviewees, however social-democrat in their views, are overwhelmed by this appeal. Years of frustration that comes from the constraints of a controlled environment with strong union dominance and hardships (be these factual or perceived – such as bringing in the 'right' staff to push out those who, according to their viewpoint, slow the system down, oppose change and innovation, or even cause harm) bring the participants in this study to embrace a corporate managerialist culture. They do not have to possess any self-aware, neoliberal understanding to do so, and perhaps the power of the corporate culture is indeed its appeal to those who declaratively and ideologically oppose it.

Conclusion: Legislation and the finite quality of power and authority

As I explained in Chapter 8, power is a finite resource, and any addition of power to one body, person, or organization requires an inescapable downsizing of power from another. Legislation has a focal, sometimes dovetailing, role in these shifts of power. Legislation allows the legislator to circumvent culture, tradition, bureaucracy, and ideology, all in the relatively tight timetable of a political regime:

> The new thing is the continuity issue between Conservatives and Labour, and there is the use of legislation, because the trouble legislation is causing … they use legislation as a high-profile tool. The Queen will say 'my government will introduce standards' – this is very powerful. It's an outlook that runs across the public sector. One that runs across Labour because power has shifted its corporate language – remodelling, foundation, commissioning, promoting – [and this is visible right from] the paper professionals, down to the local pharmacy. The interesting thing is it doesn't leave place for experiment outside. This is what Ben Levin says, his point is you have a grand theory that sweeps across different public services and across the country. It's a magnificent idea but it magnifies failure and

> magnifies success, so alternatives are excluded, quite conservative and risky, unlike a system based on incrementalism.

Legislation ignores problems of scale, and attempts to offer solutions to Bryk's (2012: 16) powerful statement that 'everything works somewhere – nothing works everywhere',[2] creating frameworks of autonomy. The various power-groups in the grid I described at the beginning of this chapter are also changing as time goes by (see Figure 10.2).

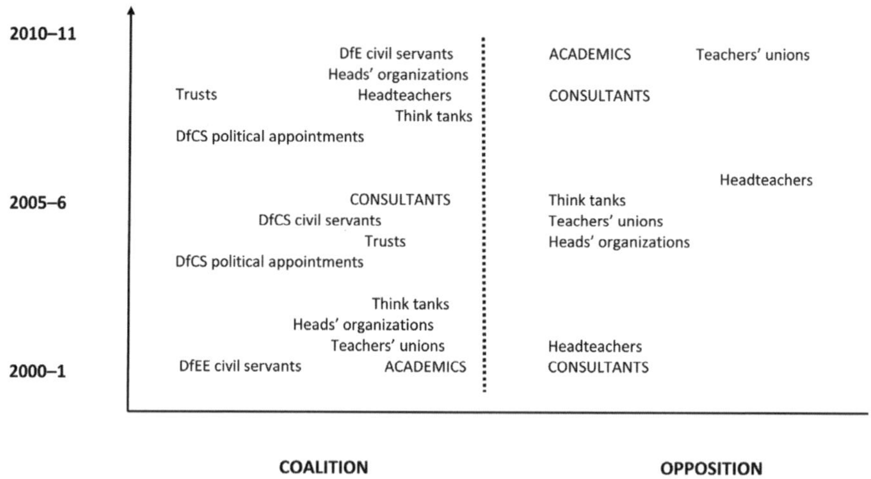

Figure 10.2: Oppositions and coalitions in law-based reform: three periods

Hancher and Moran (1989) refer to this as creating a 'regulatory space', in which individuals and organizations are divided into givers and takers of regulation. Figure 10.2 shows how all of the players have moved from coalition to opposition roles (or vice versa) with regard to creating this regulatory space through legislation. The various participants change places and alliances, and blur the boundaries between the field and the centre:

> A lot of the reform talk in the public service goes along what people call the Anglo-Saxon tradition of business that relies on continual change, and that's where all this post-'97 legislation came from. Business is different here between the US and central Europe. In Japan as well, there's more continuity and traditional values. The Anglo-Saxon tradition is about constantly challenging people, throwing things in the air and changing them. The way to develop, if you look at Japan and Germany and their model of the private sector, continuity, notions of social partnership, you don't compete in a totally cut-throat way. This is the way for a much more secure model of development.

> There is a tendency of central government to work in silos. When Peter Houston arrived he encouraged a 'don't e-mail, walk it/talk it' approach, because it took departments light years to make policy implementable, grit and the oyster, professional development. The majority of policy people found department personnel useful because over time they built trust. Advisers might stand aside and say 'I know better than you'. We moved from an imposed-prescription education policy into a collaborative partnership and the adviser was your conduit into the department. In those cases where they [the advisers' firm or group] put in bids for targeted capital to use the adviser to broker a conversation with the targeted capital people ... when they put forward their proposal, they would be more successful without hurting the rigorous evaluation proposal.

At the same time, legislation is both a tool and a creator of conditions and culture. Legislation creates terms and language. While visiting schools it has always been fascinating for me to see how the old terms remain and how officials have to re-phrase and adopt to the new term or title, often only to realize that once they have mastered the new term or title, it is already unstable and about to be redefined:

> DfS, DfE, DfEE, DfES, DCSF, 18 months ago advisers were moved from the school directorate and the children and young people and families directorate. Local transformation groups are a conduit for the engagement of the department with LEAs, cross-directorate. Children's services improvement advisers (education) were taken away: the reason was politics with a small 'p' because most of the people had an education background so the regional change advisers, who were put in place for being in charge of children's programmes with LEAs, were added. So now there are two advisers, 'you buggers are multiplying like there's no tomorrow', as someone said. More and more reaching-out services. More of the same will not deal with plateauing [of national results] we have seen. The approach in the department is that every area should develop its own programmes. There is a degree of discomfort. National strategies have moved from one contractor to another. Just legislation is not enough, you should have a framework for the local level.

The law creates an illusion of control, and when reality contradicts the illusion, the response is often further legislation. It is as if policymakers thought: 'we slipped somewhere in the last bill – we just need one more piece of legislation, one more reframing to get this right, to achieve the end result we believe will do the job' – only to awaken to a predicament of laws that pile up and create uncertainty and insecurity instead of stability, safekeeping, and confidence.

> I mean the involvement of legislation in the English education system has become markedly different during my time. I began teaching in 1972, education secretaries came and went, it was low priority, schools did pretty much what they wanted to do, good schools did a lot of curriculum development, that was a mark of good schools. If you were lucky you got to work with a HMI on curriculum development and share it on conferences. That all changed with statutory LMS, statutory Ofsted inspections, statutory NC, those are the things that introduced schools to the legislative demands in a way never done before. The legislation is forged directly through the PM and in the first administration David Milliband, then Andrew Adonis now as minister and Connor Ryan who were extremely interested in education. When Michael Bushard was permanent secretary he recruited people to give him advice, so from 1999 there were those advisers who helped in drafting the threshold assessment policy that came out of the green papers. Not all of them stayed, most of us were heads, like ... and those changes in performance were a response on the part of the PM that too many youngsters were not getting good deals and what they were taught was crap, and the teachers were crap. I'm not so close to what is happening in schools now. So the PM is enthusiastic about this. He works very closely with those of us who are on schools. He doesn't have a constituency, so on Fridays he visits schools; and they asked in the Commons how many schools he had visited and he said '49', and on Friday we went to three and he works with people like me, who have such a background. So if the secretary of state wants things to happen or not to happen he can give money, or provide some other strong steers, but legislation is his way of doing things.

Notes

[1] In this chapter, as the quotes come from the most senior and easy-to-identify participants I am not pointing at the group of interviewees each quote refers to.

[2] Bryk, A. (2012) *Accelerating Our Capacity to Learn to Improve: Networked communities engaged in improvement research.* The Carnegie Foundation.

Chapter 11

Is legislation the remedy for school reform in England? Conclusion, afterthoughts, and insights on fairness and equity

All is riddle, and the key to a riddle is another riddle.
There are as many pillows of illusion as flakes in a snow-storm.
We wake from one dream into another dream.
The toys, to be sure, are various, and are graduated in refinement to the quality of the dupe.
The intellectual man requires a fine bait; the sots are easily amused.
But everybody is drugged with his own frenzy, and the pageant marches at all hours, with music and banner and badge.

(William Faulkner, interviewed by Jean Stein, New York, 1956)

Introduction

From Poe's dream within a dream to Faulkner's riddle within a riddle, the secrets – the hopes and dissatisfactions – of England's law-based reform are slowly disclosed, though certainly not all of them. Identifying those that await further study is one of this final chapter's aims. One important point is that this book does not place education law in the broad context of the English legal system. Only short comments address that subject as it is out of my expertise and field, and beyond the scope of this study.

In accordance with this book's title, the concluding chapter will develop around the three themes of law-based reform in England: law, politics, and fairness. Finally, I shall offer some ideas for change.

Law

If you are a chief executive officer of an LEA, a headteacher of a large secondary school or indeed any school, if you are an entrepreneur who intends to establish a chain of trust schools or academies, perhaps an official in the department for education, or a social advocate in an NGO involved in education, here is what you should read: 15 primary acts of parliament that together hold 2,801 A4 pages, 4,690 sections, 222 separate schedules (some comprising dozens of articles) that refer to, and amend, previous legislation, and 1,817 repeals of parts of previous laws. This is a staggering amount by any standard. To understand the legal situation on any given issue, it is not only necessary to read a lot, but also to navigate your way through information that is not clustered together. You would need to go back to several laws and figure out what has been changed or repealed, and this is just on the primary-legislation level, not including by-laws, codes, circulars, and directives. It is clear that no single person or body can master all of these, let alone implement them or act upon them. No executive or regulatory body can assure that all of these are followed. As a leading legal adviser on education law said in 2005:

> When I began my work on education law, I had one volume. That was all the education law I needed. Now I have a whole bookcase-full.

And a senior policy adviser provides a historic timeline, and then an insider's view on legislation:

> Until 1976 PMs didn't think the law was reflected in the standing policy. The ministers were on their way up, worthy of their senior status as secretaries of state, but not dynamic politicians. Some were on their way out or pretty young, without their political teeth. Butler[1] himself was quite inexperienced. In Callaghan's government all this changed.

My study does not draw conclusions as to why this happens, but it does conclude who was responsible for it and how it evolved. Education legislation is part of the DNA of education policy in England. It is seen by decision-makers as the indispensable initial first step in any alteration. This has constitutional justification. Notwithstanding, on top of this legitimate reasoning, legislation serves other respective purposes: political, declarative, and perhaps because, as one MP is quoted as saying at the beginning of this book: 'Do you know why we legislate? Because we can.' This provides a political explanation but not a defence. Another MP said:

> The legislation is a political process of highly qualified people being consulted, sometimes listened to, sometimes ignored. ... it's a combination; the legislation doesn't mean very much if you don't back it with resources.

Besides its political role, legislation provides an association between the public and private elements of the market that has become a central tool in decentralized school systems. Controlling and retaining the public-good elements is, I believe, not just a technical function of legislation (because in a decentralized system legislation is the only form of regulation) but also a preventive and protective purpose of legislation:

> A public market ... contains 'market elements' such as choice, diversity, and completion ... it also contains 'public elements' which afford a structural position and significance to the public interest which distinguishes it from a free market model. Public elements include forms of collective action (funding and/or provision of services, framing rules for services,

> setting standards etc.), public accountability and oversight of services, and representation and participation.
>
> (Woods, 2000: 220)

In his detailed study of LEAs in England, Woods discusses the obscure association between structure and engagement. On the argument as to whether structure exists in the mind or in reality, and whether they are just perceived as such by agents and actors, Woods offers a reciprocal model in which structures both influence, and are influenced by, agents and actors, thus drawing upon dialectic dualism theory. Woods concludes the debate and explains:

> ... while without people these structures would not exist, for any one set of people at a particular time, the emergent properties generated prior to that time are 'given' structures. As such, they influence and condition (but do not determine) the actions of that set of people, who experience, draw from and interact with them. Engagement is enabled and constrained by these structures. People's actions can leave the structures unaltered or may lead to degrees of structural change.
>
> (Ibid. 222)

This model is useful for analysing and describing the mutual concomitance between the participants in this study and legislation. The policymakers and educators alike are influenced by its content but also by its mere existence. Legislation creates a culture, an ambience that is heightened by the content – in other words by the policies it carries. How can one really encompass all of this? What does it mean to work in an exceedingly over-legislated atmosphere, and what does it mean to produce this legislation?

My findings show that, as one senior DfE official explained, on the one hand, the legislation process is now influenced by many people and bodies (consultants, think tanks, headteachers, NGO/QUANGO/ALB CEOs), so supposedly the governance of legislation is flattened (Ball, 2007; Glatter, 2002). On the other hand, the involvement of these individuals, organizations, and groups creates a buffer between legislators and policymakers and the public. Although, again, to paraphrase on Ball (2007), it is doubtful whether in times where all of these were less influential on legislation it represented the public with a greater degree of fidelity.

Findings show that legislation is an engine that powers three other forces, as presented in Figure 11.1.

The first force is school funding, an obvious shaper of policy and determinant of educational priorities. The second force is that of audit, mainly through, and by, Ofsted and standards set by the ministry, OfQUAL and similar agencies. Reaching out beyond the law, redefining and expanding its boundaries, sometimes into areas uncharted by law, the audit mechanisms and the high stakes that accompany

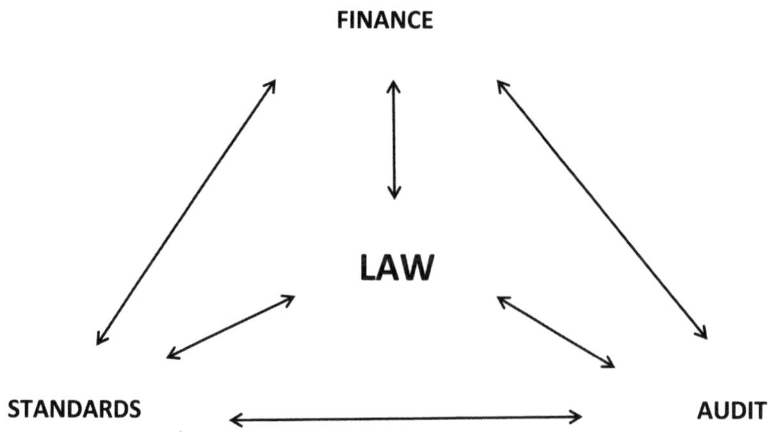

Figure 11.1: Law as the centre of policy forces

standards have a profound influence on the work of educators. The third force is that which organizes the major distinction between commissioning and delivery of education, commissioning being the organization of the system geographically and contextually, and delivery being the ownership, possession, and operation of schools and the employment of school staff. The following three accounts encompass the three forces that are powered by education law:

> What changes outcomes is law deployed carefully and skilfully – a tool in the toolkit. If you look at things tools have to be successful with poorer children so trying to effect that through the law alone is ineffective. You have to consider each issue on its merits. If you don't have to change the law it's better. It saves 18 months. Changing the law is not sufficient, it's effective with a broader programme of change implementation – of the NC, LMS, Ofsted, academies – these have a big impact in the system, the thing they have in common is that just changing the law is far from enough.
>
> (Senior ministry official, 2011)

> A cultural change is more important than legislation. Today's bill [the EA 2011] is a structural change of agencies subsidiary to the government. There's an interesting parallel today – the EBacc is not in the law but will have a consultation in the curriculum legislation, it is an important structural change like academies and free schools that don't have a legal basis but they are academies. It is a mindset and they present a cultural difference. There was a lot of controversy over trust schools but there was nothing in trust, just foundation schools and this was a variation. I said to Blair 'this is secondary legislation', and we had a talk in a back room in the Commons but he wanted to have the debate and the political power

> in legislation. And every new Queen's speech requires legislation, and there would be a panic, if there weren't a new education bill every year, so there's an exaggeration. And the white paper is far more important than legislation and a lot is not followed, but legislation is much more important in things like teaching skills and EBacc.
>
> (Senior adviser to the government, 2011)

> The biggest change in terms of multicultural issues was the work on black Caribbean children, but that was through funds and not through legislation. We had pots of money for goals we wanted to achieve, we had schools bid for that money, and there was an outcry because schools needed a lot of bureaucracy, and now the government is going the other way because you need things where money is allocated for specific interests, second-order goals like promoting a specific policy or subject, or competing priorities that will take hold and there was too little study on it.
>
> (Senior adviser to the government, 2011)

One possible role of legislation, and a potential attribute of the abundance of education law as it is created by, and derived from, central government, could be to organize power in a way that creates a relatively holistic and cohesive system. But this is often not the case. For instance, parallel to two decades of weakening LEAs, lately the government has initiated and advertised the following policy:

> Localism, localism, localism[2]
>
> The Government is overseeing a fundamental shift of power away from Westminster to councils, communities and homes across the nation. A radical localist vision is turning Whitehall on its head by decentralizing central government and giving power to the people.
>
> ...
>
> The Department sets policy on supporting local government; communities and neighbourhoods; regeneration; housing; planning, building and the environment; and fire. The Department is ending the era of top-down government by giving new powers to councils, communities, neighbours and individuals.
>
> ...
>
> Local government plays a vital role in representing the interests of its citizens, delivering and commissioning local services and promoting the Big Society. Central government will make localism real by delegating power to the lowest appropriate level. As part of this, local authorities will

> be the key player in using new delegated powers and devolving powers further down to the grassroots wherever possible.

How this vibrant vision coincides with chains and federations of schools, and the mandatory forbiddance of LEAs to set up schools and organize education, remains a riddle that this book will not solve, but it points at a second level of a conundrum that exists on top of the maze of education legislation.

There is something deterministic in the recurring usage of legislation as a tool for reforming England's education. The legality (Ewick and Silbey, 1998) that is produced by this process is confused. Parallel worlds exist between the law that, on the one hand, dominates the lives of English educators and, on the other hand, alienates them and creates an impervious barrier between them and the legislators. This results in a diluted product, creating disillusionment and suspicion, mixed with instrumentalism and lack of respect in a deep, not necessarily daily, sense:

> The development of legislation is left to lawyers when you have so many interlocking acts. … one of the interesting things is what the white papers are for. They are supposed to be white papers but they become manifestos, big chunks don't end up in the bill.
>
> (MP, 2011)

> A lot of the important parts such as section 497 of the '96 act to intervene are hardly ever used. Legislation is there to enable things to happen, in some cases it means placing duties on schools and LAs, but it needs to be combined with other things that make people work in schools.
>
> (Senior DfE official 2011)

> We realize you need new legal entities to make the most if this. And this means new legal tools and ideas, borrowed from other fields. For instance a community interest company. The kick is a normal company limited by guarantee. And all our money goes for deprived communities. This status can be taken off if we don't act like a social enterprise. It's a governmental facelift.
>
> (CEO, trust schools organization, 2011)

One change that the English system could administer, providing that a deeply-rooted political culture determined the amount and habitual updating of law, is to decide that the current method that combines omnibus legislation with lingering pieces of policy is replaced by one updated education policy and reform law valid at any given time, with all previous legislation and schedules incorporated into it. Regardless of the size of such a law, which, given the current state of things, would be huge, it could provide one single source of legitimacy and stability for the system. Its drafting may force the government and the legislators to clear a lot of clutter and solve contradictions that exemplify the current legislation and dominate the professional lives of policymakers and educators.

Law and politics

The growing link between education and politics in England (Harris, 2007; Manzer, 2003) and the growing use of legislation as part of the political process (Harris, 2007) were recurring themes among the interviewees in this study. For what type of policy change is legislation useful? How can legislation regulate education? How does legislation coexist with other forces or tools?

> There are ... important differences between conventional market transactions and political 'trade'. First, in conventional markets, when a supplier meets a consumer demand, the transaction does not give rise to any coercion – other than to require both parties to do what they voluntarily agreed. ... third parties are not affected. In a political context the end result of the 'transaction' is normally legislation which has a general coercive effect, applying to, and often imposing costs on, those who did not vote for it or did not want it.
>
> (Ogus, 2004: 59)

> Uncontroversially, it may be assumed that the legislature has neither the time nor the expertise to engage in detailed regulatory rule-making. Further, when – as is frequently the case – technical amendments are necessary, parliamentary scrutiny would impose heavy costs and serious delays. It is thus appropriate that primary legislation should concentrate on the general principles of regulatory law. The critical issue is, then, the extent to which detailed rule-making should be delegated to the executive, or rather, to an agency which is, to a greater or lesser degree, independent of government.
>
> (Ibid. 105)

England's unique interpretation of the structure and role of primary legislation produces legal structure that includes *both* immensely detailed primary legislation *and* equally immense secondary legislation (such as the admissions codes). Ogus ponders further the pros and cons of extensive and comprehensive primary legislation versus regulation through a selected regulatory agency. The latter can develop expertise and adapt more quickly than the sometimes cumbersome parliamentary process. Regulatory bodies are also (relatively speaking) less under the influence of 'political interference, encourage a long-term perspective and (perhaps) facilitate consultations and more open-ended decision-making' (ibid. 106). This, however, should be balanced with 'residual parliamentary powers of intervention and supervision'.

> To me, this is a function of the tension between the 10 Downing Street agenda and the other agenda, there is an inclusion agenda, and another agenda that is neoliberal consumerist, and contestability, destabilization, and competition that public bodies should be enablers or providers. Why? They have done so for a hundred years; it's tied up with this huge tension. The big problem that politicians face [regardless of] whether Conservative or Labour is trying to push through an ideologist interventionist agenda, is they don't know how to push change in such a large public sector and their intervention has been largely dysfunctional rather than functional. What you say about professionals you can say the same about politicians. They have the power but they don't have the understanding to make a service function better.
>
> (Senior adviser to the ministry, 2005)

> More broadly the cons are that legislation doesn't do anything unless it's enforced and implemented, and the pros are that it's cheap, it's an easy way of signalling your intent without actually doing it. There are things that are observed in the breach, things like the annual general meeting, no one ever turned up, they were completely hopeless, and were repealed.
>
> (Senior DfES official involved in drafting legislation, 2005)

Judging by the findings of this study, there is a serious attempt, however, to strengthen regulatory bodies without weakening parliamentary (and therefore public and democratic) control over education policy and reform. But the main drawback of the government's belief in regulation is the total attribution of advanced economic thinking patterns to parents and educators. This stream of thought is often disguised or justified as being opposed to paternalism by a presupposition (or illusion?) that all 'consumers' will quickly master the rules of engagement in the education market. This belief is wrong, not only because when discussing a public good such as education, the ability to gather, interpret, and understand the relevant information essential to survive in the market is fundamentally biased by variables including social class, language, culture, and cultural and social capital, but also because, as Green (2005) (see also Ben-Porath, 2010) explains, most people just want a decent school in their area. Furthermore, as I outlined in Chapter 2, there is never a genuine neoclassic market in education and similar human services. The illusion may be true when the issue is about choosing a new washer-dryer, but the consequences of bad choices in the case of education are more severe, and gathering and understanding the data is much more complex.

> … although governments are more concerned about the nature and extent of regulation than they once were, such concern appears to focus

> on economic impacts of regulation rather than the legal effectiveness of different forms of regulatory strategy.
>
> (Partington, 2010: 1021)

Here Partington addresses the linear schema that governments hold, and their disregard for the mediating variables that affect the impact of legislation on its way from the parliament floor to the classroom. Winship's (2006) model of public policy is about fitting together pieces of a puzzle and reconciling alternative solutions or problems. English primary legislation in education does not do that, although its engineers attempt to. The participants in this study explain that, too often, a new law either discards the previous solution outright (much too soon for the pace of the pedagogical and cultural 'clock', as explained earlier) or disregards it, thus creating insurmountable clashes between policies at the local and schools levels. The nature of legislation and its volume and frequency render the minimizing of these two negative effects almost impossible.

Kingdon explains that policy is not one thing but is constituted of isolated 'streams' that sometimes combine together. It is unclear how one certain problem becomes positioned at the focus of public concern and evolves into a crisis that requires government reaction – this being the first stream. The second stream comes from the policy community that 'have their pet ideas or axes to grind' (ibid. 87). The third stream is political/public and includes 'swings of national mood, vagaries of public opinion, election results', and other things. Once in a while the streams merge into a river. But many policies evolve from one stream, and then clash with another. Analysing education legislation in England shows a definite wake of these streams and the clashes between them.

Law, politics, and fairness

> The demands for equality and increased opportunity in the 1950s and 1960s led to the introduction of comprehensive schools. All-in secondary schooling rightly became the normal pattern, but the search for equality of opportunity in some cases became a tendency to uniformity. The idea that all children had the same rights to develop their abilities led too easily to the doctrine that all had the same ability. The pursuit of excellence was too often equated with elitism.
>
> (DfEE, 1997,[3] sec. 12)

It is tempting to draw upon the American model of desegregation and offer this as a remedy to England's problems of segregation. But several problems arise out of such a slant. First, the interviewees – all knowledgeable in education policy, and many contenders for social justice and genuinely concerned with the fate of minorities, immigrants, and disenfranchised ethnic groups – insist that the clear-cut lines of segregation in the US are quite unlike those in England and warn of a 'cut and paste' approach on this delicate and potentially explosive issue. Second, in the US itself the picture has changed considerably – demographically, legally, and pedagogically (Morris, 2009; Perea, 2004). Straightforward mandated integration is replaced by complex ways in which the stronger groups resegregate themselves through a variety of paths that include magnet schools and in-school tracking (Morris, 2009; Smrekar and Goldring, 2009). In addition, straightforward integration is not necessarily realized as the equitable tool that can lead to a fair system, both pedagogically and in essence. At the same time, some processes of in-school segregation occur in England as well, through what Gillborn and Youdell (2000: 98–115) referred to as 'tier systems'.

> The first thing is that law is not on its own when it comes to equality and social justice. Changing the law doesn't impact on these things. What makes a difference is the practice in schools and local areas, and the law can only influence that with a strong implementation policy. Admissions are not an answer to anything at all although of course they shouldn't be discriminatory. We did a big piece of research about segregation and how segregated the system would be if pupils went to the nearest school. And we found the overall effect of segregation was nearly zero. Like Catholic schools that have other patterns of admissions. But that people think that admissions policy will crack segregation issues is untrue. It's more about practice issues: how it's important who can go to which schools, but if you want to shift that it's not just admissions. Did children with FSM do better in schools where children are middle class? Absolutely no. They do better in city schools. It's a big challenge to let people know: hang on to these students, we can provide support and ideas but we don't have to second-guess what you do. It's an impressionistic effect on what people think.
>
> (Senior ministry official, 2006)

Even in the US, with the strong heritage of the Brown ruling, research in the last two decades shows that a lot of the immediate 'constituents' of integration do not expect desegregation policy, but rather accessible, quality education. This understanding presents serious challenges to policymakers, for if 'technical' desegregation, on the one hand, and choice, on the other hand, have failed in achieving equality of outcomes, then what is there left? The asset of England's legislative education policy is its power to offer an overall look at the whole system. The downside is that legislation is a one-size-fits-all arrangement that ignores local discrepancies that can be significant, especially in decentralized systems that include multiple providers and modes of delivery (Wong and Shen, 2008). Therefore the question arises: how can this framework assist or hinder fairness in education? I believe that fairness is a key factor in securing the legitimate status of educational legislation.

Strike (2003) discusses the role of legitimacy in education policy. This is especially important when discussing legislation. He distinguishes between 'objective legitimacy' – the obvious ingredients of a legislative process in a parliamentary democracy such as England – and 'subjective legitimacy' that evolves in the hearts and minds of citizens: participants in this study as well as parents, for instance. Legitimacy, Strike explains, is often mistaken for economic or organizational efficiency.

> A conception of equality is worthless unless it describes not only an ideal egalitarian distribution, but what counts as an egalitarian improvement in a patently unequal distribution. So our next assignment is to compose a theory of improvement that suits equality of resources and can act as a guide for making our society more egalitarian than it is. We need terms of accounting, though these may seem strange in the context of political philosophy. We might define a person's equity deficit as the amount or degree by which he has less than he would have, or is otherwise in worse circumstances than he would be, under an ideal egalitarian distribution in his community.
>
> (Dworkin, 2000: 164)

This call by Dworkin echoes Ogus's (2004) call for 'substantive accountability' (ibid. 111) that reflects the addressing of regulation, with an objective of accomplishing, in the deepest sense, the fulfilment of a public interest over and above financial or procedural accountability, which are easier to secure and rank high on the neoliberal and managerial value scale. In terms of this study I am convinced that this means having a strong law-based equity tool, especially when in many ways the structure is counter to equality:

> We wanted not to have a debate on admissions to grammar schools: there were 166 grammar schools and if we wanted to focus on GM schools and not grammar schools that would take up all of our time, and required a battle over each school. But actually in the south-east the rules on grammar schools' ballots are loose, and the view was that we need a mechanism but that if there isn't an overwhelming feeling on selection, there is little we can do. So where there was partial selection it's fine, exception on specialties and activities ... but it wasn't a big issue with New Labour voters and we had a 20 per cent threshold [allowance for schools to choose] and we wanted to get on with other reforms that were important for us and it worked.
>
> (Senior education adviser to the government, 2011)

This statement reminisces and refers to the early days of the New Labour administration in 2000, when the Prime Minister and his team were debating how to address the admissions policy. Equity tools have to work across the system, for if large pockets or areas of untouched segregation are retained, the effect of equity tools withers down:

> Well it [legislation] failed in bringing social justice to admissions. If you have money you will get your child to a good school either by playing the admissions game or by buying a house in the right area. The schools may have 35–37 per cent who have A-star grades, and not 9 per cent but you would have a large percentage of children on FSM. You have steadily grown numbers of schools that are not ethnically balanced at all, how can you describe your education as inclusive if you allow Muslims to build their own schools? Will this allow them to improve their quality of education? I sat next to Tony Blair and someone asked about admissions and he said 'we are absolutely not going down there'. And this is quite clear.
>
> (Superhead, 2006)

The amount of legislation creates an expectation that it will address the issues of fairness, but the comments deliver a mixed response, at best:

> A lot of New Labour's legislation and reform has been aimed at equality, social justice, and inclusion. The holy grail was to find a system that can sit together equity and excellence. One cannot argue against it but we haven't got there. Inclusion has been seriously misused. Every young person should have opportunities but it doesn't mean they should not all go to the same schools. How do you manage admissions? We have never managed equity in school admissions which is because the white paper [Higher Standards, Better Schools For All, 2005] is not doing that as well.
>
> (DfES official, 2005)

> Legislation is much more focused on undernourished and disadvantaged groups than it was before but there are issues of personal and human liberties and long-range programmes that are unaddressed, it's a volatile area like a bar of soap that slips through your hand.
>
> (LEA chief education officer, 2001)

> We now have 43 per cent who don't get 5 A–C grades. This has gone down about 10 per cent and banding can help to strengthen the middle. We have been experiencing numbers from good families leaving for private schools – when you have flare there is a distinct flow. The estate population has become weaker and larger. If you look at government policy even the policy targeted at minimizing gaps has not worked; we have some poor families in the most horrendous conditions, malnourished, almost Dickensian, and this is from a government committed to getting people out of the deep end. Gordon Brown is committed but it doesn't seem to

> be working. We have 210 places and 510 applications for Year 7. Because within our LEA there are several schools that can select 10 per cent, and foundation schools that select according to music.
>
> (Superhead, 2006)

These words bring me to the final question on fairness. In light of the new (but evolutionary, not revolutionary) legal arrangements, who will be responsible and how will they manage the task of promising and providing quality education for English children? Perhaps what can help, in terms of legislation, is to add a fourth side to the triangle presented in Figure 11.1, in the manner presented in Figure 11.2.

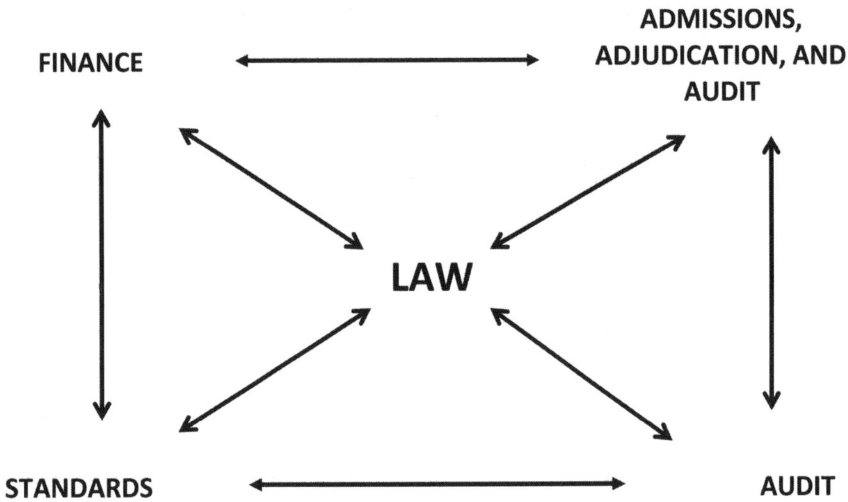

Figure 11.2: Law as the centre of policy forces – a proposed model

Studying the views of the cohort in this study, my conclusion is that most of them demand and expect the law to be not only a regulating force in the quasi-market of education but also an equity tool. In light of the growing decentralization and quasi- or complete privatization of England's public education, and keeping in mind that there is no going back to a past that never existed, one solution could be to create a fourth power under law. That is the power of a school adjudications and admissions authority. This power already exists, in the office of the school adjudicator. Regrettably it is the current Conservative–Liberal-Democrat government that, while accelerating the process of marketization and privatization, has weakened this office. But the idea I am proposing here is not to return the powers the adjudicator had under New Labour either, but to establish a strong admissions audit, perhaps equivalent in powers and public impact to those of Ofsted and standards agencies.

Looking at two decades of education reform legislation in England shows that in addition to the problems analysed and presented in this book, the power of the law was not harnessed with committed intent to create strong equity tools for schools. This is not to say that these were not created at all, but in comparison to the unequivocal language of the law in other areas, expressly in the creation of new forms of commission and delivery, the absence of this aspect is worrying. It is so not only because of the severe imbalance between equity, privatization, and competition, but also because of the dangers of creating a law-based system that does not secure quality education for all students. My suggestion of administering admissions auditing in a resilient manner is also based on the suspicion, backed by findings in this study and others in England (Ball, 2007; Bangs *et al.*, 2010; Bottery, 2000; Fitz *et al.*, 2006; Gillborn, 2008; MacBeath *et al.*, 2007) and elsewhere (Berends *et al.*, 2011; Darling-Hammond, 2010; Olsen *et al.*, 2004; Smrekar and Goldring 2009), that equity is not a foremost concern of some education regimes. Picking up on Theodore Parker's words, in 1965 the Rev. Dr Martin Luther King Jr. said that 'the arc of the moral universe is long, but it bends towards justice'. The experience of England's extreme law based-reform is, at present, one of a long arc, and it remains unclear as to how, and in which direction, it bends.

Notes

[1] Richard Austen Butler, cabinet member and President of the Board of Education, initiated the 1944 Education Act named after him.

[2] www.gov.uk/government/news/bob-neill-set-outs-the-future-of-local-planning (accessed 15 March 2013).

[3] Excellence in Schools, 1997 white paper, section 12.

Appendix:

The methodological–conceptual framework and the structure of the study

The methodological–conceptual framework: A personal account

The study presented in this book is the result of my three terms as a research fellow at the Institute of Education, University of London (IOE), in 2000–1, 2005–6, and 2010–11. My initial interest was in the link between education law and the work of policymakers and implementers, an interest that materialized in my first book on the subject (Gibton, 2004b). My first contacts at the IOE, professors Ros Levačić and Peter Earley, took me down the path of learning about educational administration and policy in England. Later, connecting with the Policy Studies group and the work of Stephen Ball, David Gillborn, Geoff Whitty, and Carol Vincent added the necessary policy angle to this work. I came to understand the special role of the law in what Ball (2008a: 39) defines as a 'policy epidemic', by no means an exclusively English phenomenon.

> Every day as I work with teachers and administrators in schools, I see the effects of a policy system that has run amok. There is no political discipline among elected officials and their advisers. To policymakers, every idea about what schools should be doing is as credible as every other idea, and any new idea that can command a political constituency can be used as an excuse for telling schools to do something. Elected officials – legislators, governors, mayors, school board members – generate electoral credit by initiating new ideas, not by making the kind of steady investments in people that are required to make the education sector more effective. The result is an education sector that is overwhelmed with policy, conditioned to respond to the immediate demands of whoever controls the political agenda, and not invested in the long term health of the sector and the people who work in it.
>
> (Elmore, 2011: 34)

The abundance of education law in England adds its power to the policy pressure, and the intersection between policy and law is the focus of this study.

> Rather than imagining law as existing apart from social relations … or conceiving of it as produced solely by groups of powerful law 'makers' … much law and society research portrays law from the 'bottom up' as a continuous production of practical reason and action. This research provides a view of law emerging from the routine, often discretionary, encounters among professional and non-professional actors. It depicts a legal system with numerous actors, involved in diverse projects, employing different legitimating discourses, material resources, and political power to achieve a wide range of goals. Emerging from these interactions, the practices and ideals to which the term 'law' might be applied are understandably variable, complex, and sometimes contradictory.
>
> (Ewick and Silbey, 1998: 19)

The method I chose for accomplishing this target is a socio-legal qualitative research design.

Research method and the structure of the study

Legal studies adopt a linear approach that presupposes a world with separately controlled denominators. Qualitative research, in contrast, with its main sub-streams – interpretive (Bernard, 2010; Moran, 2002; Smith *et. al.*, 2009) and constructivist and grounded theory (Corbin and Strauss, 2008; Charmaz, 2006, the latter both a sub-stream and an analysis method) – assumes a multi-layered, complex, narrative–based interdependent world in which :

> … studied experience is embedded in larger and, often, hidden positions, networks, situations, and relationships. Subsequently … hierarchies of power, communications and opportunity that maintain and perpetuate such differences and distinctions.
>
> (Charmaz, 2006: 130–1)

> In interpretative phenomenological analysis we are assuming that our data … can tell us something about people's involvement in and orientation towards the world, and/or about how they make sense of this.
>
> (Smith *et al.*, 2009: 46)

Policy analysis evolves around ideology (Floden, 2007), economics (Levačić, 2008), organizational and political theory (Kingdon, 2003; Manzer, 2003), and critical theory (Torres and Van Heertum, 2009). Legislation is part of all three: it rearranges school finance and redirects resources; it redefines targets and contents of education; it influences social mobility and can promote or curb desegregation and education for disenfranchised groups (Gillborn, 2008; Karen, 2008; Weitz-White and Rosenbaum, 2008); it centralizes or decentralizes power and changes models of governance, choice, and public involvement in education (Boyd, 2003; Strike, 2003; Hill, 2003; Ingersoll, 2008; Mickelson and Southworth, 2008). As education is politically driven and controlled (McDonnell, 2007, 2009; Sadovnik *et al.*, 2008; Spillane, 2007; Wong and Shen, 2008),

> ... policy making is now viewed as a much more complicated and messy process, one that involves continual negotiation, redefinition, and tinkering rather than one that involves selecting from among clearly defined alternatives one that best matches a clearly defined goal.
>
> (Kennedy, 1999: 58)

Such messy situations call for new approaches and angles of research:

> ... policy scholarship continues to be located in how policy antecedence and discourse is charted and theorized. It enables ideas to be valued evidence in analyzing how complex events and practices can be understood, and it foregrounds the need to work for conceptually informed policy and practice where intellectuals work is rehabilitated.
>
> (Gunter and Rayner, 2006: 48)

Qualitative and interpretive methods are useful for studying such 'messy' situations (Ball, 1994; Gibton, 2004b). Uncovering the politics of supposedly linear processes such as law-based reform, and disclosing the views of main players in the field (Cizek and Ramaswamy, 1998) are such tasks.

Methodological and ethical issues: problems and solutions

I would like now to share some of the problems and deliberations I had while designing and carrying out this study.

Problem 1: How can legal concepts and knowledge be incorporated into a qualitative interpretive study? Perhaps legal studies can be part of the content analysis. It is interesting to compare the ideas of critical law theory (e.g.: Nussbaum, 2006) with critical social and educational theory (e.g.: Gunter and Rayner, 2006). For instance, the use of Nussbaum's 'human capabilities' for studying issues of social justice in public education, and using theories of social justice (Barry, 2005; Brighouse, 2006) to analyse the school choice arrangements in the 2006 EIA or the EA 2011.

Problem 2: A possible discourse mismatch between law as a discipline, and gathering data from interviewees who come from multiple professions, both legal and educational. Problems included the gap between professional legal knowledge and 'lay' knowledge. Terms like 'law' (does it include legislation and case law?); 'right' (constitutional or according to popular or philosophical views?); the distinctions that need to be drawn between primary versus secondary legislation, administrative and constitutional law; and procedural issues. Of course the purpose of this study is not to examine legal knowledge of educators but to convey the interviewees' 'mindscapes' (Gibton, 2003), accurately reflecting how they see the law within their school and throughout the system. At the same time I tried to incorporate educators' views on policy, governance, equity, and equality into the discussion on education law and its role in all of these.

Problem 3: How should one build cohorts of interviewees for studying law-based reform? A meticulous mapping of the various individuals – whether in government-level policymaking or in field-level policy implementation – who influence or are influenced by legislation is necessary. This included the definition of twelve major groups of informants in government departments, in NGOs and QUANGOs, and in schools. The interviewees were located through a 'snowball technique'. Five leading professors, all experts on educational policy and administration in the UK, after being briefed in detail on the aims of the study, were asked to name senior figures who had, or had had, influence over law-based reform between 1997 and 2011. The five figures are all involved in research, auditing, consulting, advising, giving evidence before, and sitting on parliamentary and other committees on school reform, policy, and legislation, both under New Labour and Conservative governments; have written extensively on these issues throughout the last decade; and have worldwide status as experts in the field. These five key informants were not aware of the names suggested by their counterparts (the lists were disclosed only afterwards). Altogether, 60 names featured on all five lists, a further 30 on three lists and 35 more on two lists; consequently the consensus among the five 'raters' was quite high. All prospective participants who came up on two lists or more were approached. Those who refused did not belong disproportionately to any one group of interviewees. Their reasons for refusal varied. The complete detailed groups are presented in the findings of chapter five, under 'the figures of law-based reform'.

Problem 4: Is educational law part of the conceptual framework of this study, an empirical background, a baseline, or a text to be fragmented, categorized, and analysed? How should legal documents be analysed with qualitative data-analysis tools? Are they artefacts? Religious documents? Narratives? How should legal documents and interviews with legislators be combined together in the various levels of analysis? Are the thoughts and opinions of legislators an interpretive tool? Are legislators' views a rationalization of the political and social agendas that hide within legal documents? How are the opinions of those responsible for applying legislation (LEA officials, headteachers and so on) part of the *bricolage* (Denzin and Lincoln, 2000) of law-based educational reform?

Problem 5: As research on law-based reform involves public figures, and tends to disclose critical, perhaps negative or delicate opinions, thought should be given to issues of ethics, informed consent and protection of sources vis-à-vis the need to present valid findings that are often strengthened by the specific identity of the informants. Numerous ethical issues emanate from the study presented in this book. The participants were asked to be quite critical of their government. Informed consent seemed relatively easy, because due to their seniority one could assume they were well aware of the implications of being interviewed. As explained, the response rate was high. But the issue of privacy was delicate. The people interviewed were well known to each other and to the public. They were frequently quoted in newspapers and seen on television. Therefore the individuals were not given information on who the other interviewees were, and to avoid mutual identification could not even be invited, as a group, to a university symposium in which the preliminary findings were presented. I have done my best to conceal identities while presenting quotes in this book.

Research tools and population

A total of 110 in-depth interviews with 101 senior educational figures in England were conducted in 2001, 2005–6, and 2010–11.

Appendix Table: Population of interview cohort

PARTICIPANTS	POPULATION
Senior government officials	20
Government 'political' appointments	6
Teachers'/headteachers' associations/unions – senior personnel	5
Consultants to ministry officials/departments	10
Directors/CEOs of education for LEAs	10
'Superheads'	15
Senior Ofsted personnel	6
Legal advisers	2
Members of Parliament	2
NGOs/QUANGOs/think tanks – heads/CEOs	12
Senior academics involved in policymaking	3
Privately-financed foundations/think tanks – CEOs	10
Total	**101/110 interviews**

Units of analysis included phrases, vignettes, complete interviews, sub-groups within the cohort, and the three periods in which the data were gathered. The complete data was 'cut up' into phrases and vignettes (short complete accounts, 'stories' that depict a point or phenomenon), and some analyses included whole interviews or figures. A two-stage qualitative content analysis (Ritchie and Spencer, 2002) was implemented to reach grounded theory through categorization (Charmaz, 2006; Smith *et al.*, 2009; Bernard, 2010).

Three levels of analysis were applied. The first level, known as 'emic', included blind categorization of data, a process validated by two independent researchers in addition to myself. In the second level, known as 'etic', legislation and interviews were analysed in terms of equality – as a value of providing equal conditions and resources for all, equity and fairness – as processes that attempt to promise equal outcomes for all (for instance in an education system, Barry, 2005). Another criterion in the second level of analysis is in the political sphere and includes an attempt to map the interviewees as a 'policy community' (Kingdon, 2003) along a timeline of political stands and viewpoints. A third level maps the narrative of legislation and its interpretation by players in the field: those who plan it and draft it, those who influence the planners, those who implement, and those who are at the receiving end. All units and levels of analysis are represented in the book.

References

Abu-Asba, H. (2006) 'Unsettled issues in the Arab-Israeli education system before and after the Dovrat report'. In Inbar, D. (ed.), *Toward Educational Revolution?* (248–61). Jerusalem: Van Leer Institute (in Hebrew)

Baker, D.P. (2009) 'The invisible hand of world education culture: Thoughts for policy makers'. Ch. 74 in Sykes, G., Schneider, B., and Plank, D. (eds), *Handbook of Education Policy Research* (958–68). New York: AERA/Routledge

Balarin, M., Brammer, S., James, C.R., and McCormack M. (2008) *The School Governance Study.* London: Business in the Community

Balkin, J.M. (2002) 'Brown as icon'. Ch. 1 in Balkin, J.M. (ed.), *What Brown v. Board of Education Should Have Said: The nation's top legal experts rewrite America's landmark civil rights decision* (3–28). New York: New York University Press

Ball, S. (1994) 'What is policy? Texts, trajectories and toolboxes'. Ch. 2 in *Education Reform: A critical and post-structural approach* (15–27). Buckingham: Open University Press

– (2003) 'The teacher's soul and the terrors of performativity'. *Journal of Educational Policy,* 18 (2), 215–28

– (2007) *Education Plc.: Understanding private sector participation in public sector education.* London: Routledge

– (2008a) *The Education Debate.* Bristol: Policy Press

– (2008b) 'The legacy of ERA, privatization and the policy ratchet'. *Education Management, Administration & Leadership,* 36 (2), 185–200

– (2012) *Global Education Inc.: New policy networks and the neo-liberal imaginary.* London: Routledge

Bangs, J., MacBeath, J., and Galton, M. (2010) *Reinventing Schools, Reforming Teaching: From political visions to classroom realities.* London: Routledge

Barber, M. (1996) *The Learning Game: Arguments for an education revolution.* London: Victor Gollancz

Barry, B. (2005) *Why Social Justice Matters.* Cambridge: Polity Press

Ben-Porath, S.R. (2010) *Tough Choices: Structured paternalism and the landscape of choice.* Princeton, NJ: Princeton University Press

Berends, M., Cannata, M., and Goldring, E.B. (2011) 'School choice debates, research, and context'. In Berends, M., Cannata, M., and Goldring, E.B. (eds), *School Choice and School Improvement* (3–16). Cambridge, MA: Harvard Education Press

Berends, M., Springer, M.G., Ballou, D., and Walberg, H.J. (2009) (eds), *Handbook of Research on School Choice.* New York: Routledge

Bernard, R.H., and Ryan, G.W. (2010) *Analyzing Qualitative Data Systematic Approaches.* Thousand Oaks, CA: Sage

Bottery, M. (1992) *The Ethics of Educational Management: Personal, social and political perspectives on school organization.* London: Cassell

– (2000) *Education, Policy and Ethics.* London: Continuum

– (2003) 'Globalization and the educational policy context'. Ch. 16 in Davies, B. and West-Burnham, J. (eds), *Handbook of Educational Leadership and Management* (155–64). London: Pearson

– (2005) 'The individualization of consumption: A Trojan horse in the destruction of the public sector?' *Educational Management Administration & Leadership*, 33 (3), 267–88

Bottery, M. and Wright, N. (2000) *Teachers and the State.* London: Routledge

Bourdieu, P. (1987) 'The force of law: Towards sociology of the juridical field'. *Hastings Law Journal*, 38, 814–53

Bovill, C. and Leppard, M. (2006) 'Population policies and education: Exploring the contradictions of neo-liberal globalization'. *Globalization, Societies and Education*, 4 (3), 393–414

Bowen, S.W. (2011) 'No more adhocracies: Reforming the management of stabilization and reconstruction operations'. *Prism*, 3 (2), 3–18

Boyd, W.L. (1988) 'Policy analysis, educational policy, and management: Through a glass darkly?' In Boyan, N. (ed.), *Handbook of Research on Educational Administration* (501–22). New York: Longman

– (2003) 'Public education's crisis of performance and legitimacy: Rationale and overview of the yearbook'. Ch. 1 in Boyd, W.L. and Miretzky, D. (eds), *American Educational Governance on Trial: Change and challenges – the 102nd Yearbook of the National Society for the Study of Education* (NSSE) (1–19). Chicago: Chicago University Press

Brighouse, H. (2006) *On Education.* Abingdon, Oxfordshire: Routledge

Brighouse, T. and Fullick, L. (eds) (2007) *Education in a Global City: Essays from London.* London: IOE

Brighouse, T., Howell, T., and Water, M. (2002) 'The learning city: Before, during, after'. Paper presented at the annual conference of the British Educational Leadership, Management, and Administration Society (BELMAS), Birmingham, 20–22 September

Brown v. Board of Education, 347 U.S. 483 (1954)

Burbules, N.C. and Torres, C.A. (2000) 'Globalization and education: An introduction'. Ch. 1 in Burbules, N.C. and Torres, C.A. (eds), *Globalization and Education: Critical perspectives* (1–26). New York: Routledge

Calhoun, D. (2002) 'Evaluating a systemic reform project at the school district level'. Paper presented at the Annual Meeting of the American Educational Research Association, New Orleans, 1–5 April

Campbell, C. and Whitty, G. (2007) 'The governance of urban education in the UK: A public, private or partnership future?' In Pink, W.T. and Noblit, G.W. (eds), *International Handbook of Urban Education*, 1123–38. Springer International Handbooks of Education (19). Dordrecht: Springer Netherlands

Charmaz, K. (2006) *Constructing Grounded Theory: A practical guide through qualitative analysis.* Los Angeles, CA: Sage

Chubb, J.E. and Moe, T.M. (1990) *Politics, Markets & America's Schools.* Washington, DC: Brookings Institution

Cibulka, J.G. (1999) 'Moving toward an accountable system of K-12 education: Alternative approaches and challenges'. Ch. 8 in Cizek, G.J. (ed.), *Handbook of Educational Policy* (184–213). San Diego: Academic Press

– (2003) 'Educational bankruptcy, takeovers, and reconstitution'. Ch. 13 in Boyd, W.L. and Miretzky, D. (eds), *American Educational Governance on Trial: Change and challenges – the 102nd Yearbook of the National Society for the Study of Education* (NSSE) (271–90). Chicago: Chicago University Press

Cizek, G.J. and Ramaswamy, V. (1999) 'American educational policy: Constructing crises and crafting solutions'. Ch. 20 in Cizek, G.J. (ed.), *Handbook of Educational Policy* (498–522). San Diego: Academic Press

Cohen, D.K., Moffitt, S.L., and Goldin, S. (2007) 'Policy and practice'. In Fuhrman, S.H., Cohen, D.K., and Mosher, F. (eds), *The State of Educational Policy Research.* Mahwah, NJ: Lawrence Erlbaum, 63–86

Cohen, M., March, J., and Olsen, J. (1972) 'A garbage can model of organizational choice'. *Administrative Science Quarterly,* 17, 1–25

Coleman, J., Campbell, E., Hobson, C., McPartland, J., Mood, A., Weinfeld, F., and York, R. (1966) *Equality of Educational Opportunity.* Washington, DC: Department of Health, Education and Welfare, Office of Education

Corbin, J. and Strauss, A. (2008) *Basics of Qualitative Research* (3rd edition). Los Angeles: Sage

Corcoran, S.P., Schwartz, A.E., and Weinstein, M. (2012) 'Training your own: The impact of New York City's aspiring principals program on student achievement'. *Educational Evaluation and Policy Analysis,* 34 (2), 232–53

Cuban, L. (1990) 'Reforming again, again, and again'. *Educational Researcher,* 19 (1), 3–13

Darling-Hammond, L. (2010) *The Flat World and Education: How America's commitment to equity will determine our future.* New York: Teachers College Press

DeBray, E.H. (2006) *Politics, Ideology & Education: Federal policy during the Clinton and Bush administrations.* New York: Teachers College Press

Deleon, P. (2006) 'The historical roots of the field'. Ch 2 in Moran, M., Rein, M., and Goodin, R. (eds), *The Oxford Handbook of Public Policy* (39–57). Oxford: Oxford University Press

DeMitchell, T.A. and Fossey, R. (1997) 'Improving our children's future: Looking beyond law-based school reform'. Ch. 12 in *The Limits of Law-Based School Reform* (183–93), Lancaster, PA: Technomic

Denzin, K. and Lincoln, Y.S. (2000) 'The future of qualitative research'. In Denzin, N.K. and Lincoln, Y.S. (eds), *Handbook of Qualitative Research* (2nd edition) (1019–23). Thousand Oaks, CA: Sage

Diamond, P. and Giddens, A. (2005) 'The new egalitarianism: Economic inequality in the UK'. Ch. 6 in Giddens, A. and Diamond, P. (eds), *The New Egalitarianism* (101–19) Cambridge: Polity Press

Dolan, T.E. (2010) 'Revisiting Adhocracy: From rhetorical revisionism to smart mobs'. *Journal of Futures Studies,* November, 15 (2), 33–50

Dror, Y. (2007) *'National Education' through Mutually Supportive Devices: A case study of Zionist education.* Bern: Peter Lang

Dworkin, R. (2000) *Sovereign Virtue: The theory and practice of equality.* Cambridge, MA: Harvard University Press

Earley, P. (2000) 'Monitoring, managing or meddling? Governing bodies and the evaluation of school performance'. *Educational Management & Administration,* 28 (2), 199–210

Earley, P. and Creese, M. (2003) 'Lay or professional? Re-examining the role of school governors in England'. Ch. 24 in Davies, B. and West-Burnham, J. (eds), *Handbook of Educational Leadership and Management* (246–55). London: Pearson

Earley, P., Evans, J., Collarbone, P., Gold, A., and Halpin, D. (2002) *Establishing the Current State of School Leadership in England.* Norwich/London: Institute of Education, University of London/DfES

Earley, P. and Weindling, D. (2004) *Understanding School Leadership.* London: Sage

Eden, B. and Klinov, R. (1995) 'The effects of different financial methods on the extent of school integration'. In Kahane, R. (ed.), *Educational Advancement and Distributive Justice: Between equality and equity* (358–74). Jerusalem: Magnes Press

Elmore, R.F. (2004) *School Reform from the Inside Out: Policy, practice, and performance.* Cambridge, MA.: Harvard Education Press

– (ed.) (2011) *I Used to Think... And Now I Think...: Twenty Leading Educators Reflect on the Work of School Reform.* Cambridge, MA.: Harvard Education Press

Ewick, P. and Silbey, S.S. (1998) *The Commonplace of Law: Stories from everyday life.* Chicago: University of Chicago Press

Feuer, M. (2006) *Moderating the Debate: Rationality and the promise of American education.* Cambridge, MA: Harvard Education Press

Fitz, J., Davies, B., and Evans, J. (2006) *Educational Policy and Social Reproduction: Class inscription and symbolic control.* Abingdon, Oxfordshire: Routledge

Floden, R. (2007) 'Philosophical issues in education policy research'. Ch. 1 in Fuhrman, S.H., Cohen, D.K., and Mosher, F. (eds), *The State of Educational Policy Research* (3–18). Mahwah, NJ: Lawrence Erlbaum

Ford, J., Hughes, M., and Ruebain, D. (2005) *Education Law and Practice.* London: Jordans

Foster, C. (2005) *British Government in Crisis.* Portland, Oregon: Hart Publications

Fuhrman, S.H., Goertz, J.M.E., and Weinbaum, E.H. (2007) 'Educational governance in the United States: Where are we? How did we get here? Why should we care?' Ch. 3 in Cohen, D.K., and Mosher, F. (eds), *The State of Educational Policy Research* (41–62). Mahwah, NJ: Lawrence Erlbaum

Galligan, D.J. (2010) 'Legal theory and empirical research'. Ch 40 in Cane, P. and Kritzer, H.M. (eds), *The Oxford Handbook of Empirical Legal Research* (976–1001). Oxford: Oxford University Press

Gewirtz, S. (1998) 'Post-welfarist schooling: A social justice audit'. *Education and Social Justice,* 1 (1), 52–63

Gibton, D. (2003) 'Educational leadership and the tensions and dilemmas of decentralization and centralization'. Ch. 65 in Davies, B. and West-Burnham, J. (eds), *Handbook of Educational Leadership and Management* (671–84) London: Pearson

– (2004a) 'Minding the gap: Principals' graphic mindscapes on educational policy and law-based reform: A qualitative technique for evaluation and policy analysis'. *Studies in Educational Evaluation,* 30, 37–59

– (2004b) *Legalized Leadership: Law-based educational reform in England and its effect on headteachers.* London: Institute of Education

– (2011) 'Post-2000 law-based educational governance in Israel: From equality to diversity?' *Education Management, Administration & Leadership,* 39 (4), 434–54

Gibton, D. and Goldring, E. (2002) 'The role of legislation in educational decentralization: The case of Israel and the United Kingdom'. *Peabody Journal of Education,* 76 (3 and 4), 81–101

Giddens, A. (1998) *The Third Way.* Cambridge: Polity Press

– (2002) *Runaway World: How globalization is reshaping our lives.* London: Profile Books

Gillborn, D. (2008) *Racism and Education: Coincidence or conspiracy?* Abingdon, Oxfordshire: Routledge

Gillborn, D. and Youdell, D. (2000) *Rationing Education: Policy, practice, reform and equity.* Buckingham, UK: Open University Press

Glatter, R. (2002) 'Governance, autonomy and accountability in education'. Ch. 14 in Bush, T. and Bell, L. (eds), *The Principles and Practice of Educational Management* (225–40). London: Paul Chapman/Sage

– (2003) 'Governance and educational innovation'. Ch. 22 in Davies, B. and West-Burnham, J. (eds), *Handbook of Educational Leadership and Management* (228–37). London: Pearson

Goldring, E., Crowson, R., Laird, D., and Berk, R. (2002) 'Unmaking desegregation policy and "going unitary": The loss of a sense of place'. Paper presented at the Annual Meeting of the American Educational Research Association, New Orleans, 1–5 April

Goldring, E. and Rallis, S.F. (1993) *Principals of Dynamic Schools: Taking charge of change,* Newbury Park CA: Corwin-Sage

Goldspink, C. (2007) 'Rethinking Educational Reform: A loosely coupled and complex systems perspective'. *Educational Management Administration & Leadership,* 35, 27–50

Green, C. (2005) *The Privatization of State Education: Public partners, private dealings.* London: Routledge

Gunter, H.M. (2005) 'Conceptualizing research in educational leadership'. *Educational Management Administration & Leadership,* 33, 165

– (2008) 'Policy and workforce reform in England'. *Education Management, Administration and Leadership,* 36 (2), 253–70

Gunter, H.M. and Rayner, S. (2006) 'The researcher, research and policy in education in England'. *International Studies in Educational Administration,* 34 (3), 37–50

Hacker, D. (2008) 'A legal field in action: The case of divorce arrangements in Israel'. *International Journal of Law in Context,* 4 (1), 1–33

Hancher, L. and Moran, M. (1989) 'Organizing regulatory space'. In Hancher, L. and Moran, M. (eds), *Capitalism, Culture, and Regulation* (271–99). Oxford: Clarendon Press

Hannaway, J. (2003) 'Accountability, assessment, and performance issues: We've come a long way – or have we?' In Boyd, W.L., and Miretzky, D. (eds) *American Educational Governance on Trial: Change and Challenges – the 102nd Yearbook of the National Society for the Study of Education (NSSE).* Chicago: Chicago University Press

Harris, N. (1993) *Law and Education: Regulation, consumerism and the education system.* London: Sweet & Maxwell

– (2007) *Education, Law, and Diversity.* Oxford: Hart

Harvey, D. (2005) *A Brief History of Neoliberalism.* Oxford: Oxford University Press

Hess, F.M. and Petrilli, M.J. (2006) *No Child Left Behind.* New York: Peter Lang

Heubert, J.R. (1997) 'Schools without rules? Charter schools, federal disability law, and the paradoxes of deregulation'. *Harvard Civil Rights – Civil Liberties Law Review,* 32 (2), 301-353

– (1999) 'Six law-driven reforms: Developments, lessons, and prospects'. Ch. 1 in Heubert, J.R. (ed.) *Law and School Reform: Six strategies for promoting educational equity* (1–38). New Haven, CT: Yale University Press

Heyneman, S.P. (2009) 'International perspectives on school choice'. In Berends, M., Springer, M.G., Ballou, D., and Walberg, H.J. (eds), *Handbook of Research on School Choice.* New York: Routledge, 79–96

Hill, P.T. (2003) 'What's wrong with public education governance in big cities and how should it be fixed?' Ch. 4 in Boyd, W.L. and Miretzky, D. (eds), *American Educational Governance on Trial: Change and challenges – the 102nd Yearbook of the National Society for the Study of Education (NSSE)* (57–81). Chicago: Chicago University Press

Hill, P.T. and Lake, R.J. (2008) 'Charter school governance'. In Berends, M., Springer, M.G., and Walberg, H.J. (eds), *Charter School Outcomes* (113–30). New York: Lawrence Erlbaum Associates

Hill, P.T., Pierce, L.C., and Guthrie, J.W. (1997) *Reinventing Public Education: How contracting can reform America's schools.* Chicago: University of Chicago Press

Houser, E.R. (1996) 'A framework for appraising educational reforms'. *Educational Researcher,* 25 (7), 6–14

Ichilov, A. (2010) 'The establishment of public education in Israel and the withdraw from it'. In Ichilov, A. (ed.), *Privatization and Marketization in Public Education in Israel* (21–51). Tel-Aviv: Ramot/Tel-Aviv University (in Hebrew)

Imber, M. and van Geel, T. (2010) *Education Law* (4th edition). New York: Lawrence Erlbaum

Ingersoll, R.M. (2008) 'Teacher Quality, Educational Inequality, and the Organization of Schools'. Ch. 8 in Sadovnik, A.R., O'Day, J.A., Bohrnstedt, G.W., and Borman, K.M. (eds), *No Child Left Behind and the Reduction of the Achievement Gap* (153–77). New York: Routledge

Jackson, B. (1985) *Semiotics and Legal Theory.* London: Routledge and Kegan Paul

Jakobi, A.P. (2009) 'Global education policy in the making: International organizations and lifelong learning'. *Globalization, Societies and Education,* 7 (4), 473–87

James, C., Brammer, S., Conolly, M., Fertig, M., James, J., and Jones, J. (2011) 'School governing bodies in England under pressure: The effects of socio-economic context and school performance'. *Educational Management Administration & Leadership,* 39 (4), 414–34

Jencks, C.S. (1972) *Inequality: A Reassessment of the Effect of Family and Schooling in America.* New York: Basic Books

Karen, D. (2008) 'No Child Left Behind? Sociology Ignored'. Ch. 1 in Sadovnik, A.R., O'Day, J.A., Bohrnstedt, G.W., and Borman, K.M. (eds), *No Child Left Behind and the Reduction of the Achievement Gap* (13–24). New York: Routledge

Kelly, A. (2009) 'Globalisation and education: A review of conflicting perspectives and their effect on policy and professional practice in the UK'. *Globalisation, Societies and Education,* 7 (1), 51–68

Kennedy, M. (1999) 'Infusing educational decision making with research'. Ch. 3 in Cizek, G.J. (ed.) *Handbook of Educational Policy* (54–81). San-Diego: Academic Press

Kingdon, J.W. (2003) *Agendas, Alternatives, and Public Policies* (2nd ed.). Addison-Wesley

Kirst, M. (2003) 'Mayoral influence, new regimes, and public school governance'. Ch. 10 in Boyd, W.L. and Miretzky, D. (eds), *American Educational Governance on Trial: Change and challenges – the 102nd Yearbook of the National Society for the Study of Education (NSSE)* (196–218). Chicago: Chicago University Press

Kuo, V. (1998) 'Political influence networks and Kentucky school finance reform'. Paper presented at the Annual Meeting of the American Educational Research Association, San Diego, CAL, 13–17 April

LaFever, K. (2006) 'NCLB: Nexus of citizens learning the business, neoliberalism, and the No Child Left Behind act'. Ch. 5 in Peotter, T.S., Wegwert, J.C., and Haerr, C. (eds), *No Child Left Behind and the Illusion of Reform* (49–62). Lanham, MD: University Press of America

La Morte, M. (2002) *School Law: Cases and concepts* (7th ed.). Boston: Pearson

– (2011) *School Law: Cases and concepts* (10th ed.). Boston: Pearson

Lauen, D.L. and Tyson, K. (2009) 'Perspectives from the disciplines: Sociological contributions to education policy research and debates'. In Sykes, G., Schneider, B., and Plank, D. (eds), *Handbook of Education Policy Research* (71–82). New York: AERA/Routledge

Lawton, D. (2005) *Education and Labour Party Ideologies 1900–2001 and Beyond.* London: Routledge

Le Grand, J. (2005) 'Inequality, choice and public services'. Ch. 12 in Giddens, A. and Diamond, P. (eds), *The New Egalitarianism* (200–10). Cambridge: Polity Press

Leithwood, K., Jantzi. D., and Steinbach, R. (1999) *Changing Leadership for Changing Times* Buckingham, UK: Open University Press

Levačić, R. (2002) 'Efficiency, equity and autonomy'. Ch. 12 in Bush, T. and Bell, L. (eds), *The Principles and Practice of Educational Management* (187–206). London: Paul Chapman/Sage

– (2008) 'Financing schools: Evolving patterns of autonomy and control'. *Education Management, Administration, and Leadership*, 36 (2), 221–35

Levačić, R. and Dawnes, P. (2004) *Formula Funding of Schools, Decentralization and Corruption.* Paris: UNESCO International Institute for Educational Planning

Levačić, R., Simmons, K., and Smales, L. (2003) 'The missing Bucks: Buckinghamshire Upper Schools Forum campaign for fair funding and the use of research evidence'. Paper presented at the annual conference of the British Educational Leadership, Management, and Administration Society (BELMAS), Kents Hill, UK, 3–5 October

Levačić, R. and Woods, P.A. (2000) 'The impact of quasi-markets and performance regulation on socially disadvantaged schools'. Paper presented at the annual meeting of the American Educational Research Association, New Orleans, 24–28 April

Levin, B. (2005) *Governing Education.* Toronto: University of Toronto Press

Levin, B. and Fullan, M, (2008) 'Learning about System Renewal'. *Educational Management Administration & Leadership*, 36 (2), 289

Liss, B., Moskovitch., Sadovnik, A., and Tractenberg, P. (2006) *Don't Forget the Schools: Legal considerations for tax reform.* Newark, NJ: IELP

Lubienski, C. (2002) 'The politics of the public in public education'. Paper presented at the annual meeting of the American Educational Research Association, New Orleans, 1–5 April

Lundqvist, L.J. (2001) 'Implementation from above: The ecology of power in Sweden's environmental governance'. *Governance: An International Journal of Policy and Administration*, 14 (3), 319–37

MacBeath, J., Gray, J., Cullen, J., Frost, D., Steward, S., and Swaffield, S. (2007) *Schools on the Edge: Responding to challenging circumstances.* London: Paul Chapman

MacDonald, B. (1991) 'Critical introduction: From innovation to reform – a framework for analysing change'. In Rudduck, J. *Innovation and Change* (1–13). Buckingham: Open University Press

Manzer, R. (2003) *Educational Regimes and Anglo-American Democracy.* Toronto: University of Toronto Press

McDonnell, L.M. (2007) 'The Politics of Education: Influencing policy and beyond'. Ch. 2 in Fuhrman, S.H., Cohen, D.K., and Mosher, F. (eds), *The State of Educational Policy Research* (19–40). Mahwah, NJ: Lawrence Erlbaum

– (2009) 'A political science perspective on education policy analysis'. In Sykes, G., Schneider, B., and Plank, D., *Handbook of Education Policy Research* (57–70). New York: AERA/Routledge

McLaren, P. (2005) 'Critical pedagogy in the age of global imperialism: Dispatches from headquarters'. Ch. 1 in Satterthwaite, J. and Atkinson, E. (eds), *Discourses of Education in the Age of Imperialism* (3–24). Stoke-on-Trent: Trentham Books

McUsic, M.S. (1999) 'The law's role in the distribution of education: The promises and pitfalls of school finance litigation'. Ch. 3 in Heubert, J.R. (ed.), *Law and School Reform: Six strategies for promoting educational equity* (88–159). New Haven, CT: Yale University Press

– (2004) 'The future of Brown v. Board of Education: Economic integration of the public schools'. *Harvard Law Review*, 117 (3), 1334–77

Mickelson, R.A. and Southworth, S. (2008) 'When school choice leaves many children behind: Implications for NCLB from the Charlotte-Mecklenburg Schools'. Ch. 11 in Sadovnik, A.R., O'Day, J.A., Bohrnstedt, G.W., and Borman, K.M. (eds), *No Child Left Behind and the Reduction of the Achievement Gap* (227–42). New York: Routledge

Minow, M. (2001) 'Surprising legacies of Brown v. Board'. In Carter, D.J., Flores, S.M., and Reddick, R.J. (eds), *Legacies of Brown: Multiracial equity in American education.* (9–36). Cambridge, MA: Harvard Educational Review

Mintzberg, H. (1979) *The Structuring of Organizations: A synthesis of the research.* Englewood Cliffs, NJ: Prentice Hall

Miron, G. and Nelson, C. (2002) *What's Public about Charter Schools? Lessons learned about choice and accountability.* Thousand Oaks, CA: Corwin Press

Mitchell, D.E. and Encarnation, D.J. (1984) 'Alternative state policy mechanisms for influencing school performance'. *Educational Researcher*, 13 (5), 4–11

Moran, D. (2002) *Introduction to Phenomenology.* London: Routledge

Morris, J.E. (2009) 'Racial realities across different places: Dual directions in recommitting to the promises of Brown'. In Smrekar, C.E. and Goldring, E.B. (eds), *From the Courtroom to the Classroom: The shifting landscape of school desegregation* (271–82). Cambridge, MA: Harvard Education Press

Nussbaum, M.C. (2006) *Frontiers of Justice: Disability, nationality, species membership.* Cambridge, MA: Belknap – Harvard University Press

Ogus, A.I. (2004) *Regulation, Legal form, and Economic Theory.* Oxford and Portland, Oregon: Hart

Olsen, M., Codd, J., and O'Neill, A. (2004) *Education Policy, Globalization, Citizenship and Democracy.* London: Sage

Oplatka, I. (2010) *The Legacy of Educational Administration.* Frankfurt: Peter Lang

Orfield, G. (1999) 'Conservative activists and the rush toward resegregation'. Ch. 2 in Heubert, J.R. (ed.), *Law and School Reform: Six strategies for promoting educational equity* (39–87). New Haven, CT: Yale University Press

Orton, J.D. and Weick, K.E. (1990) 'Loosely coupled systems: A reconceptualization'. *Academy of Management Review*, 15 (2), 203–23

Partington, M. (2010) 'Empirical legal research and policy-making'. Ch. 41 in Cane, P. and Kritzer, H.M. (eds), *The Oxford Handbook of Empirical Legal Research* (1002–24). Oxford: Oxford University Press

Payne, C.M. (2008) *So much reform – so little change: The persistence of failure in urban schools.* Cambridge. MA: Harvard Education Press

Perea, J. (2004) 'Buscando America: Why integration and equal protection fail to protect Latinos'. *Harvard Law Review*, 117 (3), 1420–69

Phillips, D. and Ochs, K. (2004) 'Researching Policy Borrowing: Some methodological problems in comparative education'. *British Educational Research Journal*, 30 (6), 773–84

Plank, D.N. and Keesler, V. (2009) 'Education and the shrinking state'. Ch. 53 in Sykes, G., Schneider, B., and Plank, D. (eds), *Handbook of Education Policy Research* (694–704). New York: AERA/Routledge

Rallis, S.F. and Goldring, E.B. (2000) *Principals of Dynamic Schools: Taking charge of change* (2nd ed.). Newbury Park, CA.: Corwin-Sage

Ranson, S. (2011) 'School governance and the mediation of engagement'. *Educational Management Administration & Leadership*, 39 (4), 398–413

Rawls, J. (1971) *A Theory of Justice*. Cambridge, MA: Harvard University Press

Reglin, G.L. (1992) 'Public school educators' knowledge of selected supreme court decisions affecting daily public school operations'. *Journal of Educational Administration*, 30 (2), 26–31

Reilly, E. (2000) 'Education and The Constitution: Shaping each other and the next century'. *Akron Law Review*, 34 (1), 1–19

Riley, K.A. (1998) *Whose School is it Anyway?* London: Falmer Press

Ritchie, J. and Spencer, L. (2004) 'Qualitative data analysis for applied policy research', Ch. 12 in Huberman, M.A. and Miles, M.B. (eds), *The Qualitative Researcher's Companion* (305–30). Thousand Oaks, CA: Sage

Rizvi, R. and Engel, L.C. (2008) 'Neo-liberal globalization, educational policy, and the struggle for social justice. Ch. 34 in Ayers, W., Stovall, D., and Quinn, T. (eds), *Handbook of Social Justice in Education* (529–41). New York: Taylor & Francis

Robertson, R. (1995) 'Glocalization: Time-space and homogeneity-heterogeneity'. In Featherstone, M., Lash, S., and Robertson, R. (eds), *Global Modernities* (25–44). London: Sage

Rosen, L. (2009) 'Rhetoric and symbolic action in the policy process'. In Sykes, G., Schneider, B., and Plank, D. (eds), *Handbook of Education Policy Research* (267–85). New York: AERA/Routledge

Ruff, A. (1999) 'Admissions appeals in 1999: The impact of the 1998 regulations and R. v. Birmingham city council ex parte'. *Education and the Law*, 11 (4), 77–87

– (2002) *Education Law: Text, cases and materials*. Oxford: Oxford University Press

Sadovnik, A.R., Dworkin, G.A., Gamoran, A., Hallinan, M., and Scott, J. (2008) 'Conclusion: Sociological perspectives on NCLB and federal involvement in education'. Ch. 18 in Sadovnik, A.R., O'Day, J.A., Bohrnstedt, G.W., and Borman, K.M. (eds), *No Child Left Behind and the Reduction of the Achievement Gap* (359–74). New York: Routledge

San Miguel, G. and Valencia, R.R. (2004) 'From the treaty of Guadalupe Hidalgo to Hopwood: The educational plight and struggle of Mexican Americans in the southwest'. In Carter, D.J., Flores, S.M., and Reddick, R.J. (eds), *Legacies of Brown: Multiracial equity in American education* (121–80). Cambridge, MA: Harvard Education Press

Satterthwaite, J. and Atkinson, E. (eds) (2005) *Discourses of Education in the Age of Imperialism*. Stoke on Trent: Trentham Books

Smith, J.A., Flowers, P., and Larkin, M. (2009) *Interpretative Phenomenological Analysis: Theory, method, and research*. Los Angeles, CA: Sage

Smrekar, C.E. and Goldring, E.B. (eds) (2009) *From the Courtroom to the Classroom: The shifting landscape of school desegregation*. Cambridge, MA: Harvard Education Press

Spillane, J.P. (2007) 'The making and effects of education policy: Commentary/policy, politics, institutions, and markets'. Ch. 6 in Fuhrman, S.H., Cohen, D.K., and Mosher, F. (eds), *The State of Educational Policy Research* (129–36). Mahwah, NJ: Lawrence Erlbaum

Stein, M.L., Goldring, E.B., and Cravens, X. (2011) 'Do parents do as they say? Choosing Indianapolis charter schools'. In Berends, M., Cannata, M., and Goldring, E.B. (eds), *School Choice and School Improvement* (105–24). Cambridge, MA: Harvard Education Press

Stevens, P.A. (2007) 'Researching race/ethnicity and educational inequality in English secondary schools: A critical review of the research literature between 1980 and 2005. *Review of Educational Research*, 77 (2), 147–85

Stewart, C. (ed.) (2007) *Creolization: History, ethnography, theory*. Walnut Creek, CA: Left Coast Press

Stoll, L. and Stobart, G. (2005) 'Informed consent? Issues in implementing and sustaining government-driven educational change'. In Bascia, N., Cumming, A., Datnow, A., Leithwood, K., and Livingstone, D. (eds), *International Handbook of Educational Policy* (153–72). Dordrecht: Kluwer

Strike, K.A. (2003) 'Liberty, democracy, and community: Legitimacy in public education'. Ch. 3 in Boyd, W.L. and Miretzky, D. (eds), *American Educational Governance on Trial: change and challenges – the 102nd Yearbook of the National Society for the Study of Education (NSSE)* (37–56). Chicago: Chicago University Press

Superfine, B.M. (2008) *The Courts and Standards-based Education Reform*. New York: Oxford University Press

Taylor, C. and Ryan, C. (2005) *Excellence in Education: The making of great schools*. London: David Fulton

Teubner, G. (1986) *Dilemmas of Law in the Welfare State*. Berlin: de Gruyter

Thompson-Ford, R. (2004) 'Brown's ghost'. *Harvard Law Review*, 117 (3), 1305–33

Tichy, N.M., Tushman, M.L., and Fornbrun, C. (1979) 'Social network analysis for organizations'. *The Academy of Management Review*, 4 (4), 507–19

Torres, C.A. and Van Heertum, R. (2009) 'Education and domination: Reforming policy and practice through critical theory'. In Sykes, G., Schneider, B., and Plank, D. (eds), *Handbook of Education Policy Research* (221–39). New York: AERA/Routledge

Tractenberg, P. (2006) 'Education'. In Tarr, A.G. and Williams, R.F. (eds), *State Constitutions for the Twenty-First Century*, vol. 3 (241–306). Albany: State University of New York Press

– (2006) *Don't Forget the Schools: Fiscal, budget, and policy considerations for tax reform*. Newark, NJ: Institute on Education Law and Policy, Rutgers University

Wasserman, S. and Faust, K. (1994) *Social Network Analysis: Methods and applications*. Cambridge: Cambridge University Press

Weckstein, P. (1999) 'School reform and enforceable rights to quality education'. Ch. 7 in Heubert, J.R. (ed.) *Law and School Reform: Six strategies for promoting educational equity* (306–93). New Haven, CT: Yale University Press

Weitz-White, K. and Rosenbaum, J.E. (2008) 'Inside the black box of accountability: How high-stakes accountability alters school culture and the classification and treatment of students and teachers'. Ch. 5 in Sadovnik, A.R., O'Day, J.A., Bohrnstedt, G.W., and Borman, K.M. (eds), *No Child Left Behind and the Reduction of the Achievement Gap* (97–116). New York: Routledge

Welner, K. (2000) 'Reclaiming a refuge: Can equity-minded education policies once again be promoted through the judiciary?' Paper presented at the annual Meeting of the American Educational research Association, New Orleans, 24–28 April

– (2008) *NeoVouchers: The emergence of tuition tax credits for private schooling*. Lanham, MD: Rowman & Littlefield

– (2012) 'Scholars as policy actors: Research, public discourse, and the zone of judicial constraints'. *American Educational Research Journal*, 49 (1), 7–29

Welner, K., Hinchey, P.H., Molnar, A., and Weitzman, D. (2010) *Think Tank Research Quality Lessons for Policy Makers, the Media, and the Public*. Charlotte, NC: Information Age

Welner, K. and Molnar, A. (2010) 'Junk social science: Its patrons and its audience'. In Hinchey, P.H., Molnar, A., and Weitzman, D. (eds), *Think Tank Research Quality Lessons for Policy Makers, the Media, and the Public* (311–16). Charlotte, NC: Information Age

Whitty, G. (2008) 'Twenty years of progress? English education policy 1988 to the present'. *Education Management, Administration & Leadership*, 36 (2), 165–84

Whitty, G., Power, S., and Halpin, D. (1998) *Devolution and Choice in Education: The school, the state and the market.* Buckingham, UK: Open University Press

Wilkins, D.B. (2004) 'From "separate is inherently unequal" to "diversity is good for business": The rise of market-based diversity arguments and the fate of the black corporate bar'. *Harvard Law Review*, 117 (3), 1548–1615

Winship, C. (2006) 'Policy analysis as puzzle solving'. In Moran, M., Rein, M., and Goodin, R. (eds), *The Oxford Handbook of Public Policy* (109–23). Oxford: Oxford University Press

Wong, K.K. (2011) 'Redesigning urban school districts in the USA: Mayoral accountability and the diverse provider model'. *Educational Management Administration & Leadership*, 39 (4), 486–500

Wong, K.K. and Shen, F.X. (2008) 'Charter law and charter operation: Re-examining the charter school marketplace'. Ch. 6 in Berends, M., Springer, M.G., and Walberg, H.J. (eds), *Charter School Outcomes* (131–62). New York: Lawrence Erlbaum Associates

Woods, P. (2000) 'Varieties and themes in producer engagement: Structure and agency in the schools public-market'. *British Journal of Sociology of Education*, 21 (2), 219–42

Woods, P., Woods, G., and Gunter, H. (2005) 'Academy schools: Challenges and prospects for educational leadership and public education'. Paper presented at the annual meeting of the British Educational Leadership, Management and Administration Society (BELMAS), Kents Hill, UK, 23–25 September

– (2007) 'Academy schools and entrepreneurialism in education', *Journal of Educational Policy*, 22 (2), 237

Yogev, A. (1997) 'Autonomy and choice as school strategies for peripheral communities in Israel'. In Shapira, R. and Cookson, P.W. (eds), *Autonomy and Choice in Context: An international perspective* (177–201). Oxford: Pergamon Press

Young, O.R. (2006) 'Choosing governance systems: A plea for comparative research'. Ch 41 in Moran, M., Rein, M., and Goodin, R. (eds), *The Oxford Handbook of Public Policy* (844–857). Oxford: Oxford University Press

Zhao, Y. and Lei, J. (2009) 'New technology'. Ch. 52 in Sykes, G., Schneider, B., and Plank, D. (eds), *Handbook of Education Policy Research* (671–93). New York: AERA/Routledge

Index